Corporate Governance in Lithuania

OECD
BETTER POLICIES FOR BETTER LIVES

This work is published under the responsibility of the Secretary-General of the OECD. The opinions expressed and arguments employed herein do not necessarily reflect the official views of OECD member countries.

This document, as well as any data and any map included herein, are without prejudice to the status of or sovereignty over any territory, to the delimitation of international frontiers and boundaries and to the name of any territory, city or area.

Please cite this publication as:
OECD (2018), *Corporate Governance in Lithuania*, OECD Publishing, Paris.
http://dx.doi.org/10.1787/9789264302617-en

ISBN 978-92-64-30260-0 (print)
ISBN 978-92-64-30261-7 (PDF)

Series: Corporate Governance
ISSN 2077-6527 (print)
ISSN 2077-6535 (online)

The statistical data for Israel are supplied by and under the responsibility of the relevant Israeli authorities. The use of such data by the OECD is without prejudice to the status of the Golan Heights, East Jerusalem and Israeli settlements in the West Bank under the terms of international law.

Corrigenda to OECD publications may be found on line at: *www.oecd.org/about/publishing/corrigenda.htm*.

Foreword

This report on *Corporate Governance in Lithuania* was prepared in the context of Lithuania's accession process to the OECD, which was launched in April 2015 by decision of the OECD Council. On 3 May 2018, the OECD Council decided to invite Lithuania to accede to the OECD Convention and thereby become a Member of the Organisation, upon formal deposit of its instrument of accession to the OECD Convention, which was pending at the time of publication. As part of its OECD accession process, Lithuania underwent an assessment against the OECD's corporate governance standards for listed companies and state-owned enterprises (SOEs), namely the *G20/OECD Corporate Governance Principles* and the *OECD Guidelines on Corporate Governance of State-Owned Enterprises*. The assessment was undertaken by the two OECD bodies responsible for developing these standards, the Corporate Governance Committee and its Working Party on State Ownership and Privatisation Practices.

This report presents the positive overall results of that assessment and highlights the significant reforms undertaken by Lithuania – both prior to and during the OECD accession process – to better align its practices with internationally-agreed corporate governance standards. Prior to the launch of its OECD accession process, Lithuania was already cooperating closely with the OECD Working Party on State Ownership and Privatisation Practices in the context of its state ownership reforms and underwent a separate assessment against the *OECD Guidelines on Corporate Governance of State-Owned Enterprises*, which was published in 2015. This separate assessment recognised measures already initiated in Lithuania to professionalise state ownership practices and improve SOEs' corporate governance and disclosure arrangements. It also made recommendations for additional reform, which Lithuania began implementing and which informed the subsequent assessment and recommendations made during the accession review process.

Over the course of the accession review process, Lithuania continued to take important measures to better align its corporate governance legislation and practices with OECD standards and good practices. These included upgrading the companies law to strengthen the responsibilities and independence of listed companies' boards, curtail the risk of abusive related party transactions and ensure that minority shareholders have equal access to corporate information. This has laid the groundwork for establishing a more modern corporate governance model in Lithuania, with the aim to attract private investors – including foreign investors – to Lithuania's capital markets, in support of broader economic development. Lithuania has also maintained a commitment to implementing state ownership reforms, including through measures to professionalise state ownership practices, shield SOEs' from political interference and strengthen their performance and transparency. These measures attest to Lithuania's commitment to promote the efficient operation and transparency of SOEs and a level playing field with private companies.

This report also includes a number of recommendations for continued improvement, with a view to ensuring that companies and markets create optimum value for the

Lithuanian economy and society. As an OECD member country, Lithuania will have the opportunity to benefit from the reform experiences and expertise of its peers as it continues to embark on corporate governance reforms.

This report was approved for public release by the Corporate Governance Committee in April 2018. The information is current through February 2018. Successive versions of the report informed six separate accession discussions on Lithuania held by the OECD Corporate Governance Committee and its Working Party on State Ownership and Privatisation Practices between November 2016 and April 2018. The principle author of this report is Korin Kane, building on an initial assessment of Lithuania against the *G20/OECD Principles of Corporate Governance* prepared by Mary Crane-Charef and with oversight by Daniel Blume, all of the OECD Directorate for Financial and Enterprise Affairs.

Table of contents

Tables

Figures

Boxes

Acronyms

AGM	Annual general meeting of shareholders
BAS	Business Accounting Standards (Lithuania)
CGC	Corporate Governance Committee
CSD	Central Securities Depository (Nasdaq Baltic CSD)
CSDL	Central Securities Depository of Lithuania (Branch of Nasdaq Baltic CSD)
EBRD	European Bank for Reconstruction and Development
EU	European Union
FCIS	Financial Crime Investigation Service
GCC	Governance Coordination Centre
IAS	International Accounting Standards
IFRS	International Financial Reporting Standards
MMF	Money market fund
OECD	Organisation for Economic Co-operation and Development
SOE	State-owned enterprise
WPSOPP	Working Party on State Ownership and Privatisation Practices

Executive summary

This report was developed as part of Lithuania's OECD accession process. It assesses Lithuania's corporate governance arrangements – the laws, regulations and institutions that shape company oversight – for listed and state-owned enterprises (SOEs) against the standards of the *G20/OECD Principles of Corporate Governance* (the *Principles*) and the *OECD Guidelines on Corporate Governance of State-Owned Enterprises* (the *SOE Guidelines*). The report reaches a positive overall assessment of Lithuania's ability and willingness to implement these OECD corporate governance standards and makes recommendations for continued improvement.

Lithuania's corporate governance landscape for listed and state-owned enterprises

The corporate governance framework for Lithuania's 27 listed companies is largely consistent with the *Principles.* The institutional structure for capital market oversight in Lithuania is generally sound, with active market surveillance by an independent regulator, the Bank of Lithuania, and courts that have ruled in favour of minority shareholders in several cases. The Nasdaq Vilnius Corporate Governance Code, applicable to listed companies, establishes corporate governance standards that are consistent with good practice. There is scope for strengthening compliance with its voluntary standards.

Lithuania has undertaken significant reforms to its state ownership practices over the past decade. These include notably the establishment of sound governance and disclosure standards applicable to all SOEs and the establishment of Governance Coordination Centre to monitor and report publicly on related compliance. These measures have introduced more professional and harmonised state ownership practices across the various sectoral line ministries responsible for overseeing Lithuania's 66 SOEs (and 5 listed subsidiaries). About 60% of SOEs by value are incorporated as limited liability companies, while the remainder are statutory corporations whose legal form accords the state direct authority over many corporate decisions, such as CEO hiring and dismissal.

Assessment relative to the core principles on corporate governance

Ensuring the enforcement of shareholder rights and equitable treatment

Lithuania has the basic legal requirements in place to enforce the rights and equitable treatment of shareholders with respect to most of the relevant areas of the *Principles.* A number of recent legislative reforms have strengthened minority shareholders' rights and equitable access to information. These include new procedures for board and audit committee review of material related party transactions – to help ensure that transactions are undertaken in the interest of the company and all shareholders – and the elimination of a legal provision that granted controlling shareholders privileged access to corporate information.

Timely and reliable disclosure in accordance with international standards

Lithuania has a robust legal framework for listed companies' disclosure and has recently taken steps to strengthen reporting requirements related to board composition, executive remuneration and the content of shareholders' agreements. Listed companies are not required to report in accordance with IFRS, but in practice all currently listed companies do so and the Lithuanian authorities are in the process of addressing remaining material inconsistencies between IFRS and local accounting standards. Concerning disclosure related to SOEs, Lithuania publishes annual reports on the performance and governance of SOEs whose content and frequency are above-average in comparison with international practices. Concerning disclosure by individual SOEs, the state recently made its related standards mandatory (not "comply-or-explain") for all large SOEs, consistent with OECD recommendations. This triggered the requirement for several large SOEs to prepare their accounts in accordance with IFRS.

Effective separation of the government's ownership and regulatory roles

While this report finds that some vulnerabilities to clear separation of the government's ownership and regulatory functions remain, Lithuania has made significant progress in recent years to professionalise and harmonise state ownership and corporate governance practices across the numerous line ministries responsible for overseeing the country's 66 SOEs. These steps include the development of high standards of governance and disclosure for all SOEs and the establishment of an ownership coordination function (the Governance Coordination Centre) to monitor – and report publicly on – compliance with these standards by SOEs and their ownership ministries. The recent transfer of the Governance Coordination Centre to a public institution (it was previously housed within an SOE), together with the doubling of its operational budget, have strengthened its capacity to monitor and help enforce the state's governance and disclosure standards.

Ensuring a level playing field between state-owned and private enterprises

SOEs in Lithuania are not formally exempt from the application of laws and regulations applicable to private companies, including those bearing on competition. The competition authority has undertaken a number of investigations involving SOEs, pointing to fruitful efforts to separate the state's roles as regulator and owner. Some differences in SOEs' operational conditions can nonetheless distort the competitive landscape, including rate-of-return requirements that are not market-consistent and preferential loans between SOEs that have occurred in some cases. Other issues affecting the level playing field are specific to statutory SOEs, whose legal form accords the state decision-making powers that should be the purview of boards of directors. Lithuania recently adopted plans to convert several commercially-oriented statutory SOEs into limited liability companies, which would help level the playing field between these SOEs and private companies.

Recognising the duties, rights and responsibilities of boards

Recently enacted legislative reforms have strengthened the legal responsibilities of listed companies' boards as well as their ability to effectively monitor management in the interest of companies and their shareholders. Under the new legislation, the boards of all Lithuanian listed companies must perform certain supervisory functions – including review of related party transactions – and comprise a minimum proportion of independent directors. In the SOE sector, boards have also been strengthened through new rules barring acting politicians and requiring a minimum proportion of independent directors.

Recommendations

With respect to listed companies, this report recommends that Lithuania give priority to monitoring implementation of recent legislative reforms on boards of directors and, in the medium term, consider further strengthening and clarifying their legal responsibilities. With respect to SOEs, this report recommends that Lithuania give priority to: strengthening the effectiveness of the Governance Coordination Centre; ensuring that the state's requirements on board composition and disclosure practices are fully implemented by the SOEs for which they are mandatory; and moving forward with plans to fully corporatise commercially-oriented statutory SOEs. To complement these priority recommendations, this report addresses additional recommendations to further align with good practice, which include: updating the corporate governance code for listed companies; revising the insolvency framework; and ensuring that the recently consolidated SOEs in the forestry and road maintenance sectors operate efficiently and respect high standards of governance and disclosure.

Chapter 1

Introduction to the corporate governance review of Lithuania

The review of Corporate Governance in Lithuania was prepared in the context of Lithuania's accession process to the OECD, to assess the corporate governance arrangements for listed and state-owned enterprises in Lithuania against the G20/OECD Principles of Corporate Governance and the OECD Guidelines on Corporate Governance of State-Owned Enterprises. This introductory chapter provides an overview of the process and methodology of the review, including reference to the "core" corporate governance principles used to inform the assessment. The chapter also summarises measures taken by Lithuania throughout the accession review process to implement OECD recommendations and further align Lithuanian practices with OECD corporate governance standards.

This report reviews Lithuania's implementation of the *Recommendation of the Council on Principles of Corporate Governance* (the *Principles*) and the *Recommendation of the Council on Guidelines on Corporate Governance of State-Owned Enterprises* (the *SOE Guidelines*). The report was developed in the context of Lithuania's accession process to the OECD, to support an evaluation of Lithuania's willingness and ability to implement substantive OECD legal instruments in the field of corporate governance and to compare Lithuania's policies and practices with OECD best policies and practices in this area. To this end, the report reviews Lithuania's legal, regulatory and institutional framework and implementation with respect to five "core corporate governance principles" set out in the *Roadmap for the Accession of Lithuania to the OECD Convention* (the *Roadmap*) (OECD, 2015b). These principles are:

- Ensuring a consistent regulatory framework that provides for the existence and effective enforcement of shareholder rights and the equitable treatment of shareholders, including minority and foreign shareholders;
- Requiring timely and reliable disclosure of corporate information in accordance with internationally recognised standards of accounting, auditing and non-financial reporting;
- Establishing effective separation of the government's role as an owner of state-owned companies and the government's role as regulator, particularly with regard to market regulation;
- Ensuring a level playing field in markets where state-owned enterprises and private sector companies compete in order to avoid market distortions; and
- Recognising stakeholder rights as established by law or through mutual agreements and the duties, rights and responsibilities of corporate boards of directors.

The development of this report was guided by a document entitled *Concepts to Guide Corporate Governance Accession Reviews* (the "Concept Paper").[1] The Concept Paper provides a methodology for conducting corporate governance accession examinations, identifying which *Principles* and *SOE Guidelines* recommendations are most relevant for assessing accession candidate countries against the five *Roadmap* principles.

The information included in this report draws upon Lithuania's position *vis-à-vis* the *Principles* and *SOE Guidelines* as set out in its Initial Memorandum, a document by which accession candidate countries set out their position with respect to OECD legal instruments prior to undergoing a series of technical reviews. It also draws on a more detailed self-assessment by the Lithuanian authorities against all of the *Principles*, prepared with reference to the *OECD Methodology for Implementation of the Corporate Governance Principles* and submitted to the OECD Secretariat in April 2016 (OECD, 2017); as well as responses to a standard questionnaire on the *SOE Guidelines* submitted in 2015 as part of a separate SOE review undertaken by the OECD Working Party on State Ownership and Privatisation Practices. The separate SOE review was undertaken in response to a request from the Lithuanian government made prior to the launching of Lithuania's accession process (OECD, 2015a). Its findings and recommendations have informed the parts of this report on the corporate governance of SOEs. The report also incorporates information on Lithuania's progress in implementing OECD recommendations, based notably on: letters sent by the Lithuanian Minister of Economy (dated 6 April 2016, 16 December 2016, 30 June 2017 and 30 January 2018); materials supplied by the Lithuanian authorities throughout the review process; and interviews with governmental and non-governmental counterparts held during five fact-finding visits by the OECD Secretariat in September 2015, May 2016, January 2017, August 2017 and February 2018.

Successive versions of this report were made available to support a total of six separate accession discussions held by the OECD Corporate Governance Committee and its Working Party on State Ownership and Privatisation Practices between November 2016 and April 2018.[2] Box 1.1 summarises measures taken by the Lithuanian authorities to implement the recommendations communicated to Lithuania in the context of the corporate governance accession review process.

Box 1.1 Summary of measures taken by Lithuania to implement OECD recommendations on the corporate governance of listed and state-owned enterprises

The text that follows summarises measures taken by the Lithuanian authorities to implement the recommendations of the Corporate Governance Committee and the Working Party on State Ownership and Privatisation Practices made in the context of Lithuania's corporate governance accession review process. The last set of recommendations prior to the finalisation of Lithuania's accession process was communicated to Lithuania via a letter signed by the Chairs of the Committee and the Working Party dated 1 December 2017. The letter put forth: (i) priority recommendations necessary to complete the accession review process and come to a formal opinion regarding Lithuania's willingness and ability to implement OECD corporate governance standards; and (ii) additional recommendations which the Lithuanian authorities were encouraged to implement in the future to further align with OECD corporate governance standards.

On the priority recommendations of the Corporate Governance Committee

- ***Strengthening the responsibilities and composition of boards of directors.*** Amendments to the Law on Companies were enacted in November 2017 requiring that the single-tier boards of listed companies be accorded supervisory responsibilities, including approval of related party transactions, and comprise at least one third independent directors. These measures strengthened the legal responsibilities and required composition of listed companies' boards of directors.

- ***Improving measures for review and disclosure of related party transactions.*** Amendments to the Law on Companies were enacted in November 2017 establishing requirements for board approval, audit committee review and public disclosure of material related party transactions for listed companies. These requirements, together with new Bank of Lithuania rules on audit committee composition, strengthen the scope for independent scrutiny of such transactions.

- ***Supporting more equitable disclosure and access to company information for all shareholders.*** Amendments to the Law on Companies were enacted in November 2017 removing a provision that previously granted controlling shareholders privileged access to corporate information. Amendments to the Law on Financial Statements of Entities were enacted in November 2017 requiring that companies disclose the contents of shareholders' agreements to the market. These amendments effectively support more equitable disclosure and access to information by all shareholders.

On the priority recommendations of the Working Party on State Ownership and Privatisation Practices

- ***Strengthening the ownership function.*** The ownership co-ordination body, the Governance Coordination Centre, was transferred to a separate public institution in July 2017 (it was previously located within an SOE), its annual budget was doubled to EUR 354 000 for 2018 and it has an authorisation to increase its staff from six to nine people. These steps have improved the GCC's institutional arrangements and should allow it to more effectively fulfil its monitoring and advisory functions.

- ***Increasing the operational independence of SOE boards of directors.*** Rules enacted in March 2017 bar politicians from serving on SOE boards and mandate a one half proportion of independent members. 30 SOE boards complied with these rules at the time of writing and nomination procedures were underway in an additional eight SOEs (out of the 43 for which the rules are mandatory).

- ***Streamlining SOEs' legal and corporate forms.*** Lithuania's 42 forestry SOEs and 11 road maintenance SOEs were successfully consolidated into, respectively, a single State Forest Enterprise and a single Road Maintenance SOE. Both are now overseen by boards of directors that comply with the aforementioned rules on board independence. A State Enterprise Reorganisation Plan establishes a timeline for converting 11 statutory SOEs into limited liability companies by end 2019 and undertaking other reorganisations, after which only five statutory SOEs will remain.

- ***Ensuring that SOEs are subject to high quality accounting and auditing standards.*** The state's SOE disclosure standards – which, among others, require IFRS reporting – were made mandatory (not comply-or-explain) for 13 large SOEs. Eight of those SOEs are compliant and four are foreseen to implement IFRS by 2020. The one non-compliant SOE, Ignalina Nuclear Power Plant, is in the process of being decommissioned and does not undertake any commercial activities.

- ***Enacting amendments to the Law on Companies to strengthen boards and safeguard minority shareholders' rights*** (reiterating the related concerns raised by the Corporate Governance Committee, as applicable to fully corporatised SOEs). Related amendments were enacted in November 2017 and are applicable to listed companies, including listed SOEs.

On additional recommendations to further align with OECD corporate governance standards

- ***Further strengthening the responsibilities of the boards of listed and state-owned enterprises in line with OECD standards.*** There is scope for making additional improvements to the Law on Companies in the future, notably concerning the responsibilities and functioning of boards, once the Lithuanian authorities have had some time to assess implementation of the most recent amendments.

- ***Updating the Nasdaq Vilnius Corporate Governance Code.*** The Nasdaq Vilnius stock exchange plans to revise its Corporate Governance Code in 2018, to ensure consistency with recent legal reforms, notably those concerning listed companies' boards of directors, audit requirements and disclosure rules.

- ***Improving the insolvency framework.*** The insolvency framework was still under review at the time of writing. A new unified law on insolvency and restructuring was foreseen for discussion by the Parliament in the second quarter of 2018.

- ***Addressing inconsistencies between local and international accounting standards.*** As of March 2018, the Lithuanian authorities were well advanced in updating national accounting rules to address what they considered to be the most material inconsistencies with international accounting standards.

The report is structured as follows. This introduction (Chapter 1) is followed by an overview of Lithuania's corporate governance landscape for listed and state-owned enterprises (Chapter 2). This is followed by a detailed review of Lithuania's performance against each of the five *Roadmap* core principles (Chapter 3). It ends with conclusions and recommendations for further aligning Lithuanian policies and practices with OECD corporate governance standards (Chapter 4).

Notes

1. The Concept Paper is an unpublished guidance document that was first issued in 2008 and was subsequently updated to take into account the 8 July 2015 adoption of the revised *Principles* and *SOE Guidelines*. The document takes as a main reference the OECD Council *Roadmap for the Accession of Lithuania to the OECD Convention*, as well as similar *Roadmaps* elaborated for Colombia, Latvia and Costa Rica, which set out the terms, conditions and processes for their accession to the OECD.

2. Accession discussions on Lithuania were held by the Corporate Governance Committee on 15 November 2016, 3 November 2017 and 10 April 2018 and by the Working Party on State Ownership and Privatisation Practices on 24 March 2017, 24 October 2017 and 27 March 2018.

References

OECD (2017), *Methodology for Assessing the Implementation of the G20/OECD Principles of Corporate Governance*, OECD, Paris, http://dx.doi.org/10.1787/9789264269965-en.

OECD (2015a), *OECD Review of the Corporate Governance of State-Owned Enterprises: Lithuania,* OECD, Paris, www.oecd.org/corporate/oecd-review-corporate-governance-soe-lithuania.htm.

OECD (2015b), *Roadmap for the Accession of Lithuania to the OECD Convention* (Adopted by Council at its 1320th session on 8 July 2015), OECD Council, http://www.oecd.org/officialdocuments/publicdisplaydocumentpdf/?cote=C(2015)92/FINAL&docLanguage=En.

Chapter 2

Lithuania's corporate governance landscape

This chapter describes the corporate governance arrangements – the laws, regulations and institutions that shape company oversight – for both listed and state-owned enterprises in Lithuania. Following an introductory overview of Lithuania's economic context and business climate, the chapter describes the corporate ownership and control landscape for Lithuania's 27 listed companies. It then details the laws, regulations and institutions that constitute the corporate governance framework for these companies, with an overview of recent related legislative reforms. This is followed by a descriptive overview of the corporate governance arrangements for Lithuania's 66 state-owned enterprises, including a synthesis of recent or ongoing state ownership reforms.

The statistical data for Israel are supplied by and under the responsibility of the relevant Israeli authorities. The use of such data by the OECD is without prejudice to the status of the Golan Heights, East Jerusalem and Israeli settlements in the West Bank under the terms of international law.

2.1 Economy

The Republic of Lithuania (hereafter Lithuania) regained its independence in 1991. It is a small open economy with about 3 million inhabitants. Per-capita income growth over the last 25 years was above levels in most OECD countries and exceeded levels of other economies in the region, reducing the gap relative to OECD average incomes (OECD, forthcoming). Lithuania joined the European Union (EU) in 2004 and adopted the Euro in January 2015.[1] The fast rise in living standards since 2000 was only dented by the global financial crisis of 2009, with unemployment edging up to almost 18% and, in 2015, when exports (accounting for 81% of GDP) were hit by the recession in Russia and counter-sanctions and a slowdown in other major trading partners. Lithuanian exports to Russia contracted by around one third in 2015 (OECD, 2016). Nonetheless, firms were successful in re-orienting exports to a diverse range of countries.

Lithuania's economic growth was a strong 3.8% in 2017, making it among the fastest growing economies in the EU. Buoyant exports on the back of broad based external demand recovery and a rebound in investment were the key drivers of this growth (OECD, forthcoming). Unemployment fell to 7.1% in 2017, well below the crisis highs. The Government's Economic Development Scenario for 2018-2021 foresees growth of around 3% in 2018-19 and 2.5% over the medium term (Table 2.1) (Ministry of Finance of the Republic of Lithuania, 2018).

Lithuania is generally considered to have a sound business environment and consistently ranks in the top third or higher of global cross-country economic rankings. Lithuania ranked 16th out of 190 economies in the World Bank Group's *Doing Business 2018*, an improvement over the previous year's ranking of 21st (World Bank, 2018 and World Bank, 2017). It ranked 41st in the World Economic Forum's *Global Competitiveness Report 2017-2018*, placing it in the top third of the 137 surveyed economies (World Economic Forum, 2017). Finally, Lithuania ranked 38th out of 176 countries and territories in the 2017 Transparency International *Corruption Perceptions Index* and its overall score has improved since 2012, indicating a drop in public perceptions of corruption in Lithuania (Transparency International, 2017).

Table 2.1. Key macroeconomic indicators for 2017-2021

	2017	2018	2019	2020	2021
Real GDP, rate of change, %	3.8	3.2	2.8	2.5	2.5
Real GDP, million EUR	35 854.5	37 001.4	38 033.1	38 965.8	39 935.9
Labour productivity (real GDP per one employed person), rate of change, %	4.4	3.7	3.3	3.0	3.0
Real GDP components, rate of change, %					
Household consumption expenditure	3.9	4.0	3.8	3.8	3.5
Government consumption expenditure	1.2	1.1	1.0	0.9	0.9
Gross fixed capital formation	7.3	7.6	5.3	4.8	4.0
Exports of goods and services	13.2	7.0	5.7	5.0	4.7
Imports of goods and services	12.8	7.6	6.5	5.5	5.1

Source: Ministry of Finance of the Republic of Lithuania (2018), "Economic Development Scenario for 2018-2021 (March 2018)", http://finmin.lrv.lt/en/actual-financial-data/economic-development-scenario.

2.2 Business environment and capital market

Similar to its Baltic neighbours, Estonia and Latvia, Lithuania's capital markets are small relative to OECD averages and characterised by very low liquidity and highly concentrated ownership. These traits were further exacerbated during and since the financial and economic crisis, from which Lithuania's capital markets have not fully recovered. Most Lithuanian companies (99.5%) are small- to medium-sized enterprises (SMEs).[2] Roughly 6% of all companies are registered as public limited liability companies, a category which includes listed companies.

Companies that have issued equity or tradeable debt securities in Lithuania do so via the Nasdaq Vilnius exchange. The Nasdaq Vilnius exchange, together with the exchanges in Riga and Tallinn, form the Nasdaq Baltic Market. Of the three, Lithuania is the largest, both in terms of the total number of listed companies (27) and its market capitalisation of EUR 3.9 billion, though its capitalisation as a percentage of GDP ranks in the middle (Nasdaq Baltic, 2015). (See also Table 2.4). Securities are registered via the Lithuanian branch of the Nasdaq Central Securities Depository.

The Nasdaq Vilnius regulated market is the principal market in Lithuania and comprises a main list and a secondary list for equity, as well as a bond list (made up mainly of Lithuanian government securities) and a fund list.[3] The regulated market is regulated under EU directives and is under the supervision of the Bank of Lithuania. The listing requirements are based on European standards and EU directives and intended for companies that are well established. (The listing requirements for different trading lists are shown in Table 2.2 below.) The market also includes First North Baltic, which is a multilateral trading facility, also known as the "alternative market".

As of 28 February 2018, Lithuania had 27 companies trading equity on the regulated market (12 on the main list and 15 on the secondary list), as well as two companies trading equity and two trading bonds on the Nasdaq Vilnius First North alternative market. Only one company, state-owned Lithuanian Energy, had issued bonds on the bond list ("green" bonds, which were admitted to the market in July 2017), along with 21 government securities issues. On the fund list, five funds were listed as of 28 February 2018.

Listing requirements are much less demanding for companies aiming to join the alternative First North Baltic market. To be admitted for trading on the alternative market, a company should enter into an advisory agreement with a Certified Adviser. Certified Advisers guide companies through the application process to the Nasdaq First North Baltic market and ensure that the companies fulfil all the requirements of First North on a continuing basis. As of 28 February 2018 there were two companies with listed equity and two companies with listed bonds on the Nasdaq Vilnius First North market and six Certified Advisers granted the status necessary to provide services in Lithuania.[4]

Table 2.2.Requirements for admission to Nasdaq Vilnius trading lists

Market	Market cap min. (EUR)	Free float minimum	Operating history	Reporting frequency	Accounting standards2	Report on compliance with Nasdaq Vilnius Corporate Governance Code required?	Disclosure language
Equity – main list	4 mill.*	25% free float or market cap at least EUR 10 million	3 years*	Audited annual reports; quarterly financial statements; material events	Lithuanian accounting regulations and legislation	✓	Lithuanian & English
Equity – secondary list	1 mill.*	No minimum	2 years*	Audited annual reports; quarterly financial statements; material events	Lithuanian accounting regulations and legislation	✓	Lithuanian & English
Bond List	200 000	N/A	2 years	Audited annual reports; quarterly financial statements; material events	Lithuanian accounting regulations and legislation	✓	Lithuanian & English
Fund List	See Note 1.	-	-	-	-	-	-
First North Baltic	No minimum	No min.	No min.	Audited annual set of financial reports; semi-annual financial statements; material events	Lithuanian accounting regulations and legislation		Lithuanian or English

1. Units or shares issued by collective investment undertakings, for which admission into the Fund Trading List is sought, shall meet the requirements of the Law on Collective Investment Undertakings of the Republic of Lithuania and other legal acts.
2. For issuers seeking to list equity on the main and secondary lists, the company's financial statements for at least the year preceding the issuance of new shares must be drawn up according to IFRS.

* The NASDAQ rules allow for exceptions to be made to minimum market capitalisation levels but in practice all listed companies meet these standards.

Source: Lithuanian authorities; Listing Rules of Nasdaq OMX Vilnius

Main and secondary listed companies in Lithuania, as well as Bond List companies, are expected to comply with the Nasdaq Vilnius Corporate Governance Code and to include a report on their compliance with the Code in their annual reports. (See Chapter 2, section 2.5 on the legal and regulatory framework for more on the Code.) Representatives from the private sector and civil society report that the culture of corporate governance in Lithuania is still nascent compared to other economies in the EU area. Based on a review of listed companies' compliance with the Corporate Governance Code compiled by the Bank of Lithuania in 2010 and data provided by Nasdaq Vilnius on listed companies' corporate governance disclosures in annual reports from 2015, most companies are generally compliant with the Code. Market observers report that, while weaknesses remain (see next paragraph), compliance with the Code has generally improved since it was last updated in 2010.[5] In addition, several Lithuanian companies have won annual "Nasdaq Baltic Market Awards" distinctions for best or most improved investor relations in the period from 2014 to 2016 (namely Apranga, Energijos Skirstymo Operatorius, Klaipėdos nafta, Litgrid and TEO LT). These awards highlight the best investor relations in financial and non-financial reporting and improve the overall standard of investor relations among listed companies in the Baltic region.

Broadly, weaknesses remain in companies' ability to explain areas of non-compliance with the Code. This includes, in particular, disclosures related to practices for the composition and responsibilities of the supervisory and management boards, the application of director independence rules and disclosure of executive remuneration policies. (See Table 2.3 for a summary of the exchange's compilation of 28 listed companies' disclosures on compliance with the Code in 2015. The reported compliance percentages are an average of the compliance percentages of several sub-recommendations under each Principle. See Chapter 3, section 3.2 for more on corporate governance disclosure practices by listed companies.)

The Nasdaq Vilnius Corporate Governance Code was last revised in 2010. Given the extensive recent legislative changes concerning listed companies' corporate governance and disclosure requirements (discussed in detail in the Chapter 2.5 section on recent legal and regulatory changes), a new revision to the Code would be warranted to ensure consistency with the legislative framework.

Table 2.3. Average compliance with the Nasdaq Vilnius Corporate Governance Code in 2015

Principle	Fully comply	Partially comply	Do not comply	Not applicable
PRINCIPLE I. BASIC PROVISIONS The overriding objective of a company should be to operate in common interests of all the shareholders by optimizing over time shareholder value.	98%			
PRINCIPLE II. THE CORPORATE GOVERNANCE FRAMEWORK The corporate governance framework should ensure the strategic guidance of the company, the effective oversight of the company's management bodies, an appropriate balance and distribution of functions between the company's bodies, protection of the shareholders' interests.	71%	8%	22%	
PRINCIPLE III. THE ORDER OF THE FORMATION OF A COLLEGIAL BODY TO BE ELECTED BY A GENERAL SHAREHOLDERS' MEETING The order of the formation a collegial body to be elected by a general shareholders' meeting should ensure representation of minority shareholders, accountability of this body to the shareholders and objective monitoring of the company's operation and its management bodies.	49%	9%	27%	10%
PRINCIPLE IV. THE DUTIES AND LIABILITIES OF A COLLEGIAL BODY ELECTED BY THE GENERAL SHAREHOLDERS' MEETING The corporate governance framework should ensure proper and effective functioning of the collegial body elected by the general shareholders' meeting, and the powers granted to the collegial body should ensure effective monitoring of the company's management bodies and protection of interests of all the company's shareholders.	53%	12%	31%	5%
PRINCIPLE V. THE WORKING PROCEDURE OF THE COMPANY'S COLLEGIAL BODIES The working procedure of supervisory and management bodies established in the company should ensure efficient operation of these bodies and decision-making and encourage active co-operation between the company's bodies.	86%	2%	7%	5%
PRINCIPLE VI. THE EQUITABLE TREATMENT OF SHAREHOLDERS AND SHAREHOLDER RIGHTS The corporate governance framework should ensure the equitable treatment of all shareholders, including minority and foreign shareholders. The corporate governance framework should protect the rights of the shareholders.	92%	1%	6%	3%

Principle	Fully comply	Partially comply	Do not comply	Not applicable
PRINCIPLE VII. THE AVOIDANCE OF CONFLICTS OF INTEREST AND THEIR DISCLOSURE The corporate governance framework should encourage members of the corporate bodies to avoid conflicts of interest and assure transparent and effective mechanism of disclosure of conflicts of interest regarding members of the corporate bodies.	97%			3%
PRINCIPLE VIII. COMPANY'S REMUNERATION POLICY Remuneration policy and procedure for approval, revision and disclosure of directors' remuneration established in the company should prevent potential conflicts of interest and abuse in determining remuneration of directors, in addition it should ensure publicity and transparency both of company's remuneration policy and remuneration of directors.	11%	9%	43%	46%
PRINCIPLE IX. THE ROLE OF STAKEHOLDERS IN CORPORATE GOVERNANCE The corporate governance framework should recognise the rights of stakeholders as established by law and encourage active co-operation between companies and stakeholders in creating the company value, jobs and financial sustainability. For the purposes of this Principle, the concept "stakeholders" includes investors, employees, creditors, suppliers, clients, local community and other persons having certain interest in the company concerned.	100%			
PRINCIPLE X. INFORMATION DISCLOSURE AND TRANSPARENCY The corporate governance framework should ensure that timely and accurate disclosure is made on all material information regarding the company, including the financial situation, performance and governance of the company.	89%	6%	4%	2%
PRINCIPLE XI. THE SELECTION OF THE COMPANY'S AUDITOR The mechanism of the selection of the company's auditor should ensure independence of the firm of auditor's conclusion and opinion.	77%	5%	6%	13%

Source: Nasdaq Vilnius

2.3 Corporate ownership and listing trends

As noted above, Lithuania's capital market today is small and ownership is highly concentrated. As of February 2018, only 31 companies (roughly a third less than in 2004) were listed on Nasdaq Vilnius with a total market capitalisation of EUR 3.9 billion (this figure includes the 27 on the main list and the four with listed equities or bonds on the alternative First North Baltic market). One private company has issued listed bonds on the regulated market's Bond List. Consistent with global trends, it appears that the capital market continues to shrink despite Lithuania's overall post-crisis economic recovery (described in Chapter 2.1). According to the Bank of Lithuania's 2015 annual report, the total number of trades on the primary and secondary markets decreased by 28.2% in 2015, year-on-year, and the turnover decreased by 23.7% (Bank of Lithuania, 2016).

In terms of overall ownership, 59% of listed companies have a controlling shareholder holding more than 50% of company shares. In six of these companies, the controlling shareholder holds more than 90% of all shares. Four of these six companies are majority-owned by the state (ESO and Lietuvos Energijos Gamyba on the main list and Amber Grid and Litgrid on the secondary list). The markets are also highly illiquid: 56% of companies have a free float rate below 20% and the average level of free float is 14%. Only two listed companies have a free float equal to or above 50%.

Table 2.4. Listed companies according to market capitalisation and turnover (2007-17)

	2004	2005	2006	2007	2008	2009	2010	2011	2012	2013	2014	2015	2016	2017	Baltic total (2017)	Percentage Vilnius (2017)
Number of listed companies	43	43	42	40	40	39	39	33	33	32	33	30	27	27	Total: 68 *Riga: 24* *Tallinn: 17*	40%
Main list companies	8	10	11	13	17	15	18	18	18	16	16	14	13	12	Total: 32 *Riga: 5* *Tallinn: 15*	40%
Secondary list companies	35	33	31	27	23	24	21	15	15	16	17	16	14	15	Total: 36 *Riga: 19* *Tallinn: 2*	42%
Debt securities	37	37	28	25	31	39	24	28	28	28	26	20	21	20	Total: 71 *Riga: 48* *Tallinn: 3*	28%
Funds listed	0	0	0	0	0	0	0	1	1	5	5	5	5	5	Total: 11 *Riga: 5* *Tallinn: 1*	45%
Market capitalisation (EUR millions)	4 753	6 937	7 728	6 892	2 608	3 220	4 220	3 139	2 992	2 907	3 330	3 379	3 496	3 784	Total: 7261 *Riga: 973* *Tallinn:2504*	52%
Market capitalisation, % GDP	29	31	34	26	8	12	15	9	9	8	9		9	9		
Turnover (EUR millions)	313	588	1607	757	332	214	224	176	129	92	79	74	87	98	Total: 299 *Riga:* 49 *Tallinn:* 151	33%

Note: The last column averages total figures for all three Nasdaq Baltic markets: Vilnius, Tallinn, and Riga.
Source: Lithuanian authorities and Nasdaq Vilnius.

As of end-2017, the ten largest listed companies made up 84% of Lithuania's total market capitalisation, 90% of total turnover and 83% of the total number of transactions. Three listed companies— Energijos Skirstymo Operatorius (distribution and public supply of electricity), Telia Lietuva (telecommunications) and Šiaulių bankas (a bank) — accounted for 38% of total market capitalisation, 58% of total market turnover and 46% of total transactions concluded on the regulated market. Energijos Skirstymo Operatorius is 94.98%-owned by the state-owned group of energy companies, Lithuanian Energy Group. (See Table 2.5 and Figures 2.1-2.3.)

Regarding sectoral breakdown, 41% of the total market capitalisation in Lithuania as of end-2017 belonged to listed companies operating in the utilities sector: Energijos Skirstymo Operatorius (distribution and public supply of electricity, natural gas distribution), Lietuvos Energijos Gamyba (generation of electric and heat power), LITGRID (electricity transmission) and Kauno Energija (manufacture of electricity and thermal energy, supply to the customers). All of these companies are majority state-owned, including Kauno Energija, which is owned by the municipality of Kaunus city. The second- and third-most active sectors are telecommunications (represented by Telia Lietuva, the largest telecommunication company in Lithuania) and consumer goods (represented by 12 different companies) (see Figure 2.4).

Table 2.5. Top 10 listed companies, according to total capitalisation, turnover and number of transactions as of end-2017

	Capitalisation		Turnover		Transactions	
No.	Company	EUR millions	Company	EUR millions	Company	No
1.	Energijos Skirstymo Operatorius	812.32	Šiauliu bankas	44.52	Šiauliu Bankas	18 342
2.	Telia Lietuva	608.83	Apranga	8.5	Klaipedos nafta	5 330
3.	Lietuvos Energijos Gamyba	390.58	Telia Lietuva	6.5	Energijos Skirstymo Operatorius	4 044
4.	LITGRID	353.03	Energijos Skirstymo Operatorius	5.9	Telia Lietuva	3 513
5.	Šiauliu bankas	276.32	Klaipedos nafta	5.1	Grigeo	3 280
6.	Amber Grid	258.65	Pieno žvaigždes	4.8	Vilkyškiu Pienine	2 951
7.	Klaipedos nafta	194.11	Grigeo	4.0	Panevežio statybos trestas	2 808
8.	Apranga	143.76	Vilkyškiu pienine	3.3	Apranga	2 643
9.	AUGA group AB	108.70	Panevežio statybos trestas	3.1	Rokiškio suris	2 392
10.	Linas Agro Group	107.28	Rokiškio suris	2.7	AUGA group	1 773
	Total (top 10)	*3 253.59*	*Total (top 10)*	*88.36*	*Total (top 10)*	*47 076*
	Total (market)	*3 872.44*	*Total (market)*	*97.70*	*Total (market)*	*56 450*
	Percentage:	*84%*	*Percentage:*	*90%*	*Percentage:*	*83%*

Source: Lithuanian authorities and Nasdaq Vilnius

Figure 2.1. Top 10 listed companies, in terms of % of total market capitalisation, February 2018

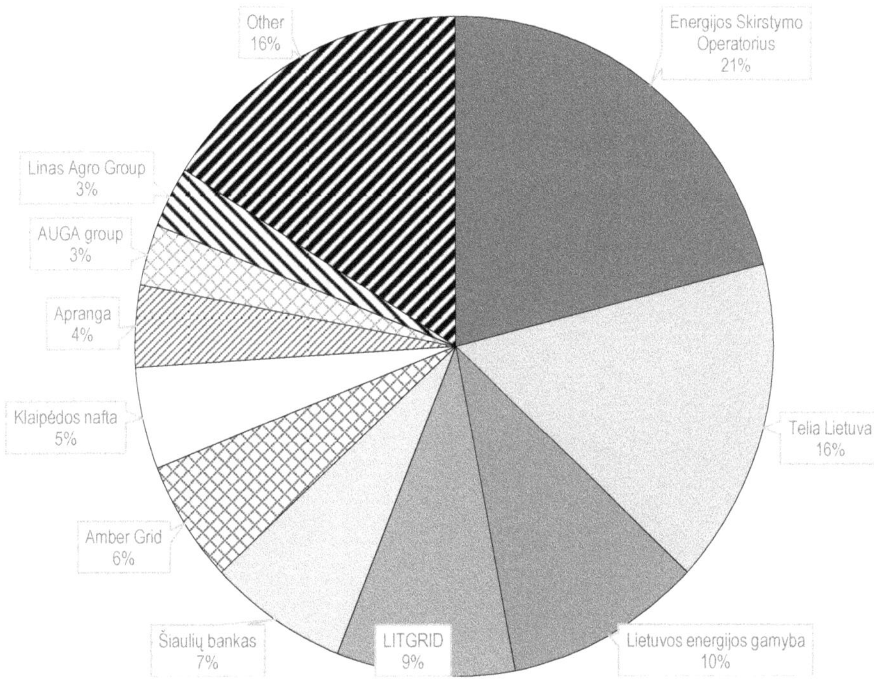

Source: Lithuanian authorities and Nasdaq Vilnius

Figure 2.2. Top 10 listed companies, in terms of % of total market turnover, 2017

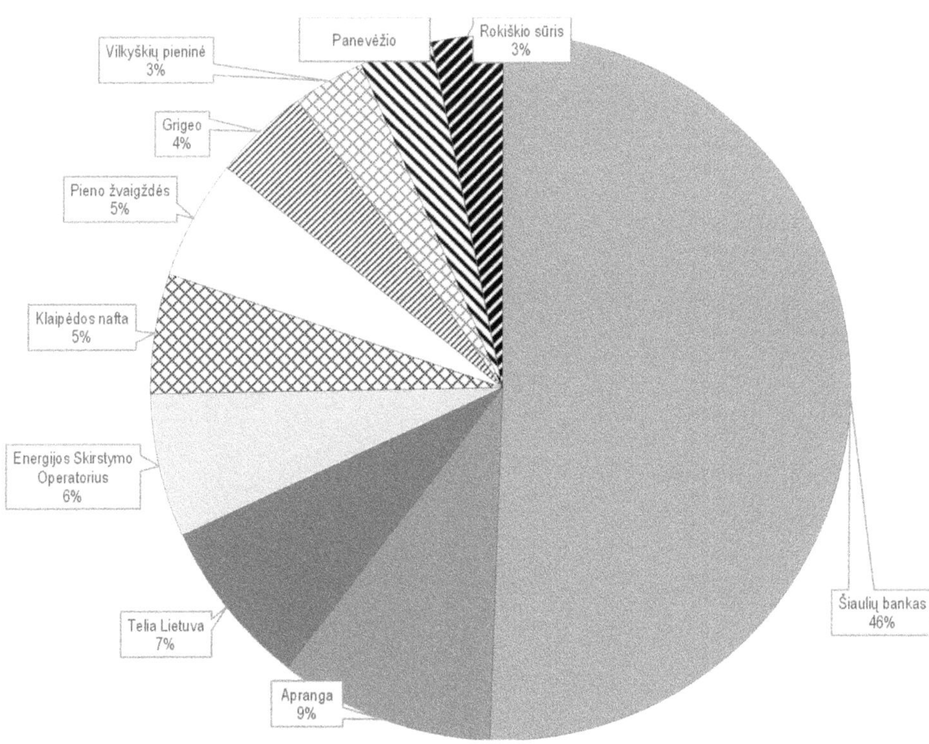

Source: Lithuanian authorities and Nasdaq Vilnius

Figure 2.3. Top 10 listed companies, in terms of % of total market transactions, 2017

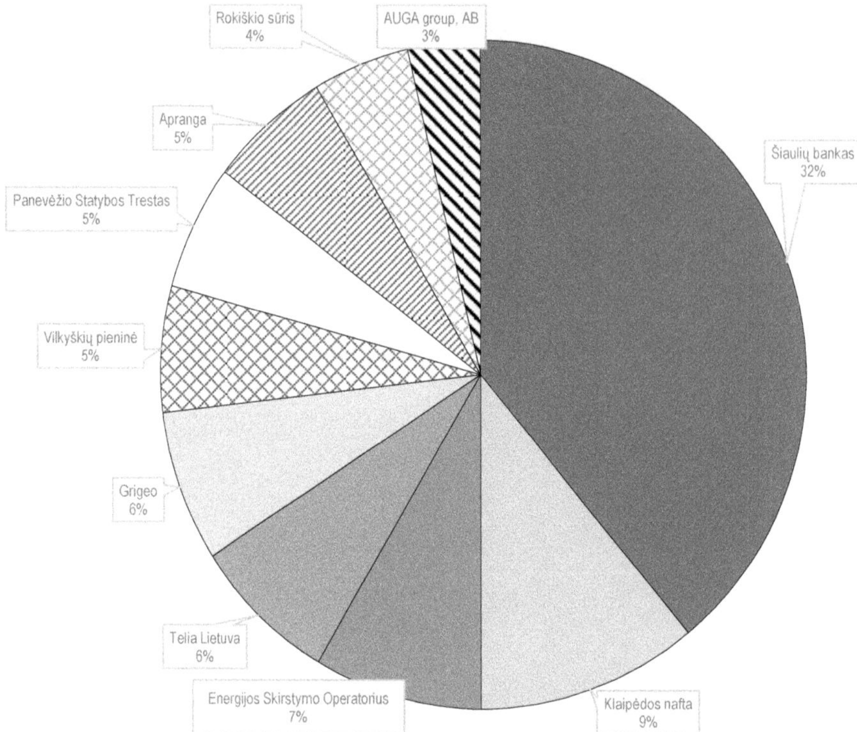

Source: Lithuanian authorities and Nasdaq Vilnius

Figure 2.4. Market capitalisation by industry, end 2017

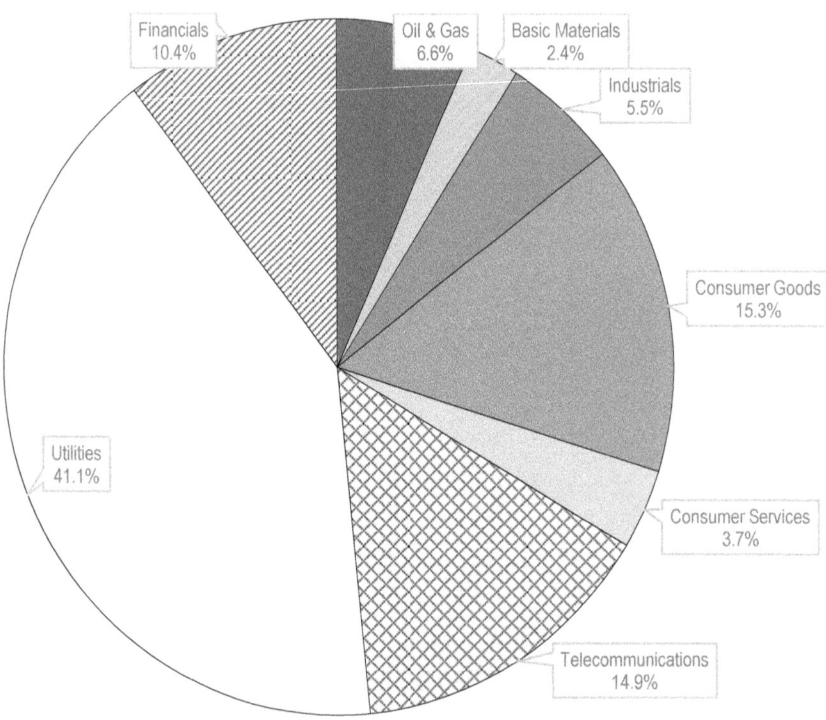

Source: Lithuanian authorities and Nasdaq Vilnius

Institutional investors – such as mutual funds, pension funds, insurance companies and hedge funds – do not play a major role in the Lithuanian capital market. Based on data from the Lithuanian authorities, private non-financial institutional owners account for roughly 17% of all shareholders (Table 2.6). The majority of shareholders in Lithuania are legal persons; households hold only 8.75% of all shares, a level that has remained steady since 2009.

In the Baltic region, generally, the percentage of shares owned by foreign shareholders is high by international standards, partly due to the small size of the economies (Nasdaq Baltic, 2015). Lithuania is no exception: according to data from the Central Securities Depository (CSD) of Lithuania, 59% of all equity in Lithuanian listed companies is held by resident shareholders, a 14% decrease *vis-à-vis* foreign investors since 2009. Of foreign investors investing in Lithuania's capital markets, 48% are domiciled in Sweden, 8% in Canada, 8% in Russia and 8% in Poland. In most cases, these investments represent foreign companies that have acquired substantial stakes in listed Lithuanian companies (See Table 2.6).

Table 2.6. Main resident shareholders of listed companies as of 31 May 2014

No	Investors	EUR million	%
1.	National private non-financial corporations	1 300.47	16.61
2.	State non-financial corporations	1 212.27	15.48
3.	Central government	1 160.10	14.89
4.	Households	685.04	8.75
5.	Local government	185.57	2.37
6.	Foreign controlled non-financial corporations	46.73	0.60
7.	Deposit-taking corporations, except the central bank	44.18	0.56
8.	Money markets funds (MMF)	22.96	0.29
9.	Other financial intermediaries, excluding insurance corporations and pension funds	7.40	0.09
10.	Pension funds	3.09	0.04
11.	Non-MMF investment funds	2.71	0.03
12.	Insurance corporations	2.63	0.03
13.	Financial auxiliaries	2.62	0.03
14.	Non-profit institutions serving households	1.35	0.02
15.	Social insurance funds	0.75	0.01
16.	Captive financial institutions and money lenders	0.00	0.00
17.	Central bank	0.00	0.00
18.	State government	0.00	0.00

Source: Lithuanian authorities

Table 2.7. Nasdaq CSD Lithuania branch participants, February 2018

Participants	Number
Brokerage firms	4
Commercial banks	14
Other participants	4
Total	22

Source: Lithuanian authorities and Nasdaq CSD Lithuania branch.

Overall, most Lithuanian companies reportedly see raising capital via an initial public offering (IPO) as too burdensome and expensive; the preferred source of capital, authorities and private sector representatives report, is bank credit. (Lithuanian authorities report that the total stock of loans to companies equals 20.5% GDP versus 9.4% of GDP for listed equity.) Beyond traditional bank loans, the role of venture capital is still small but growing as an alternative source of financing. Venture capital fund investments include investments made since 2010 via venture capital instruments financed from European Union structural funds. For example, 90 investments were made by Lithuanian venture capital firms in SMEs operating in high value-added economic sectors. An additional EUR 130 million in venture capital financing has been collected under the Baltic Innovation Fund, established in 2012 under a joint contract jointly signed by Lithuania, Latvia, Estonia and the European Investment Fund.

As of October 2016, the Lithuanian Government was considering or preparing to implement a number of measures to improve Lithuanian companies'—in particular SMEs'—access to finance beyond bank loans. So far, these measures appear to be mainly focused on debt markets, but also increasing access to venture capital funds (including through EU-subsidised funds) and crowd funding. In June 2016, the Parliament enacted reforms to facilitate the issuance of corporate bonds (by ensuring higher level of protection of bondholders' interests; see Chapter 2.5 section on recent legal and regulatory changes) and had adopted amendments to the Law on Companies to make it easier for private companies to offer their bonds publicly. These amendments entered into force in November 2016. Finally, the Ministry of Finance—in partnership with the European Bank for Reconstruction and Development (EBRD)—also initiated in April 2015 a review of Lithuania's national legal system to facilitate securitisation and covered bond issuances in the country. The joint Ministry of Finance/EBRD review was completed in April 2017 and includes proposals for improving related Lithuanian legislation (EBRD, 2017). The Lithuanian authorities report that draft legislation is being prepared on the basis of these proposals and is foreseen for adoption by end 2018.

2.4 Supervisory boards, management boards and CEOs of listed companies

The legal framework under the Law on Companies provides for considerable flexibility regarding both the board structures put in place and the respective responsibilities of companies' governance organs (namely the supervisory board, management board, CEO and general meeting of shareholders, or AGM). Throughout this report, the terms "supervisory board" and "management board" are used to describe the governance structures of companies adopting a two-tier board structure. For companies adopting a one-tier board structure with only a management board in place, the term "one-tier management board" is used. This section provides an overview of how public LLCs—the corporate form of listed companies—may organise their governance structures and responsibilities under the Law on Companies, discussed further in Chapter 2.5. Amendments to the Law on Companies that were enacted in November 2017 and enter into force on 1 July 2018 establish some additional rules concerning governance structures and responsibilities that are specific to *listed* public LLCs. These are specified as relevant throughout the text.

To provide some context to this section, it should be noted that, prior to earlier amendments to the Law on Companies which came into force in July 2015, Lithuanian listed companies were not required to establish boards of directors at all; the only required governance organs were the AGM and the CEO. In July 2015, amendments came into force requiring listed companies to establish either a supervisory or a management board. The additional amendments enacted in November 2017 further require that when listed companies opt for the one-tier management board model, this board must be accorded certain supervisory powers and comprise a minimum proportion of independent directors. These legislative reforms are examples of steps taken in recent years to clarify and strengthen the role of boards of directors in monitoring management. Traditionally, decision-making powers within Lithuanian corporations have been shared largely between the AGM and company CEOs.

Table 2.8. Possible board structures and responsibilities in Lithuanian listed companies before and after entry into force of November 2017 legislative reform

Type A (executive) management board + CEO	Type B (mixed) management board + CEO	Supervisory board + Type A (executive) management board + CEO	Supervisory board + CEO
Before July 2018 entry into force – and subsequent implementation – of Law on Companies amendments			
This structure is adopted by 19 out of 29 listed companies in Lithuania The management board performs mostly executive functions, including approval of the business strategy and deciding on transactions beyond a certain threshold. Supervisory functions are limited to some basic CEO oversight (hiring, dismissal and remuneration decisions). The AGM undertakes most other supervisory functions, including selecting the auditor, approving the financial statements and electing and revoking management board members.	This structure is not adopted by any listed companies in Lithuania but is permitted by the Law on Companies. The management board performs both executive and some (limited) supervisory functions. These supervisory functions include more explicit CEO oversight responsibilities than under the Type A structure, e.g. monitoring the CEO's activities, submitting related advice to the AGM and considering the CEO's suitability for office if the company is loss-making. More than half of the management board must be outside directors (not employees of the company).	This structure is adopted by 10 out of 29 listed companies in Lithuania The supervisory board performs some (limited) supervisory functions, including electing and revoking the members of the management board. Most other functions of the supervisory board are advisory in nature. The management board performs only management functions, including approval of the business strategy. More than half of the supervisory board must be outside directors (not employees of the company).	This structure is not adopted by any listed companies in Lithuania The supervisory board performs some (limited) supervisory functions, including selecting and dismissing the CEO. Most other functions of the supervisory board are advisory in nature. More than half of the supervisory board must be outside directors (not employees of the company).
After July 2018 entry into force – and subsequent implementation – of Law on Companies amendments			
The Type A structure will no longer be possible for listed companies in Lithuania. Single-tier management boards will have to be accorded additional CEO oversight responsibilities, effectively transforming them into Type B (mixed) management boards.	All listed companies that opt for a one-tier management board structure will have a Type B (mixed) management board. This management board will have the additional responsibility of approving related party transactions. At least one third of management board members must be independent.	For listed companies that opt for a two-tier structure, the supervisory board will have the additional responsibilities of approving operating strategy and related party transactions. At least one third of supervisory board members must be independent.	For listed companies that opt for a one-tier supervisory board structure, the supervisory board will have the additional responsibilities of approving operating strategy and related party transactions. At least one third of supervisory board members must be independent.

Table 2.8 provides an overview of the different governance structures and responsibilities that a listed company's AGM may (or, in some cases, *must*) establish via the company's articles of association. Implementation of the aforementioned Law on Companies amendments related to board responsibilities and composition can only be assessed beginning in July 2018 when they enter into force. The provisions on board composition are to be implemented as new boards (or board members) are elected, since the boards in place at the time of the July 2018 entry into force can serve until the expiry of their terms. Table 2.8 first provides an overview of the possible board structures and

responsibilities according to the legislation in force before July 2018 and then highlights changes in the required governance structures and responsibilities that will be triggered by the entry into force and subsequent implementation of the amendments.

Governance structures

The Law on Companies sets forth the legal foundation for the structure for boards of Lithuanian public limited liability companies ("public LLCs"), which as previously mentioned are the legal form of companies that may list shares on Lithuania's capital markets.[7] According to the Law, the general meeting of shareholders decides whether a public LLC will have a one- or two-tier board. Depending on the shareholders' decision in this regard, public LLCs can organise themselves according to different governance structures. Every public LLC must also have a "manager of the company" (hereinafter a chief executive officer, or CEO). In public LLCs with a one-tier board, the CEO cannot be a member of the management board if the AGM has assigned the management board supervisory (in addition to executive) functions, and in two-tier companies, the CEO cannot be a member of the supervisory board. To recall, the AGM *must* assign the management board supervisory functions if the public LLC is listed on the stock exchange.

According to data provided by Nasdaq Vilnius (also reported in Table 2.8), as of end-2015, 34% of listed companies had established two-tier boards, while a greater number (66%) had established one-tier management boards.[8] According to listed companies' corporate governance reports, the primary reason for opting for a one-tier management board is that supervisory boards are often considered a source of unnecessary cost. The Law on Companies also sets out some governance provisions specific to *listed* public LLCs. These include the recently introduced requirement (entering into force in July 2018) that one-tier management boards of listed companies (when such a structure is adopted) must be accorded certain supervisory functions and must comprise a minimum proportion of independent directors.

Governance responsibilities

The Law on Companies sets forth the minimum responsibilities assigned to the general meeting of shareholders, the supervisory board (where applicable), the management board and the CEO. The general meeting of shareholders may assign further supervisory functions to a company's supervisory or management board in a company's articles of association, if not in contradiction with other provisions of the Law.

General meeting of shareholders

The general meeting of shareholders has a number of exclusive rights, including revising the company's articles of association, making decisions on the company's share capital and dividend distribution and approving the annual financial statements. It is also responsible for electing and dismissing the supervisory board members or, if no supervisory board is in place, the management board members. Finally, the general meeting is responsible for electing and determining the remuneration of the company's auditor or audit firm.

Supervisory boards

Supervisory boards are primarily responsible for electing and removing members of the management board, including before the expiry of their term of office. The supervisory board's additional responsibilities have traditionally been mostly advisory in nature, for example submitting opinions and proposals to the general meeting of shareholders on the company's business strategy, annual financial statements, profit/loss distribution and annual report (Law on Companies Art. 32). The amendments to the Law on Companies that enter into force in July 2018 expand the supervisory board's oversight responsibilities to include approving the operating strategy and, for listed companies, deciding on related party transactions. Under the Law on Companies, a supervisory board must have between 3 and 15 members, more than half of whom must be non-executive (or, more specifically, must have no employment relationships with the company [Art. 31]). A company's CEO and management board members cannot sit on the supervisory board. The amendments to the Law on Companies further stipulate that for listed companies, the supervisory board must comprise at least 1/3 independent members.

The Nasdaq Vilnius Corporate Governance Code (described further in the Chapter 2.5 section on the legal and regulatory framework) recommends that listed companies establish a two-tier structure with both a supervisory board and an executive management board (Principle II.1.), noting: "The setting up of collegial bodies for supervision and management facilitates clear separation of management and supervisory functions in the company, accountability and control on the part of the chief executive officer, which, in its turn, facilitates a more efficient and transparent management process." The Code further adds in Principle II.3 that, where a company applies a one-tier structure, "it is recommended that [the collegial body] should be a supervisory body, i.e. the supervisory board. In such a case, the supervisory board is responsible for the effective monitoring of the functions performed by the company's chief executive officer." As of end-2015, ten out of 29 listed companies had two-tier boards. No listed companies had adopted the one-tier approach with only a supervisory board. Some market experts observe that this is for the better, given that the supervisory board under the Law on Companies has limited decision-making powers, allowing CEOs in these situations to operate with little direct supervision.

Management boards

The responsibilities of management boards vary somewhat depending on whether a supervisory board is also in place. If a supervisory board is not in place, the management board may – and in the case of listed companies, *must* – undertake two main supervisory functions that would otherwise be the purview of the supervisory board, namely (i) supervising the CEO's activities and submitting related feedback to the general meeting and (ii) deciding on related party transactions for listed companies (Box 2.1). Beyond these two possible supervisory functions, management board responsibilities in any board system include direct CEO oversight (hiring, dismissal and remuneration) as well as approval of the company's annual report, management structure and positions of employees (Law on Companies Art. 34). The management board is also accorded the power to decide on company investments, acquisitions and divestitures that exceed certain minimum thresholds, with the caveat that a company's articles of association can require that the management board obtain approval from the AGM (or in two-tier structures, from the supervisory board) before adopting related decisions (Law on Companies Art. 34.5).

Management boards of public LLCs can perform either purely executive functions or, if no supervisory board is in place, also (some) supervisory functions, namely those enumerated in the Law on Companies. With the entry into force and implementation of the recent amendments to the Law on Companies, listed companies will no longer be allowed to operate under a one-tier management board with purely executive functions, i.e. the board structure referred to as "Type A (executive)" in the below descriptions.

- **Type A (executive functions):** Management boards in this category perform primarily executive functions. There are no independence requirements for members of these boards. No collegial body is assigned supervisory functions (as defined in the Law on Companies), which are instead undertaken by the general meeting of shareholders. Most listed Lithuanian companies, at the time of writing, follow this model.
- **Type B (mixed executive and supervisory functions):** Management boards in this category (which currently no listed companies implement) perform both executive and supervisory functions, but supervisory functions are limited to those outlined in Art. 34.11 (Box 2.1). These functions include the ability to more closely oversee the functions and performance of the CEO, a responsibility that was strengthened with 2014 amendments to the Law on Companies. At least half of Type B management board members must have no employment relationships with the company (Art. 33.7). CEOs are barred from sitting on management boards that are assigned supervisory functions.

Box 2.1 Supervisory responsibilities of "Type B" management boards assigned both executive and supervisory responsibilities

Art. 34.11 of the Law on Companies lists the following supervisory responsibilities that must be assigned to listed companies' management boards if no supervisory board is in place. (For public LLCs that are not listed on a regulated market, these supervisory responsibilities "may" be assigned to the management board via the articles of association.)

1. Take decisions on transactions with related parties (this provision enters into force in July 2018);
2. Supervise the activities of the manager of the company, submit to the general meeting of shareholders feedback and proposals concerning the activities of the manager of the company;
3. Consider the suitability of the manager of the company for his office if the company operates at a loss;
4. Submit proposals to the manager of the company to revoke his decisions which are in conflict with laws and other legal acts, the articles of association of the company, decisions of the general meeting of shareholders or the board;
5. Address other issues regarding the supervision of the activities of the company and the manager of the company assigned to the remit of the board by the articles of association of the company, also by decisions of the general meeting of shareholders.

Source : Lithuanian Law on Companies, including official translations provided by the Lithuanian authorities of the amendments enacted in November 2017.

The recent Law on Companies amendments that prevent listed companies from operating under the Type A management board introduce a great deal more consistency to a system that has historically been perceived as confusing by business partners and investors, including sought-after foreign investors. The previous system did allow for Type-A management boards to operate, at least partially, on a "de-facto" Type B basis, through the presence of independent directors. However, the outside oversight that these directors could exercise was weakened by limitations in the supervisory responsibilities of management boards. The recent amendments appear to largely address this issue, by requiring that listed companies' management boards be accorded certain supervisory functions, including notably approval of related party transactions. (See also Chapter 3.5 assessment section on the rights, duties and responsibilities of boards).

CEO

Finally, every company incorporated under the Law on Companies must have a manager of the company (CEO). The CEO is elected and removed from office by the management board, or, if the management board is not formed, by the supervisory board. If neither board is formed (which is only possible for non-listed companies), the CEO is elected and removed from office by the general meeting of shareholders. The CEO traditionally has wide-ranging executive powers and, in many companies, can execute these powers fairly independently. Under the Law on Companies, the CEO of a public LLC is responsible for the daily activities of the company and, in acting on behalf of the company, is entitled to enter into transactions at her or his own discretion. The CEO's responsibilities include: organising the activities of the company; preparing annual and interim financial statements and reports; concluding contracts with an auditor or audit firm where external audit is required; submitting required information and documents to the general shareholders' meeting, the Enterprise Register, the securities regulator and the CSD of Lithuania (which, since September 2017 operates as a branch of the Nasdaq Baltic CSD); and publishing company information as required. The AGM may choose to require that the CEO check with the AGM before executing certain decisions on behalf of the company. One of the motivations for the 2014 amendments to the Law on Companies, as described further in Chapter 2.5, was to introduce the ability of the AGM to somewhat curb CEOs' wide-ranging powers. As of amendments to the Law on Companies enacted in November 2017, the CEO of a listed company is required to obtain the approval of the supervisory body (either the supervisory board or the management board with supervisory functions) prior to entering into transactions with related parties.

2.5 The corporate governance framework for listed companies

Lithuania is a civil law country. Its legal system, which is based on continental European legal traditions, has been significantly reformed since the country's independence was restored in 1991. Many of the reforms leading up to and since joining the European Union in 2004 have been undertaken to align Lithuania's legal and regulatory framework with the EU *acquis communautaire* (EU law). Basic rights, freedoms and duties of citizens are set forth in the Constitution of the Republic of Lithuania. Under the Constitution, the state's power is vested in Lithuania's citizens and exercised by the *Seimas* (Parliament), the President of the Republic, the Government and Lithuania's courts. The hierarchy of laws consists of the Constitution, followed by constitutional laws, resolutions of the *Seimas* or the Government of the Republic of Lithuania and acts of other governmental institutions and local municipal authorities.

Legal and regulatory framework

Civil Code

The Lithuanian Civil Code came into force in June 2000. It includes a special section on legal persons and how they should be run, including commercial entities and citizens' rights *vis-à-vis* these entities, for example the right to seek redress in Lithuania's courts.

The Civil Code supersedes other legal acts, in the event that there are contradictions between the Civil Code and other laws, except in cases where the Civil Code gives priority to the provisions of other laws.

Of the Civil Code's six "books", the second concerning "persons" is especially important to company law. It includes provisions defining a legal person, contractual liability, terms of activities of legal persons, what to include and how to disclose information in certain documents, as well as rules for the incorporation of legal persons, including registration with the Register of Legal Persons. The Civil Code's second book also includes rules applicable to the companies' managing bodies (defined as the company's CEO and/or the board of directors), including their rights and duties.

Law on Companies

The Law on Companies entered into force on 1 January 2004. It regulates the incorporation, management, activities, reorganisation, conversion, split-off and liquidation of public limited liability companies (whose shares may be publicly traded) and private limited liability companies (whose shares are not publicly traded)[9]; the composition and responsibilities of corporate organs; the rights and duties of shareholders; as well as the opening of branches of foreign companies and termination of their activities. The provisions of the Law on Companies are complemented, where applicable, by the rules set forth for companies that have issued securities as laid down in the Law on Securities.

The Law on Companies was last amended in November 2017 and the new provisions are set to enter into force in July 2018. Amendments were notably made to strengthen shareholders' equal access to corporate information, to increase board oversight responsibilities and independence and to strengthen procedures for board review of related party transactions. These recent amendments are discussed in more detail in the Chapter 2.5 section on "Recent legal and regulatory changes". The Law on Companies previously underwent amendments in June 2014, notably to include a new requirement that public LLCs have at least one collegial body, i.e. either a management board or a supervisory board and a management board.[10] The reason for this change was twofold, according to the Lithuanian authorities. First, the amendment was made to align Lithuanian company law with international practices, following an assessment of EU members' legislation that indicated Lithuania was the only EU country without an obligation for limited liability companies to establish at least one collegial body. Second, the amendments were made to strengthen shareholder rights and their ability to supervise the actions of a company's CEO and the overall supervision of a company's corporate governance.

Law on Markets in Financial Instruments

Financial markets in Lithuania are regulated by the Law on Markets in Financial Instruments, which entered into force in January 2007. The purpose of the Law is to ensure a fair, open and efficient functioning of markets in financial instruments, the protection of investor interests and the prudential management of systemic risk. Its other stated objective is to harmonise Lithuanian financial markets regulation with relevant EU legal acts. The law applies primarily to financial brokerage firms and regulated markets, as well as to the natural and legal persons participating in the regulated markets. It sets forth the rules for trading in a regulated market; rules against market abuse; rules for accounting of financial instruments; and rules for supervising markets in financial instruments, undertaken by the Bank of Lithuania (see section on the institutional framework for corporate governance below).

Law on Securities

The Law on Securities also came into force in January 2007. It sets forth rules for the offering and admission of securities to trading on Lithuania's regulated markets, for the disclosure of periodic and current information by issuers and for takeover bids. Like the Law on Markets in Financial Instruments, the government agency responsible for enforcing the Law on Securities is the Bank of Lithuania.

Other relevant laws

Other relevant laws include: the Law on Accounting, which sets forth the rules and procedures for accounting; the Law on Financial Reporting by Undertakings, which establishes the rules for the preparation and disclosure of financial and company reports; the Law on Consolidated Financial Reporting by Groups of Undertakings, which sets forth accounting rules and procedures for parent companies with subsidiaries; and the Law on Audit, which sets forth the rules and procedures for the audit of financial statements, as well as for the professionalisation of the audit profession in Lithuania.

Some recent amendments affecting the accounting and audit landscape for Lithuanian listed companies merit mentioning here, prior to describing their provisions in more detail in the relevant sections of the Chapter 3.2 assessment. Amendments to the Law on Audit were adopted by the Parliament on 15 December 2016 and entered into force on 1 March 2017. The amendments were elaborated to implement the EU Audit Directive (2014/56/EU) and Regulation (EU) No 537/2014 on specific requirements regarding statutory audits of public interest entities. The changes introduce more stringent requirements for auditor independence and also provide specific, additional requirements for auditors and audit firms that carry out audits of public interest entities, a category which notably includes listed companies and large SOEs.[11] The amendments also strengthen the role of audit committees, including requirements pertaining to audit committees' composition, formation, activities and functions, particularly in their selection of external auditors. In particular, the new functions accorded to audit committees include assessing the provision of non-audit services, monitoring auditor remuneration and playing a stronger role in selecting the auditor or audit firm. In parallel, the Bank of Lithuania adopted a Resolution on 24 January 2017 outlining requirements applicable to the audit committees of listed companies, to complement the Law on Audit provisions. The Resolution notably states that the majority of audit committee members, including its chair, must be independent. The Resolution entered into force on 1 March 2017. These provisions are reviewed in greater detail in the Chapter 3.2 assessment of accounting and audit standards and the Chapter 3.5 assessment of boards of directors.

On 21 November 2017, amendments to the Law on Financial Reporting by Undertakings were enacted by the Parliament. Their provisions must be implemented by companies in disclosures for the 2018 financial year. These amendments are described in the relevant sections of this review and notably include new requirements for listed companies to include in their annual reports information on related party transactions, board member remuneration and the content of shareholders' agreements. All companies are furthermore required to disclose details on any other management positions held by board members or the CEO.

Prior to this most recent phase of revisions, amendments to the Law on Financial Reporting by Undertakings and to the Law on Consolidated Financial Statements of Groups of Undertakings were enacted by the Parliament on 15 December 2016 and entered into force on 1 January 2017. The amendments were adopted to implement Directive 2014/95/EU on disclosure of non-financial and diversity information by certain large undertakings and groups.[12] The Directive requires large public interest companies (a category which, as mentioned earlier, notably includes listed companies and large SOEs) with more than 500 employees to disclose in their management report information on policies, risks and outcomes regarding environmental matters, social and employee issues, respect for human rights and anti-corruption and bribery issues. The Directive also requires listed companies to disclose information on diversity in their boards of directors. This information is to be disclosed in companies' non-financial statements.

The Nasdaq Vilnius Corporate Governance Code for the Companies Listed on Nasdaq Vilnius (Nasdaq Vilnius Corporate Governance Code) and the Listing Rules of AB Nasdaq Vilnius ("listing rules") also constitute important components of the corporate governance legal framework (Nasdaq Vilnius, 2009 and Nasdaq Vilnius, 2016, respectively). The former codifies the principles and standards of corporate governance that companies listed on Nasdaq Vilnius are recommended to apply to their activities. These standards are primarily related to the protection of shareholders' interests, adequate balance and distribution of functions between corporate bodies and adequate disclosure of corporate information. The Code was drafted with reference to the *G20/OECD Principles of Corporate Governance* and was first adopted by Nasdaq Vilnius and the supervisory authority in 2006 and updated in 2010. The Code is enforced on a comply-or-explain basis. Issuers must include in their annual reports a notification that they comply with the Code with an explanation of the exceptions specifying which provisions they do not comply with and for what reasons (Law on Securities, Art. 22.3). A similar requirement is included in the listing rules (paragraph 24.5), which was complemented with the introduction of an amended *Form of Disclosure of Compliance with the Corporate Governance Code for the Companies Listed on Nasdaq Vilnius.*[13] The Bank of Lithuania and the management board of Nasdaq Vilnius approved the form in March 2015 in order to comply with the European Commission Recommendation 2014/208/EU on the quality of corporate governance reporting. Nasdaq Vilnius reported plans to revise the Corporate Governance Code during the first half of 2018 to take into account – and ensure consistency with – recent Law on Companies amendments and other relevant legal reforms, discussed in the section that follows.

The Nasdaq Vilnius listing rules establish: (i) the procedure, conditions and periods for admission of financial instruments to trading lists on Nasdaq Vilnius and delisting thereof; (ii) terms and conditions of suspension and resumption of trading in the financial instruments; and (iii) requirements related to the obligations and supervision of Nasdaq Vilnius issuers. The legal basis for the listing rules is the Law on Markets in Financial Instruments (Art. 53.1, 54 and 55).

Recent legal and regulatory changes

Recent changes to the Law on Companies

A number of amendments to the Law on Companies were adopted by the Parliament in November 2017. What follows is a non-exhaustive overview of changes to the Law on Companies concerning board responsibilities and composition, procedures for the review of related party transactions and shareholders' access to information, which were all the subject of recommendations addressed to Lithuania by the Corporate Governance Committee (CGC) in the context of Lithuania's OECD accession process.

On board responsibilities

The amendments expand the responsibilities of companies' supervisory bodies (i.e. supervisory boards in two-tier systems or management boards that are accorded supervisory responsibilities in one-tier systems). Supervisory bodies' responsibilities are notably expanded to include the explicit power to approve a company's operating strategy and, for listed companies, to review and decide on related party transactions. In cases where a supervisory board is not formed, the amendments accord the responsibility for approving related party transactions either to the management board (if it is accorded supervisory powers) or to the general meeting (if the management board is not accorded supervisory powers). Importantly, listed companies are required by other new provisions in the Law on Companies to ensure that if only a one-tier management board is in place, it must be accorded supervisory responsibilities, including CEO oversight tasks and the right to approve related party transactions. This means that in practice, related party transactions for listed companies can no longer be subject only to approval by the CEO and/or the AGM. The amendments stipulate that related parties ("associated parties" according to the official translation provided by the Lithuanian authorities) are to be defined by the accounting standards adopted by the company in question. Related party transactions are subject to detailed review and disclosure procedures if they fulfil certain materiality criteria. Material related party transactions must be reviewed by listed companies' audit committees.

On board composition and independence

The amendments also seek to increase board independence, notably by: (i) requiring that all companies' supervisory bodies (i.e. the supervisory board if established or the management board if accorded supervisory powers) comprise at least 1/3 independent members; (ii) prohibiting a company's auditor from serving on supervisory bodies; and (iii) prohibiting the management board members of subsidiary companies from serving on parent companies' supervisory bodies. These amendments, together with the expanded responsibilities of boards, constitute important steps towards implementing the CGC's recommendation to establish stronger independent oversight over listed companies' CEOs and management.

On shareholders' equal access to information

Finally, the amendments also strengthen minority shareholders' equitable treatment, by removing a provision that explicitly accorded controlling shareholders privileged access to corporate information. The provision that was removed accorded controlling shareholders the explicit right to access any company documents upon request, provided they sign a written pledge that they would not disclose any commercial secrets. The amendments allow *all* shareholders to access any company documents, with the proviso that companies can refuse requests for information if they concern commercial or industry secrets or confidential information. Related disputes are to be settled in court. The removal of this provision is in line with the CGC's recommendation that legal provisions according controlling shareholders privileged access to information should be addressed.

Proposed changes to the Law on Markets in Financial Instruments

Lithuania reports that it has implemented the EU Market Abuse Regulation (MAR) and is preparing to implement the Markets in Financial Instruments Directive and Regulation (MiFID2/MiFIR).[14] Draft amendments to the Law on Markets in Financial Instruments, including MiFID2 requirements on corporate governance, are currently under consideration and the Lithuanian authorities report that the draft amendments are foreseen for adoption by Parliament in 2018.

Law on Bondholder Interest Protection

The aim of this law, which was enacted by the Parliament in June 2016 and entered into force on 1 November 2016, was to reform existing regulation on bondholders' protection, which was considered to not be concrete or effective enough to sufficiently protect bondholders' interests.[15] The law applies to companies issuing bonds. It extends the powers of bond intermediaries and bondholders and more clearly defines the duties of bond intermediaries (for example, to take measures in order to meet the company's obligations to the bondholders, to organise bondholders' meetings, to carry out decisions adopted in bondholders' meetings, etc.) Furthermore, the new law establishes a bondholders' meeting and defines its competence. The law was introduced, in part, to address past bond-issuers' failures to redeem bonds at maturity (namely bonds issued by AB Snaigė and AB Agrowill).

Changes to the insolvency framework

The Chapter 3.5 assessment section on stakeholder rights provides a detailed overview of changes that were previously under consideration to the main laws bearing on insolvency in Lithuania, namely the Law on Enterprise Bankruptcy and the Law on Restructuring of Enterprises. On 13 May 2016, the Parliament adopted a decision to return the draft amendments to these two laws to their "initiators" for improvement, among other reasons with a view to elaborating one unified law concerning insolvency. According to the Lithuanian authorities, the new unified draft law is expected to be submitted to the Parliament in the second quarter of 2018.

Institutional framework

The main government institutions responsible for the legal and regulatory framework for the corporate governance of listed companies in Lithuania are the Ministry of Economy and the Ministry of Finance (with the newly created Authority of Audit, Accounting, Property Valuation and Insolvency Management, which was established in January 2016, replacing the former Authority of Audit and Accounting). The Ministry of Justice is involved to the extent that it is responsible for overseeing Lithuania's court systems and for ensuring that draft laws and legislative amendments are coherent with Lithuania's overall body of law. The latter is also responsible for overseeing the national Register of Enterprises.

Active enforcement of the corporate governance rules for listed companies is largely undertaken by the Bank of Lithuania's Supervision Service (specifically, the service's Financial Services and Markets Supervision Department) and, to a lesser extent, Nasdaq Vilnius. A description of these bodies and their legally established scope of responsibilities is provided in this section, while a further discussion of enforcement in Lithuania is provided in relevant sections of Chapter 2.6 on the effectiveness of the corporate governance framework.

Box 2.2 Financial market supervision responsibilities tasked to the Bank of Lithuania

The Law on the Bank of Lithuania establishes the Bank and its responsibilities under Lithuanian law, including the responsibility to supervise Lithuania's financial markets. These responsibilities are further defined in the Law on Securities and the Law on Markets in Financial Instruments, included below.

Law on Securities

Under Art. 46.1 of the Law on Securities, the Supervisory Institution (i.e. the Bank of Lithuania) is responsible for "the drawing up, approval and publication of the prospectus, the publication of the periodic and current information, [and] execution of takeover bids":

- *Issuer prospectuses:* Prior to the public offering and admission of securities to trading on the regulated market, the Bank of Lithuania is responsible for ensuring the correctness and completeness of information presented in an issuer's prospectus, for approving an issuer's prospectus, and for maintaining on its website the list of prospectuses approved during the last 12 months (Section II).
- *Disclosure of periodic and current information:* Issuers that have admitted securities to trading on the regulated market must draw up and make public, post in the Central Storage Facility and submit to the Bank of Lithuania annual reports and periodic information (i.e. quarterly financial statements and other material events) in a manner established by the Bank (Section III).
- *Takeover bids:* The Bank of Lithuania is responsible for establishing the procedure for submitting, implementing and suspending takeover bids (voluntary and mandatory)[1], as well as the procedure for the approval and publication of the circular and the settlement for the purchased securities, the information to be disclosed, and the cases where the terms of the takeover bid may be modified or the takeover bid voided. It is also responsible for supervising compliance with the Law on Securities' provisions related to such bids (Section IV).

Law on Markets in Financial Instruments

Under Art. 69 of the Law on Markets in Financial Instruments, the purposes of the Bank of Lithuania's supervisory functions are to: ensure a fair, transparent and efficient function of markets in financial instruments; ensure protection of investors' interests; and reduce systemic risk in markets in financial instruments. To this end, Art. 70 of the law assigns the Bank of Lithuania the following tasks and functions.

Tasks:

In fulfilling its purpose under the Law, the Bank of Lithuania is expected to supervise the observance of the rules of fair trading in respect of circulation of financial instruments; undertake the measures ensuring an efficient functioning of markets in financial instruments and protection of investors; submit proposals regarding the formation of the state economic policy promoting development of markets in financial instruments; disseminate information about the principles of functioning of markets in financial instruments; and undertake other measures for implementation of this Law and other legal acts related to a market in financial instruments.

Functions:

To carry out these tasks, the Bank of Lithuania is expected to perform the following functions:

- Draft, approve, amend and declare as void the rules regulating the licensing and activities of regulated markets, financial brokerage firms, financial adviser companies and brokers, circulation of financial instruments;
- Provide explanations and recommendations on issues of circulation of financial instruments;
- Issue or revoke licenses of regulated markets, financial brokerage firms, financial adviser undertakings, brokers;

- Monitor, analyse, inspect and otherwise supervise the activities of financial brokerage firms, financial adviser undertakings, regulated markets and members thereof, the Central Depository and managers of accounts;
- Perform the functions assigned to the competent authority under Regulation (EC) No 1060/2009[2];
- Impose the sanctions specified in this Law and other laws of the Republic of Lithuania on the persons that have violated this Law and resolutions of the supervisory institution;
- Prepare or participate in the preparation of publications about the functioning and regulation of markets in financial instruments;
- Organise examinations and performance appraisals to assess the knowledge and competence of financial brokers;
- Co-operate with associations of financial brokerage firms;
- Conclude agreements with appropriate institutions of other states on co-operation and exchange of information;
- Co-operate and exchange required information with appropriate institutions of other states;
- Co-operate with the European Securities and Markets Authority under Regulation (EU) No 1095/2010 and with the European Banking Authority under Regulation (EU) No 1093/2010 and immediately provide them with the entire information necessary for the achievement of their tasks;[3]
- Exercise supervision on a consolidated basis;
- Perform other functions specified by this Law and other laws of the Republic of Lithuania.

1. Law on Securities Art. 2.41 defines a "mandatory takeover bid" as a bid "submitted by a person who has acquired over 1/3 of votes in the general meeting of shareholders of the offeree company to the holders of the remaining securities of the offeree company, to buy up the remaining voting securities of the offeree company and securities representing the right to acquire such voting securities".
2. Regulation (EC) No 1060/2009 of the European Parliament and of the Council of 16 September 2009 on credit rating agencies: http://eur-lex.europa.eu/LexUriServ/LexUriServ.do?uri=OJ:L:2009:302:0001:0031:EN:PDF
3. Regulation (EU) No 1095/2010 of the European Parliament and of the Council of 24 November 2010 establishing a European Supervisory Authority (European Securities and Markets Authority): http://eur-lex.europa.eu/legal-content/EN/TXT/PDF/?uri=CELEX:32010R1095&from=EN; Regulation (EU) No 1093/2010 establishing a European Supervisory Authority (European Banking Authority): http://www.esrb.europa.eu/shared/pdf/EBA-en.pdf?f28519d76ca89a9eaad5c92280b24212

Source : Information provided by the Lithuanian authorities, the Bank of Lithuania website (www.lb.lt) and the legal texts cited here.

Established under the Law on the Bank of Lithuania, the Bank is vested with a wide range of tasks and duties related to oversight and management of the banking system, including implementing policies to protect and ensure the stability of financial markets (i.e. macro-prudential policy), among other measures related to the implementation of the Law on the Bank of Lithuania and other legal acts (Law on Bank of Lithuania Art. 8). Most importantly for the purposes of this review, the Law on the Bank of Lithuania assigns the Bank the responsibility for financial market supervision (Art. 8.2.2) and for settling disputes between the consumers and financial market participants out of court (Art. 8.2.3), responsibilities that the Bank took over from the former Securities Commission in 2012. Since taking over these functions, the Bank is also vested with powers under the Law on Securities and the Law on Markets in Financial Instruments. These responsibilities are described in Box 2.2 and are fulfilled by the Bank of

Lithuania's Supervision Service, in particular its Financial Services and Markets Supervision Department.

The regulated market is managed by Nasdaq Vilnius, which along with Nasdaq Riga and Tallinn, make up the Nasdaq Baltic Securities Market. The Nasdaq Central Securities Depository's Lithuania branch is the national depository responsible for custody and settlement of all publicly issued and circulated securities issued in Lithuania. The Nasdaq CSD Lithuania branch was previously owned by Nasdaq Vilnius but was since merged with the securities depositories of Estonia and Latvia and is now 100% owned by Nasdaq Nordic Oy (Finland). The Nasdaq CSD was established through the merger of the Estonian, Latvian and Lithuanian central securities depositories in 2017. Its head office is based in Latvia. Nasdaq Vilnius is responsible for the enforcement of its listing requirements and the Nasdaq Vilnius Principles of Corporate Governance and, in so doing, co-operates regularly with the Bank of Lithuania. The tasks of the exchange and the CSD are set forth in the Law on Markets in Financial Instruments. If and when certain disciplinary measures are taken against issuers by Nasdaq Vilnius, the exchange's management board must notify the Bank of Lithuania and, at the Bank's request, provide materials related to the exchange's inspection and sanctions.

Finally, the Lithuanian Register of Legal Entities, which is a state-owned enterprise under the responsibility of the Ministry of Justice, plays an important role in that all legal entities must register their existence and all company information with the Register, which is then responsible for making this information public. The Government decides what information collected by the Register is available to users for free and what information must be paid for by users. However, the Register does not have enforcement powers. (Further discussion of the role of Lithuania's Register of Legal Entities is provided in Chapter 3.2 assessment of the framework for disclosure of company information.)

2.6 Overall effectiveness of the corporate governance framework

The Concept Paper guiding corporate governance accession reviews calls for the corporate governance landscape section to make an assessment against key recommendations in Chapter 1 of the *Principles*. This section therefore builds on the preceding introduction to Lithuania's corporate governance framework and assesses its implementation in practice, according to *Principles* 1.A to 1.F. The discussion of Lithuania's corporate governance framework for listed companies is distinct from—but linked to—Lithuania's corporate governance framework for state-owned enterprises (SOEs).

Corporate governance framework (Principle I.A)

The headline recommendation of Chapter I of the *Principles* states that "The corporate governance framework should promote transparent and fair markets, and the efficient allocation of resources. It should be consistent with the rule of law and support effective supervision and enforcement." **Principle I.A** further specifies that the corporate governance framework should be developed taking into account its impact on overall economic performance, market integrity and the incentives it creates for market participants and the promotion of transparent and well-functioning markets.

In their self-evaluation under the *Principles*, the Lithuanian authorities consider their corporate governance framework to be sound and developed to support transparent and efficient markets, as well as market integrity. They therefore consider this *Principle* fully implemented.

Every legislative initiative in Lithuania is subject to a public consultation process as per the Law on Legislative Framework. As part of this process, drafts of laws and other legal acts must be prepared electronically in the Information System of Legal Acts. The system allows participating institutions and stakeholders to review and propose changes to draft acts electronically, thereby at the same time centralising all proposed changes and comments. The entity or entities responsible for a draft legal act must assess all presented proposals and present conclusions regarding these proposals to the entity adopting the legal act (i.e. the Parliament, or *Seimas*). Once adopted, all legal acts are disclosed publicly and are stored in a Registrar of Legal Acts (https://www.e-tar.lt/portal/en/index), for which access is free of charge.

While in practice the low level of market liquidity and the absence of active institutional investors may limit the incentives for efficient functioning of Lithuania's equity market, Lithuania's legal framework and legislative processes appear to be consistent with the promotion of transparent and fair markets.

Consistency with the rule of law, transparency and enforcement (Principle I.B)

Principle I.B states that the legal and regulatory requirements that affect corporate governance practices in a jurisdiction should be consistent with the rule of law, transparent and enforceable.

The Lithuanian self-evaluation report states that it fully implements this Principle. Rule of law in Lithuania is a constitutional principle protected by the Lithuanian Constitutional Court. All changes to the legislative framework must be made transparently and in alignment with the rule of law, as per the aforementioned legislative consultation process set forth under the Law on Legislative Framework. Finally, the Lithuanian authorities add that, where codes and principles are used as a standard or as an explicit substitute for legal or regulatory provisions, their status is clearly specified.

Public enforcement of the corporate governance framework

The Bank of Lithuania's Supervision Service is primarily responsible for the public enforcement of Lithuania's rules for listed companies, including rules against market abuse. To fulfil this role, the Bank has developed a surveillance system, which includes receiving signals from all market participants, including the Nasdaq Vilnius exchange. The Bank of Lithuania has developed an internal system for detecting possible market abuse, which applies to all transactions concluded and orders executed on the regulated market. Enforcement is carried out in co-operation with police, prosecutors and the exchange. This co-operation includes working via formal agreement with the Financial Crime Investigation Service (FCIS) of the Lithuanian police. As per this agreement, the Bank can cooperate with the police on investigations (i.e. police may accompany Bank officials to ensure entry into company premises for search and seizure operations) and the Bank may access FCIS resources and special means (i.e. phone surveillance in criminal cases).

The Bank of Lithuania may investigate entities under the Bank's supervision; investigation of entities outside their jurisdiction requires authorisation from the courts. Upon completion of an investigation into possible market abuse by a natural person, the Bank of Lithuania will provide the protocol to the court for a final decision; if the target of the investigation is a legal person, then the decision is made by the Board of the Bank of Lithuania. The Board is the governing body of the Bank of Lithuania and consists of a Chairman of the Board, two Deputy Chairmen of the Board and two Members of the Board. In criminal cases, investigations are undertaken in co-operation with the police and the case is submitted to the Financial Crime Investigation Service.

The Bank of Lithuania meets regularly with the Nasdaq Vilnius exchange, also, to engage with the exchange on its monitoring of issuers' compliance with exchange rules, notably the Nasdaq Vilnius listing rules and Corporate Governance Code. While Nasdaq Vilnius has authority to issue warnings, halt trading or delist companies, in practice it refers cases to the Bank, and provides reports to the Bank every six months on its surveillance activities. Nasdaq Vilnius sees its main role as developing and disseminating the Nasdaq Vilnius Corporate Governance Code, with the Bank of Lithuania taking full responsibility for enforcing the corporate governance framework.

Data provided by the Bank of Lithuania shows that it has an active public market surveillance programme (see data in Tables 2.9-2.10 and Figures 2.5-2.6 below). These data reveal a system that flagged more than 1 500 transactions per year between 2013 and 2016 as suspicious. The Bank suggested that such transactions are flagged in the system for review relatively frequently due to the low volume of trading, which can easily result in "false positives" when small transactions cause substantial changes in share prices. A small number of the flagged suspicious transactions (46 in 2013, 29 in 2014, 28 in 2015 and 20 in 2016) were then subject to more detailed analysis. These cases led to 23 verbal warnings and 22 written warnings over this same period. The Bank of Lithuania also issued two warnings to issuers in 2015 for "inappropriate disclosure of regulated information". The majority of market manipulation warnings related to potential insider trading (managers trading during closed periods) and price or order-based manipulation; the remaining warnings addressed suspicious trading at the end of a trading session ("marking the close" manipulation), auction manipulation (submitting and cancelling large orders during an auction) and front running (involving suspicious broker transactions).

The Bank of Lithuania reported that in general, it considers verbal and written warnings to be more efficient and effective in influencing and improving individual and market behaviour than fines, allowing for earlier intervention without significant harm to the market. However, the Bank of Lithuania did report separately on one insider trading case (described in Box 3.3 of this report, in the Chapter 3.1 assessment section on insider trading and abusive self-dealing) which led in 2014 to the imposition of administrative penalties of EUR 1 600 and EUR 1 500 against two individuals and EUR 20 000 against a brokerage firm for violating the Law on Markets in Financial Instruments rules' against insider trading and abusive self-dealing. Those sanctions were under appeal at the time of writing. Applicable fines were updated in July 2016 to align Lithuania's framework with EU regulations and increase sanctioning authority. In line with the updated framework, the Bank of Lithuania, in a more recent (early 2018) case, imposed a fine of EUR 200 000 on a company for not disclosing to the market information on a loan granted to another company owned by the first company's main shareholder. The company was expected to appeal the decision in court. Overall, it appears that the Bank of Lithuania, while active in surveying the market, has played a relatively limited role in terms of actual enforcement cases leading to sanctions. However, the Lithuanian authorities suggested that their framework mainly relies on private actions for enforcement of shareholder rights. Despite the limited extent and severity of enforcement actions undertaken, interviews with market participants suggested that the market regulator is considered to be even-handed and well-respected in its enforcement actions.

Table 2.9. Notifications received from the market and from the website of the supervisory authority on cases of possible market manipulation in 2013-2016

	2016	2015	2014	2013
Other notifications (email, phone, webpage)	2	3	3	5
Notifications from investment firms	5	8	10	3
Notifications from regulated market	4	1	3	13

Source: Bank of Lithuania

Figure 2.5. Number of notifications of all suspicious transactions, 2012-2017 (Bank of Lithuania internal system)

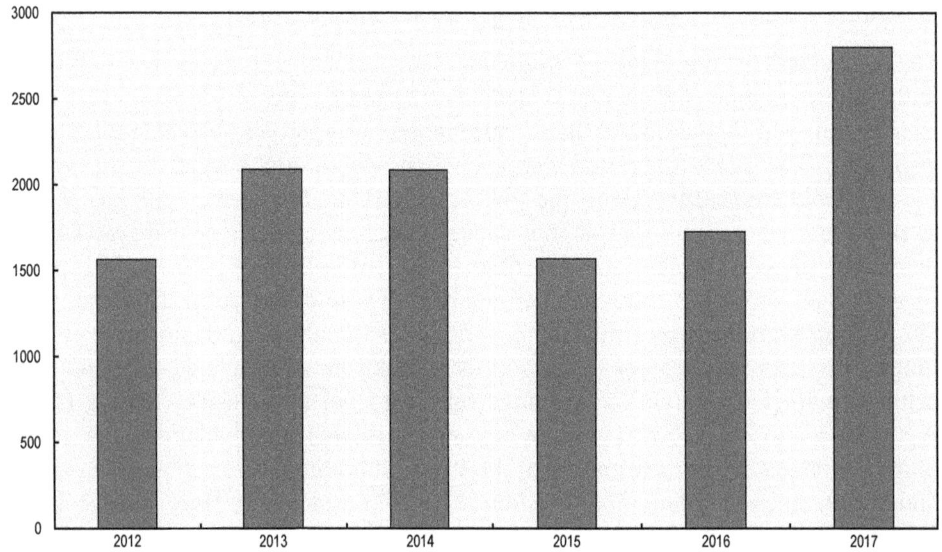

Source: Bank of Lithuania

Figure 2.6. Breakdown of all suspicious transactions per category of offence, 2013-2017

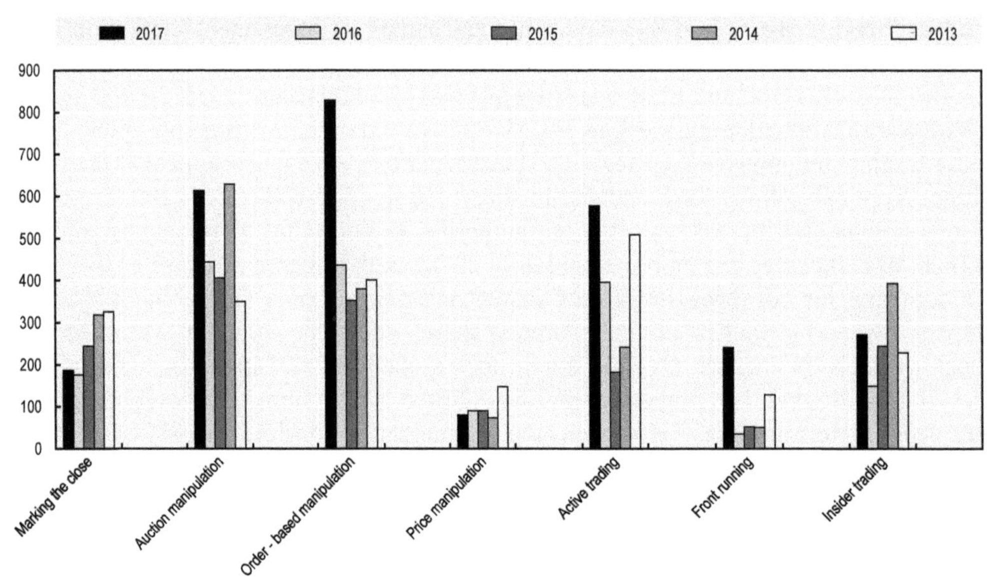

Source: Bank of Lithuania

Table 2.10. Information on reviews of suspicious transactions and the outcomes thereof, 2013-2016

	2016	2015	2014	2013
Detailed analysis (number of cases)	20	28	29	46
Verbal warnings	4	4	3	12
Warning letters (written warnings)	5	4	8	5

Source: Bank of Lithuania

Private enforcement and Lithuania's court system

Enforcement is mainly handled through private actions under civil law in Lithuanian courts. (There are no specialised courts for hearing company law matters.) The Civil Code states that subjects of civil relationships shall act according to the principles of justice, reasonableness and good faith (Art. 1.5). Furthermore, decisions of the bodies of a legal person may, in judicial proceedings, be declared void where they contravene the imperative provisions of the law, incorporation documents of a legal person or principles of reasonableness and good faith. Where the decision infringes their rights or interests, action can be taken by the creditors of a legal person, a respective managing body of a legal person, member of a legal person or other persons prescribed by the law. (See Civil Code Articles 1.5, 2.81.3 and 2.82.4.)

The Civil Code also provides for the ability of shareholders – acting alone or as part of a group – to request that the court appoint an investigator to investigate whether a company's managing body or its members acted improperly. Under this procedure, which was introduced to the Civil Code in 2001 in order to strengthen shareholder rights, an application for an investigation may be filed with the district court (depending on the location of the legal person's registered office). The application can only be made after the shareholder or shareholders have tried to resolve the question or conflict directly with the managing body or its member(s). If the court agrees to accept an application for an investigation, the court then appoints an expert investigator (which can be a confirmation of an investigator already agreed to by all parties or court-appointed). The court then reviews the report prepared by the investigator and may apply one of the following measures: (i) revoke the decisions taken by the legal person's managing body; (ii) temporarily suspend the powers of the members of company's managing body, or exclude a person from the managing body; (iii) appoint provisional members to the company's managing body; (iv) authorise non-implementation of certain provisions of incorporation documents (this provision provides the court with authority to deem certain provisions of a company's articles of corporation as unfair or unlawful and thus not legally binding); (v) oblige the making of amendments to certain provisions of incorporation documents; (vi) transfer the voting rights of a member of a legal person's body; (vii) oblige a legal person to take or not take certain actions; or (viii) liquidate a legal person and appoint a liquidator.

The Lithuanian authorities reported that in 2015, 2 288 commercial cases were filed at the county court level among five county courts; 978 cases were considered at the Court of Appeals, and 53 reached the level of the Supreme Court. However, it was not possible to obtain data on how many of these cases may have been related to shareholder or management disputes involving listed companies, or on their outcomes. The Chapter 3.1 assessment sub-section dealing with the market for corporate control and Box 3.1 highlight experience involving five specific court cases related to enforcement of takeover law provisions in Lithuania. These show a strong record of enforcement of minority shareholder interests at the Supreme Court level, but less consistent treatment of these issues at the lower court levels. For other issues, shareholder private actions appear to be less common due to the costs and time involved in pursuing such cases and the fact that damages awarded must be paid by the company rather than the controlling shareholder *per se*, undermining the incentive of the individual shareholder to take such actions, since gains and losses must be shared by all. Nevertheless, as noted in the Chapter 3.1 assessment sub-section dealing with minority shareholder protections, fact-finding interviews with representatives from the private sector indicated that, in general, minority shareholders may bring their claims to court and that Lithuanian courts can effectively deal with these disputes. Such cases are not uncommon, and have been brought by both resident and foreign shareholders.

On a more general level, external observers report that the judicial process in Lithuania has seen substantial improvements in recent years. This is due in part to judicial trainings to facilitate the judiciary's understanding and implementation of new provisions, laws and regulations introduced in Lithuania to comply with EU law (EBRD, 2012).

Division of enforcement responsibilities (Principle I.C)

Principle I.C states that the division of responsibilities among different authorities should be clearly articulated and designed to serve the public interest.

Lithuania's self-evaluation report states that, under the Law on Public Administration, public administration bodies must avoid the abuse of power and must seek proportionality and efficiency in their actions (Art 3). Therefore, public bodies are required to coordinate and to provide each other information or assistance as required.

The public agencies engaged in developing, implementing and enforcing Lithuania's legal and regulatory corporate governance framework for listed companies and their responsibilities have been described in the landscape section of this report. Their respective responsibilities appear to be clearly specified and allocated among these different bodies (see Chapter 2.5 section dealing with the institutional framework). This includes the Ministry of Economy for the Law on Companies; the Bank of Lithuania for enforcing the Law on Securities and the Law on Markets in Financial Instruments; the Ministry of Finance for developing accounting and auditing laws; the Authority of Audit, Accounting, Property Valuation and Insolvency Management for the enforcement of audit standards and the supervision of the audit profession (with some functions delegated to the Chamber of Auditors) and the enforcement of the insolvency framework; the Ministry of Justice, for oversight of the Register of Enterprises; and Nasdaq Vilnius, for monitoring trading on the exchange and enforcing the listing rules (though, as noted before, such cases are in practice referred to the Bank of Lithuania). The Bank of Lithuania is also responsible for the enforcement of accounting standards in listed companies.

Stock market regulation (Principle I.D)

Principle I.D. states that stock market regulation should support effective corporate governance.

Stock market rules supporting corporate governance, as described above (in the Chapter 2.5 section on the legal and regulatory framework) include Nasdaq Vilnius listing rules and recommendations on corporate governance contained in the Nasdaq Vilnius Corporate Governance Code. On the latter, corporate governance reports on compliance with the Code are legally required as part of listed companies' annual reports under the Law on Securities, which is enforced by the Bank of Lithuania. For its part, the Nasdaq

Vilnius exchange supervises issuers' activity as per the listing rules and Nasdaq Vilnius Corporate Governance Code. As noted above, the exchange may take certain disciplinary measures against issuers. When this happens, the exchange's management board must notify the Bank of Lithuania.

Integrity and resources of enforcement authorities (Principle I.E)

Principle I.E states that supervisory, regulatory and enforcement authorities should have the authority, integrity and resources to fulfil their duties in a professional and objective manner. Moreover, their rulings should be timely, transparent, and fully explained.

As noted in the Chapter 2.5 section on the institutional framework, public enforcement of the corporate governance framework largely rests with the Bank of Lithuania. The Bank is an independent institution established under the Law on the Bank of Lithuania (Art. 3). It appears to have both a governance structure and a budgetary process that provide it with a degree of independence from both the Government and the legislature.

The Lithuanian self-evaluation reports that the Bank exercises its powers within the remits set forth under the Law on the Bank of Lithuania and other laws and has the resources to fulfil its duties. The on-going operations of the Bank of Lithuania are managed by four services, four departments and three autonomous divisions. Most relevant to this review is the Supervision Service's Financial Services and Markets Supervision Department. Pursuant to the Law on the Bank of Lithuania, the costs of financial market supervision (around EUR 7.4 million) are funded by the contributions of supervised financial market participants (60%) and the Bank of Lithuania's own funds (40%). The Supervision Service has 126 employees, 44 of whom are employees of the Financial Services and Markets Supervision Department. The human resources and annual budget of the Supervision Service are determined by the Board of the Bank.

The Bank of Lithuania is governed by the Board of the Bank, consisting of a Chairperson, two Deputy Chairpersons and two Members. The Chair of the Board is nominated by the President and appointed by the Parliament to a five-year term. Other board members are nominated by the Chair and appointed by the President to staggered, six-year terms, which may be renewed for a second term. The current Chairman was appointed to a second five-year term in April 2016, demonstrating a history of stability within the Bank's governance structure.

Enforcement of the accounting and auditing framework, as described further in the relevant Chapter 3.2 assessment section, rests largely with the newly (as of January 2016) re-organised Authority of Audit, Accounting, Property Valuation and Insolvency Management under the Ministry of Finance. Enforcement of the accounting framework for listed companies rests with the Bank of Lithuania.

Cross-border co-operation (Principle I.F)

Principle I.F states that cross-border co-operation should be enhanced, including through bilateral and multilateral arrangements for exchange of information.

Lithuania's self-evaluation report states that Lithuanian law allows for fluid cross-border co-operation between supervisory authorities. The core coordinator for this purpose is the Bank of Lithuania. According to the Law on the Bank of Lithuania (Art. 46), the Bank has the right to conclude agreements on co-operation in the area of financial market supervision with the institutions of other states performing financial market supervision, the European Banking Authority, the European Insurance and Occupational Pensions Authority, the European Securities and Markets Authority and other institutions of the Republic of Lithuania and foreign countries. Pursuant to the Law on International Treaties, the Bank informs the Ministry of Foreign Affairs on this co-operation.

The Bank may also cooperate with supervisory institutions of other EU Member States for the purpose of performing its functions. Co-operation shall cover the exchange of information, participation in investigation or inspection activities or the performance of other supervisory functions at the initiative of any of the supervisory institutions.

Cross-border co-operation is also facilitated by bilateral and multilateral arrangements with various foreign countries. For example, Lithuania has joined the Multilateral Memorandum of Understanding (MMoU), which is the basis for co-operation and exchange of information among the International Organization of Securities Commissions (IOSCO) members and participates in the activities of the European Securities and Markets Authority, which ensures effective co-operation.

2.7 Overview of the SOE sector

This section provides an overview of the size and sectoral composition of Lithuania's state-owned enterprise sector and of the legal forms under which SOEs operate. Chapter 2.8 that follows describes the legal and regulatory framework for SOEs' corporate governance, which is assessed in Chapter 3 of this report. A review of the corporate governance of Lithuanian SOEs was undertaken in 2015 and is available on the OECD website (OECD, 2015). The main findings of that review, complemented with information on recent developments in SOEs' ownership and corporate governance arrangements, have informed related sections in this accession review.

As of end-2015, there were 128 directly-owned SOEs in Lithuania and an additional five listed subsidiaries. End-2015 figures are used throughout the report to ensure consistency and comparability of data. However, it is important to note that following a number of restructurings in the state's SOE portfolio (including mergers in the forestry and road maintenance sectors), there were 66 SOEs as of February 2018. As most of the reduction in the number of SOEs has been achieved through mergers, the end-2015 figures still broadly reflect the characteristics of the Lithuanian SOE portfolio in terms of corporate value, employment and sectoral distribution.

Lithuanian SOEs can take one of three legal forms: (i) state enterprises (*Valstybės įmonės* – statutory SOEs), which have no shares and can only be owned by the state; (ii) private limited liability companies (*Uždarosios akcinės bendrovės*) whose shares cannot be traded publicly, unless laws provide otherwise; and (iii) public limited liability companies (*Akcinės bendrovės* – joint stock companies), whose shares can be sold and traded on a stock exchange. The latter two categories are referred to as "fully corporatised SOEs" throughout this report. As of end-2015, the state was full or majority owner of 79 statutory SOEs, 19 public LLCs and 30 private LLCs. The five listed SOE subsidiaries are all incorporated as public LLCs. Table 2.11 provides an overview of Lithuanian SOEs by legal form, size and board structure. The majority of large SOEs in Lithuania (18 out of 24) have the legal form of statutory SOEs. The majority of SOEs with boards (63 out of the 70 that have established boards) have adopted a one-tier management board structure. Statutory SOEs are not legally permitted to establish two-tier boards.

Table 2.11. Overview of Lithuanian SOEs by legal form and size (end 2015)

Category	Number	Asset value as percentage of all SOEs	Number of SOEs with the following board structures		
			One-tier management	Two-tier	No board
Statutory SOEs (state enterprises)	79 (of which 18 are large SOEs)	39.32%	31	0	48
Private limited liability companies	30 (of which 2 are large SOEs)	36.24%	20	4	6
Public limited liability companies	19 (of which 4 are large SOEs)	24.45%	12	3	4
Listed subsidiaries of public limited liability companies	5	N/A	1	4	0
Totals	128 SOEs + 5 listed subsidiaries	100%	63 SOEs + 1 listed subsidiary	7 SOEs + 4 listed subsidiaries	58 SOEs

Source: OECD Secretariat calculations based on information provided by the Lithuanian authorities. Note: For the purpose of this Table, "large" SOEs are those included in the largest size categories (I and II) of the Ownership Guidelines discussed in Chapter 2.8.

Figure 2.7. Size of the state-owned enterprise sector relative to national employment

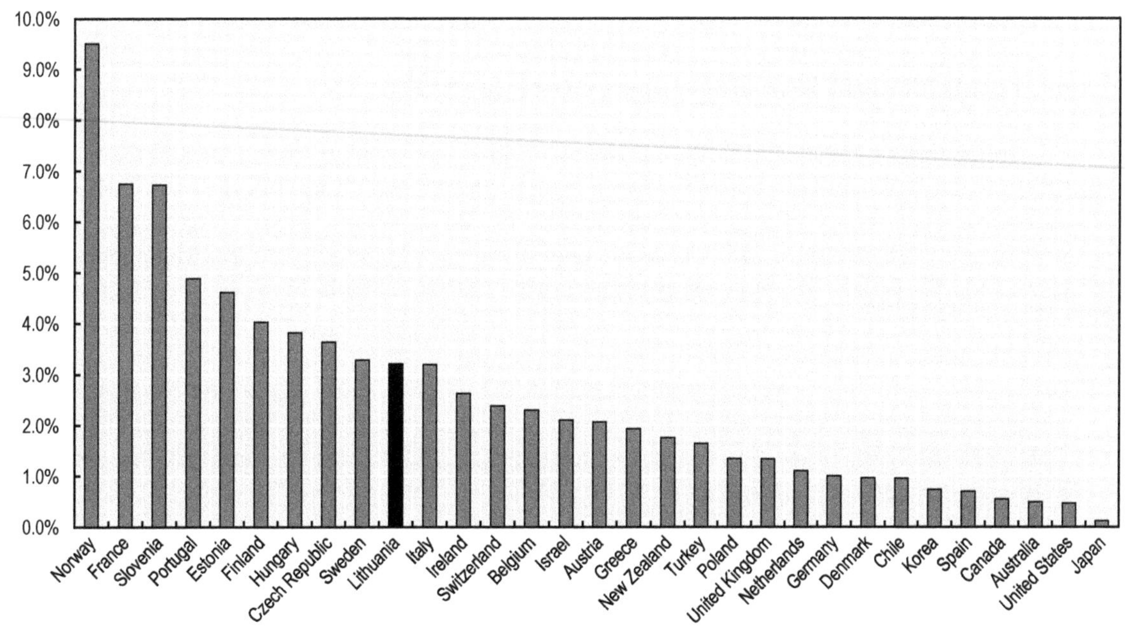

Source: OECD (2014), *The Size and Sectoral Distribution of SOEs in OECD and Partner Countries*, Paris, OECD.

SOEs in Lithuania account for approximately 3.2% of national employment. This is above the 2.4% average for all OECD countries and places Lithuania in line with the top ten OECD countries with the largest SOE sectors relative to national employment (Figure 2.7). The size and sectoral composition of the Lithuanian SOE sector is largely comparable to that of other post-transition Eastern European economies. By valuation, SOEs are most concentrated in the electricity and gas, transportation and primary sectors. The largest SOE employers are Lithuanian Railways, Lithuanian Energy and Lithuanian Post, together employing 23 401 people.

Table 2.12. Overview of the size and sectoral distribution of Lithuanian state-owned enterprises (end-2015)

Sector	Number of enterprises	Number of employees	Value of enterprises (EUR million)
Total	**128**	**40 711**	**5 165**
Primary sectors (including forestry)	42	3 642	1 156
Manufacturing	4	336	24
Finance	5	149	36
Telecoms	1	359	32
Electricity and gas	9	9 165	1 877
Transportation	18	16 290	1 858
Other utilities	1	5 766	28
Real estate	0	0	0
Other activities	48	5 004	154

Source: OECD (2017), *The Size and Sectoral Distribution of SOEs in OECD and Partner Countries*, OECD, Paris.

Lithuania has decentralised state ownership arrangements, with 12 ministries (in their own capacity, or via ministerial departments) and 5 other public institutions exercising ownership rights in SOEs. A Governance Coordination Centre (GCC) was established in 2012, to monitor and report on SOEs' compliance with the state's disclosure standards for SOEs and make recommendations for improving SOEs' governance arrangements, among other functions. One of its key tasks since its establishment has been to prepare and publish annual aggregate reports on the operations and performance of SOEs.

2.8 Legal, regulatory and governance framework for SOEs

Depending on their legal form, the two main laws governing Lithuanian SOEs are: (i) the Law on Companies, applicable to all fully corporatised SOEs and (ii) the Law on State and Municipal Enterprises, applicable to all statutory SOEs. The main law concerning the exercise of the state's ownership function is the Law on the Management, Use and Disposal of State and Municipal Assets, which notably outlines the responsibilities of the GCC.[16] These laws are complemented by a number of additional governmental resolutions pertaining to SOEs, the two most important of which are (i) the Ownership Guidelines, which establish requirements for SOEs' corporate governance arrangements, including as relates to the exercise of the ownership function; and (ii) the Transparency Guidelines, which outline the reporting and disclosure standards that large SOEs are mandated to implement.

Law on Companies

As mentioned previously, the Law on Companies, applicable to Lithuania's 49 fully corporatised SOEs, was amended in November 2017. Provisions in three areas merit mentioning here for their implications on SOEs' corporate governance arrangements. The first area concerns requirements for establishing boards of directors. As mentioned in Chapter 2.4, the Law on Companies does not require private LLCs to establish boards (applicable to 30 SOEs), whereas public LLCs are required to establish either a supervisory or a management board (applicable to 19 SOEs). In practice, as of end-2016, the majority (46 out of 49) of fully corporatised SOEs had established boards. The three without boards are private LLCs and in the smallest size category. (This constitutes an update to the end-2015 information on boards reported elsewhere in the report, notably in Table 2.11.)

The second area concerns controlling shareholders' right to privileged access to information. As detailed in the Chapter 3 assessment on shareholder rights and equitable treatment, prior to amendments enacted in November 2017, the Law on Companies accorded any shareholder or group of shareholders who held or controlled at least half of company shares the explicit right to access all company documents, pursuant to submitting a pledge to the company – in a form approved by the company – not to disclose commercial or industry secrets (former Art. 18). This means that the state as a controlling shareholder could legally access company information that was not simultaneously available to minority shareholders. This, combined with the state's representation on the boards of most SOEs, arguably increased the scope for the state's involvement in their day-to-day management. The amendments to the Law on Companies enacted in November 2017 appear to largely address this concern, since the problematic provision has since been removed and all shareholders are accorded the explicit right to access certain corporate information upon request.

The third area relates to an amendment enacted to the Law on Companies in April 2017 which introduced maximum term limits and reappointment criteria applicable only to the CEOs of SOEs. The provision notably requires that the CEOs of SOEs be dismissed after five years if they do not fulfil their objectives and places a two-term limit on their employment. (See Chapter 2.8 section on recent or ongoing reforms in the SOE sector and Chapter 3.3 assessment section on simplifying and standardising SOE legal forms. Parallel amendments were made to the Law on State and Municipal Enterprises introducing maximum term limits and reappointment criteria for the CEOs of statutory SOEs.)

Law on State and Municipal Enterprises

The Law on State and Municipal Enterprises is applicable to all statutory SOEs in Lithuania. The 79 statutory SOEs in place as of end 2015 have since been substantially reduced through the 2017 mergers of the 11 road maintenance and 42 forestry enterprises into two large SOEs. As they remained statutory enterprises, their mergers had no impact on the applicable legislation. The government has also announced plans to privatise, consolidate or convert most remaining statutory SOEs to limited liability companies or public institutions, which if implemented would result in five statutory SOEs remaining under this separate legal form by end 2019.[17] These plans are discussed in greater detail in the below section on recent or ongoing reforms in the SOE sector.

The Law on State and Municipal Enterprises includes provisions related to their creation, operations, reorganisation and liquidation. Concerning its implications on the corporate governance arrangements of statutory SOEs, the Law notably outlines their required governance organs, the criteria for (management) board composition and the respective roles and responsibilities of the ownership entity (usually the line ministry exercising ownership rights), the board and the CEO. Key provisions in these areas can be summarised as follows.

- *Governance organs*. The required governance organs of a statutory SOE are the "institution exercising the rights and duties of the owner of the enterprise" (the ownership entity) and the "single person management body" (the manager/CEO).[18] The articles of association, which are to be approved by the ownership entity, may also provide for the establishment of a one-tier management board, which may include non-executive members.[19] The Law does not allow for the establishment of a two-tier board structure. The articles of association must indicate the respective responsibilities of the enterprise's governance organs only if different from those explicitly enumerated in the Law on State and Municipal Enterprises.

- *Composition of boards.* If a management board is established through the enterprise's articles of association, it must include at least three persons and its members must be civil servants and other natural persons. The CEO of the enterprise may also be appointed a member of the management board. For large statutory SOEs, other natural persons must make up at least 1/3 of management board members, a provision intended to allow for independent directors on the boards of statutory SOEs.[20] A number of general qualifications necessary for natural persons to serve on boards are established.
- *Responsibilities of the ownership entity.* The ownership entity is responsible, among others, for approving the enterprise's strategy, appointing and dismissing the CEO, appointing and removing board members (if a board is established) and selecting the auditor or auditing firm. The ownership entity has the explicit right to remove all or some of the board members before the expiry of their four-year term of office. Where individual board members are removed or resign, new board members shall be appointed to the standing board until the expiry of the term for which the board was formed. (Large statutory SOEs are required separately by the Ownership Guidelines, discussed below, to establish boards.)
- *Responsibilities of the board.* Where a board is established, it is responsible, among others, for determining the structure of the enterprise and communicating to the ownership entity drafts (for approval) of the enterprise's strategy, activity report(s) and other operational documents outlined in the Law.
- *Responsibilities of the CEO.* The CEO ("manager" by national nomenclature) is responsible, among others, for drafting the enterprise's strategy, activity report(s) and other operational documents, and for communicating them to the board (if established) or the ownership entity.

Key differences in the legal framework applicable to statutory SOEs, as compared to the legal framework applicable to fully corporatised SOEs, are further outlined in the Chapter 3.3 assessment on simplifying and standardising SOE legal forms.

Law on the Management, Use and Disposal of State and Municipal Assets

The Law on the Management, Use and Disposal of State and Municipal Assets applies to all state assets, including securities held by the state. In essence, it stipulates that the responsibility for the ownership of state assets resides with both the *Seimas* (the Lithuanian Parliament) and the Government (the Council of Ministers). It also outlines that state and municipal assets must be used, managed and disposed of in an efficient manner and in the public interest.

As of amendments enacted on 20 April 2017, the Law also outlines the functions of the Monitoring and Forecast Agency, a public institution under the remit of the Ministry of Economy which now houses the state's SOE monitoring and coordination function, known as the "Governance Coordination Centre" (GCC). Prior to the amendments, the GCC was housed in the Bank of Property (*Turto Bankas*), a statutory SOE under the Ministry of Finance. It was transferred to the Monitoring and Forecast Agency to address a shortcoming in its institutional arrangements – which was highlighted in the OECD's

2015 SOE review – namely the fact that the GCC was located in an SOE that it was simultaneously responsible for monitoring (OECD, 2015). The Law entitles the Monitoring and Forecast Agency to receive information from ownership ministries on SOEs' compliance with the state's governance and transparency standards. It also accords the Monitoring and Forecast Agency responsibility for publishing annual and interim reports on SOEs' operations, advising SOEs on their operational strategy and governance practices and making proposals to ownership ministries on SOEs' dividend levels and public policy obligations. The amendments transferring the GCC to the Monitoring and Forecast Agency entered into force on 1 July 2017.

Law on State Enterprises and Facilities of Strategic Importance to National Security and Other Enterprises of Importance to Ensuring National Security

The Law on State Enterprises and Facilities of Strategic Importance to National Security and Other Enterprises of Importance to Ensuring National Security sets forth a number of conditions pertaining to enterprises identified as important to national security, notably regarding their share ownership, the state's power of decision when issues of national security are deemed to arise and their change in legal form (Table 2.13). Amendments to the Law were enacted on 12 January 2018, which do not appear to have any material implications for the corporate governance of SOEs.

Table 2.13. Lithuanian SOEs and other enterprises considered of importance to national security

State and municipal enterprises (statutory SOEs) that must be owned by the state	State-owned limited liability companies whose capital can be shared, provided that the state retains power of decision	Other enterprises identified of importance to national security, and for which laws may set forth additional requirements for their operation
Nuclear enterprise	Lithuanian Energy Production	ORLEN Lietuva*
Klaipeda Seaport enterprise	EPSO-G	Project implementation company defined in the Law of the Nuclear Power Plant
Oil products enterprise	Lithuanian Energy	Telia Lietuva*
Air navigation enterprise	Litgrid	Achema*
Inland Waterways enterprise	Lithuanian Electricity Distribution Network Operator	
Lithuanian Airports enterprise	Amber Grid	
Šiauliai Airport (municipality-owned enterprise)	Liquefied Natural Gas (LNG) terminal operator and project implementation company	
Enterprise responsible for the state registry	Klaipeda Oil	
Data transmission operator enterprise	Lithuanian Railways	
Forestry enterprise	Giraite Armament Factory	
Water supply and wastewater extraction service enterprise	Jonava Grains	
	Lithuanian Radio and Television Centre	
	Lithuanian Post	
	Geoterma	
	Detonas	
	Operator of electricity distribution	
	National investor	

Source: Law on State Enterprises and Facilities of Strategic Importance to National Security and Other Enterprises of Importance to Ensuring National Security, English translation provided by the Lithuanian authorities. * Companies which are not majority-owned by the Lithuanian state or municipal governments.

Ownership policy and related SOE regulations

Ownership Guidelines

The Ownership Guidelines (approved by the Government Resolution number 665 "On the Approval of the Procedure for the Implementation of the State's Property and Non-Property Rights at State-owned Enterprises", 2012) outline the rights and responsibilities of all state ownership entities regarding the implementation of SOE governance arrangements. (In Lithuania, Government Resolutions are what in many other jurisdictions would be called either "decrees" or "administrative acts".) This is the document by which the Lithuanian Government outlines its ownership policy for SOEs. It includes both mandatory standards imposed on state ownership entities – such as ensuring the establishment of management boards in all SOEs of a certain size – as well as optional provisions which state ownership entities are expected to implement on a "comply-or-explain" basis. For the purpose of this report, "state ownership entity" refers to the authority responsible for exercising the state's ownership rights in a given SOE. The main provisions of the Ownership Guidelines are outlined below.

- *The Governance Coordination Centre.* The Governance Coordination Centre (GCC) is established as an authority designated to monitor and analyse the implementation of the Ownership Guidelines by state ownership entities. Its mandate is reproduced in Box 2.3.[21]

Box 2.3 The mandate of the Governance Coordination Centre housed in the Monitoring and Forecast Ageny

The public institution "Monitoring and Forecasting Agency" shall[1]:

(1) Be entitled to receive from institutions implementing rights and duties of the state as a legal entity participant in state-owned enterprises information on the activities of these enterprises, their results and decisions related to the governance of these enterprises with the state implementing property and non-property rights; having received this information, it shall monitor and analyse the compliance of these enterprises with the requirements of governance, transparency and execution of indicators;

(2) Each year prepare and publish on its website the summary of annual and interim reports on state-owned enterprises and their activities;

(3) Advise institutions implementing rights and duties of the state as a legal entity participant in state-owned enterprises, as well as other public limited liability companies and private limited liability companies where shares owned by the state confer thereto ½ or more votes in the general meeting of shareholders (hereinafter – companies) on the efficient governance of these enterprises and companies, the implementation of strategies, long-term and short-term goals and the achieved results of implementation of specific indicators, and give recommendations on how to improve these indicators;

(4) Advise and provide methodological assistance to state-owned enterprises and companies on issues of preparation of strategies and improvement of governance of state-owned enterprises;

(5) Provide proposals to institutions implementing rights and duties of the state as a legal entity participant in state-owned enterprises and companies on issues of calculating dividends and profit contributions;

(6) Provide proposals to institutions implementing rights and duties of the state as a legal entity participant in state-owned enterprises and companies on special obligations conducted by these enterprises.

1 The Monitoring and Forecast Agency is a public institution under the Ministry of Economy to which the GCC's functions were transferred in July 2017. Reference to the GCC, rather than to the Monitoring and Forecast Agency, is maintained throughout the text as the commonly used term to refer to the unit responsible for monitoring and reporting on SOE governance practices and performance.

Source : Unofficial translation of the Law Amending Article 23 of the Law on the Management, Use and Disposal of State and Municipal Assets, provided by the Lithuanian authorities. The amendments were enacted on 20 April 2017.

- *Separation of the state's role as an owner and a regulator.* Where a state ownership entity in a given sector exercises both the state's ownership rights and a sectoral policy function, these must be carried out by separate departments to avoid conflicts of interest. It is recommended that public servants involved in sectoral policy do not serve on the boards of SOEs operating in the concerned sector.

- *Categorisation of SOEs according to their objectives.* State-owned enterprises are classified into three groups according to their objectives (those in group 1A are expected to maximise profits, those in 1B to also fulfil objectives in the national strategic interest, and those in group 2 to primarily fulfil national social or political objectives, with profit seeking taking a secondary role). State ownership entities shall, when necessary, review SOEs' objectives as well as the rationale for their continued state ownership and their legal form.

- *Objectives of individual SOEs.* State ownership entities shall ensure that SOEs in groups 1A and 1B seek growth in business value and obtain an adequate return on capital for the state, and that SOEs in group 2 seek profitability. Every three years the GCC shall calculate the target capital structures for all SOEs and, with the consent of the shareholding entity, submit them to the Government for approval. Short- and long-term financial and non-financial objectives shall be set for SOEs and their implementation monitored by their governance organs.

- *Procedures for objectives-setting.* The "relevant governance organs" of SOEs are to develop annual strategies and submit them to the GCC for review and comment, following which the state ownership entity submits the strategies to the Government for approval.

- *Supervision of implementation.* State ownership entities shall ensure that the governance organs responsible for developing SOEs' strategies report annually on strategy implementation. State ownership entities shall submit the strategy implementation reports to the GCC, who within two months shall submit a summary report on strategy implementation to the Government.

- *Sanctions in case of failure to achieve objectives.* If an SOE fails to achieve its objectives, state ownership entities shall: examine the suitability of relevant members of the management board; and ensure that the variable part of remuneration is reduced or not paid to the CEO and, where applicable, management board members.

- *Formation of boards.* SOEs are divided into five size categories according to sales revenue and assets (Table 2.14). State ownership entities shall ensure that all large SOEs (size categories I and II), or those of strategic importance to national security, at least establish one-tier management boards. Taking into account the SOEs that fall into both categories, 27 directly-owned SOEs are required to establish boards and do so in practice (the 24 large SOEs, plus Detonas, Giraitė Armament Factory and Jonava Grains) as well as four listed SOE subsidiaries in the energy sector.[22] Not counting the SOE subsidiaries separately, the SOEs in which boards are required account for 87.74% of all SOEs by asset value (as shown in Table 2.11, other SOEs have established boards, although are not mandated to do so.)

- *Board committees*. State ownership entities shall ensure that all large SOEs establish both an internal control committee and a remuneration committee. Both committees must be composed of at least three members. The internal control committee must include one independent member.
- *Ministerial selection committees for SOE boards*. A board selection committee is established comprising the Minister of Economy, the Minister of Finance and the head of the ownership entity. The GCC is invited to provide technical advice to the selection committee, where appropriate. In March 2017, this section of the Ownership Guidelines was amended and the related text was revised and essentially transferred to a separate resolution on the SOE board nomination process.
- *Duties of the state ownership entity*. State ownership entities shall appoint one employee or civil servant to oversee a specific SOE. They should ensure timely transfer of SOE dividends or profit contributions to the state budget.
- *Exercising the state's rights as a shareholder*. State ownership entities shall ensure that SOEs' articles of association empower the board to adopt specific decisions referenced in the Lithuanian Law on Companies and applicable to the boards of private enterprises. State ownership entities may nominate an authorised representative to vote on their behalf at general meetings.
- *Composition of SOE boards*. State ownership entities shall ensure that the majority of SOE board members are not employees of the enterprise and that in large SOEs one third of management board members are independent. Boards are advised not to elect the CEO as chair of the management board, unless a supervisory board is also in place. Amendments to the Ownership Guidelines which entered into force on 24 March 2017 require that all SOE boards (where they are formed) include at least one half independent members. SOEs had until January 2018 to comply with this new requirement. This applies to all SOEs that have established boards, including (but not limited to) the 24 large SOEs and the three SOEs of strategic importance that are required by other legal provisions to establish boards. In practice, the Lithuanian authorities only consider 43 SOEs to be "active" and thus under the scope of the board independence requirements, owing to the authorities' plans to privatise or convert the other 23 SOEs into other legal forms.
- *Selection criteria for board members*. General selection criteria for both board members and the CEO are established, including notably educational level and lack of criminal record. Criteria are established for board members to be considered independent, including not being an employee of the enterprise or of the state ownership entity. Ministerial selection committees are invited, where appropriate, to develop more specific selection criteria for the board members of large SOEs.
- *Process of board nomination*. The process for board nomination for large fully corporatised SOEs (categories I and II) is laid out as follows: the board conducts an annual self-evaluation; the state ownership entity sends results to the GCC; the GCC sends results and recommendations to the Ministerial selection committee; if the selection committee fails to agree then the nomination shall be decided by the Government. While this provision is only applicable to large fully

corporatised SOEs, the Lithuanian authorities have since established a more broadly applicable board nomination process to implement the March 2017 independence requirements in both fully corporatised and statutory SOEs, which is discussed in the Chapter 3.3 section on SOE board nomination processes.)

- *Remuneration of SOE board members and executives.* It is recommended that for fully corporatised SOEs, remuneration of supervisory and management board members be a fixed amount not exceeding one quarter of the CEO's remuneration. It is recommended that remuneration be reduced or discontinued for board members that do not regularly attend meetings or vote on agenda issues.

Several provisions of the Ownership Guidelines apply differently to large and smaller SOEs, defined as such using a combination of enterprises' sales revenues and assets on a scale ranging from roman numbers I to V (reproduced in Table 2.14). In most cases the highest standards of governance apply to SOEs in the two largest categories. As of end-2015, 24 individual SOEs fell under the categories I and II, representing 87.43% of all SOEs by asset value. Importantly, the Ownership Guidelines do not apply explicitly to the subsidiaries of SOEs under direct state ownership. Instead, ownership entities are encouraged to strive towards the application, within SOE subsidiaries, of those elements of the Ownership Guidelines pertaining to the establishment and monitoring (involving the GCC) of enterprise-specific objectives, return targets and strategies.

Table 2.14. Size categories of SOEs

Assets, EUR million	Sales revenues (past financial year), EUR million					
	Up to 3	3 to 6	6 to 15	15 to 30	30 to 60	60 and above
Up to 3	V	V	IV	IV	III	III
3 to 6	V	IV	IV	III	III	II
6 to 15	IV	IV	III	III	II	II
15 to 30	IV	III	III	II	II	I
30 to 60	III	III	II	II	I	I
60 and above	III	II	II	I	I	I

Source: Lithuanian Ownership Guidelines (2012)

Transparency Guidelines

The Transparency Guidelines (approved by the Government Resolution number 1052 "On the Approval of the Guidelines for Ensuring Transparency of the Activities of State-Owned Enterprises and Designating a Co-ordinating Authority", 2010) establish disclosure standards that are mandatory for Lithuania's 13 largest SOEs.[23] The Lithuanian authorities reported that they had reversed a previous decision to make the Transparency Guidelines mandatory for 85 "large and public interest" SOEs. The Transparency Guidelines also designate the Ministry of Economy as the authority responsible for formulating and coordinating the implementation of policies relating to SOE governance. Their main provisions can be summarised as follows:

- *Scope of applicability.* The disclosure standards are mandatory for 13 large SOEs identified in the Law on Financial Reporting by Undertakings as "large enterprises". All other SOEs, irrespective of size or legal form, must implement the disclosure standards on a "comply-or-explain" basis. Importantly, the subsidiaries of companies under direct state ownership are not explicitly included in the scope of applicability, but the Transparency Guidelines recommend that state-owned parent companies take action to ensure they are implemented by majority-owned subsidiaries.

- *General information disclosure requirements*. All SOEs are encouraged to implement the information disclosure standards outlined in the Corporate Governance Code for listed companies (the 13 large SOEs must implement them). All SOEs must prepare annual reports (for fully corporatised SOEs) or annual activity statements (for statutory SOEs). Large SOEs must also prepare interim (quarterly) reports and statements. Information should be publicly accessible on the website of the SOE or the state ownership entity.
- *Content of annual and interim reports*. Annual and interim reports (or activity statements for statutory SOEs) should include, among others, information on: performance against strategic objectives; social and environmental policies and initiatives; and compliance with the provisions of the Transparency Guidelines, including explanations for any provisions not implemented.
- *Accounting and auditing standards for financial statements*. SOEs shall keep accounts in accordance with international accounting standards. Financial statements should be prepared on a quarterly and annual basis and be audited in accordance with international audit standards.
- *Submission and publication of reports and financial statements*. SOEs shall publish their annual and interim reports and financial statements on their websites or that of the state ownership entity, according to a specified schedule. SOEs should also publish information on any legally prescribed "special commitments" imposed by the state to implement social, strategic or political goals. SOEs shall submit their reports and financial statements to the relevant state ownership entity, along with information on senior executive remuneration for the preceding year.
- *Drafting and publication of the state's annual aggregate report*. The state ownership entity shall send (i) the aforementioned reports and financial statements to the GCC and (ii) information on the implementation of governance policies to the coordinating authority (Ministry of Economy). The GCC shall assess SOEs' compliance with the Transparency Guidelines and draft the state's annual aggregate report on SOEs. The GCC shall also submit proposals to the Government concerning the nature of SOEs' "special commitments", related funding arrangements and impact on SOE performance indicators.

Regulatory framework

Lithuanian SOEs do not appear to enjoy regulatory exemptions compared to private enterprises. They are notably included in the scope of the following laws applicable to private enterprises: the Law on Competition, the Law on Public Procurement and and sector-specific laws such as the Law on Energy. The 2015 SOE review pointed to some potential issues with the institutional arrangements for enforcing such laws. For example, the Public Procurement Office (PPO) is responsible for the implementation of the public procurement policy set by the Ministry of Economy, which itself oversees nine SOEs as of end-2015. This introduces the potential for conflict of interest in the Public Procurement Office's application of the Law on Public Procurement, notably in instances where SOEs owned by the Ministry of Economy engage in public procurement. However, the Lithuanian authorities assert that the Public Procurement Office is an independent institution. Other instances point to apparently fruitful efforts to strengthen the independence of regulators and separate the state's ownership and regulatory functions. For example, the Competition Council is an independent competition authority financed directly from the state budget, which has in practice undertaken a number of investigations involving SOEs.

Board structures and composition in Lithuania's largest SOEs: Changes from 2015 to 2018

As noted previously, the legal framework for both fully corporatised and statutory SOEs in Lithuania provides for considerable flexibility regarding both the board structures put in place and the respective responsibilities of SOEs' governance organs (i.e. ownership ministry, AGM, supervisory board, management board and CEO). In practice, one-tier management boards are the predominant model employed within SOEs (and are furthermore the only model possible for statutory SOEs). As of end-2015, two-tier board structures (with both supervisory and management boards) had been established in four individual SOEs and four listed SOE subsidiaries, while 63 SOEs and one listed subsidiary had one-tier management boards and 58 had no board in place (see Table 2.11 in previous section). Among the 58 SOEs with no board in place, 42 were state-owned forestry enterprises, in which the boards were abolished in 2015 as part of the foreseen restructuring of the sector. As of February 2018, no major changes in SOEs' board structures had occurred, with the exception of the establishment of boards in the newly consolidated State Forest Enterprise and Road Maintenance SOEs. Fourteen SOEs, most of which were in the smallest size category, had no boards in place. Nearly all of these were foreseen to undergo reorganisation or privatisation in the near term.

Concerning SOE board composition, since the OECD first reviewed the corporate governance of Lithuanian SOEs in 2015, Lithuania has undertaken a number of reforms to equip boards with more independent directors and shield them from political interference. The most recent of these reforms is the newly introduced rule (outlined in the preceding section on ownership policy and related SOE regulations) mandating that SOE boards comprise at least one half independent directors and precluding acting politicians from serving on SOE boards. As a result, compared to the situation in 2015, the boards of Lithuania's largest SOEs currently have no acting politicians and have undergone a substantial increase in independent directors. Based on evolutions in the board structure and composition of Lithuania's largest SOEs from the time of the 2015 review to February 2018, the following general observations can be made. (Table 2.15 provides a comparison of the board composition of Lithuania's largest SOEs between December 2016 and February 2018, as well as the board composition of the newly consolidated forestry and road maintenance enterprises.)

- Boards are in place in all of Lithuania's 24 largest SOEs (those in categories I and II), as well as the recently consolidated State Forest Enterprise and Road Maintenance SOE (which entered category I following their consolidation). Two large SOEs in the energy sector that previously (at the time of the 2015 SOE review) had no board in place – EPSO-G and Lithuanian Oil Products Agency – have established boards. As of February 2018, all of these newly created boards comply with the state's SOE board independence requirements (a minimum proportion of one half independent directors and no acting politicians), with the exception of Lithuanian Oil Products Agency, which is reportedly foreseen to undergo restructuring and eventually be liquidated by December 2018.

- Among (other) large SOEs in the energy sector, most have established two-tier board structures. Supervisory boards comprise mainly representatives of ownership ministries, but most also include at least one half independent members. The only exception is Lithuanian Oil Products Agency, which as mentioned previously is foreseen to undergo restructuring.
- The large SOEs in the transportation sector have one-tier management boards.24 As of February 2018, the four large transportation SOEs whose boards were previously chaired by vice ministers or other politically-affiliated individuals (Lithuanian Airports, Lithuanian Post, Klaipėda State Seaport Authority and Lithuanian Railways) all reportedly comply with the state's board independence rules.[25]

Table 2.15. Board structures and composition in Lithuania's largest SOEs and subsidiaries (December 2016 to February 2018)

SOE name, legal form and responsible ministry	Board structure and composition		
		December 2016	February 2018
Lithuanian Railways (Public LLC) *Ministry of Transport and Communications (MoTC)*	One-tier management board	**Chair:** Romas Švedas (independent) Monika Rimkūnaitė-Bložė (independent) Rolandas Zukas (independent) Paulius Martinkus (Vice Minister, MoTC) Mantas Bartuška (CEO, Lithuanian Railways)	**Chair:** Romas Švedas (independent) Monika Rimkūnaitė-Bložė (independent) Rolandas Zukas (independent) Vladislav Kondratovič (Director of Department, MoTC) Mantas Bartuška (CEO, Lithuanian Railways) *Note: Compliant with state's rules on board composition. Two additional independent board members were reportedly elected by the nomination committee, but not yet nominated by the shareholder. After nomination 5 out of 7 board members will be independent.*
Lithuanian Energy (Private LLC) *Ministry of Finance (MoF)*	Two-tier	**Supervisory board:** **Chair:** Šarūnas Kliokys (independent) Antanas Danys (independent) Virginijus Lepeška (independent) Agnė Bagočiutė (MoF) Rasa Noreikienė (Ministry of Economy) Tomas Garasimavičius (Office of the Government of the Republic of Lithuania) **Management board:** **Chair:** Dalius Misūnas (CEO, Lithuanian Energy) Darius Kašauskas (Lithuanian Energy) Mindaugas Keizeris (Lithuanian Energy) Dominykas Tučkus (Lithuanian Energy) Ilona Daugėlaitė (Lithuanian Energy)	**Supervisory board:** **Chair:** Darius Daubaras (independent) Daiva Lubinskaitė-Trainauskienė (independent) Andrius Pranckevičius (independent) Ramūnas Dilba (Director of Department, MoF) Aušra Vičkačkienė (Director of Department, MoF) **Management board:** **Chair:** Darius Maikštėnas (CEO, Lithuanian Energy) Darius Kašauskas (Lithuanian Energy) Vidmantas Salietis (Lithuanian Energy) Dominykas Tučkus (Lithuanian Energy) Živilė Skibarkienė (Lithuanian Energy) *Note: Compliant with state's rules on board composition*

SOE name, legal form and responsible ministry		Board structure and composition	
		December 2016	February 2018
► Lithuanian Energy Production (Public LLC, subsidiary of Lithuanian Energy) *MoF*	Two-tier	**Supervisory board:** **Chair:** Mindaugas Keizeris (Lithuanian Energy) Dominykas Tučkus (Lithuanian Energy) Pranas Vilkas (Independent) **Management board:** **Chair:** Eglė Čiužaitė (Lithuanian Energy Production CEO) Management board members: Adomas Birulis (Lithuanian Energy Production) Mindaugas Kvekšas (Lithuanian Energy Production) Darius Kucinas (Lithuanian Energy Production)	**Supervisory board:** **Chair:** Mindaugas Keizeris (Lithuanian Energy) Dominykas Tučkus (Lithuanian Energy) **Management board:** **Chair:** Eglė Čiužaitė (CEO, Lithuanian Energy Production) Management board members: Nerijus Rasburskis (Lithuanian Energy Production) Mindaugas Kvekšas (Lithuanian Energy Production) Darius Kucinas (Lithuanian Energy Production) *Note: Compliance with state's rules on board composition not mandatory because enterprise is an SOE subsidiary*
► ESO (Energy Distribution Operator[26]) (Public LLC, subsidiary of Lithuanian Energy) *MoF*	Two-tier	**Supervisory board:** **Chair:** Dalius Misiūnas (Lithuanian Energy CEO) Ilona Daugėlaitė (Lithuanian Energy) Petras Povilas Čėsna (independent) **Management board:** **Chair:** Dalia Andrulionienė (CEO, ESO) Augustas Dragūnas (ESO) Rytis Borkys (ESO) Dalius Svetulevičius (ESO)	**Supervisory board:** **Chair:** Unassigned Ilona Daugėlaitė (Lithuanian Energy) Petras Povilas Čėsna (independent) **Management board:** **Chair:** Dalia Andrulionienė (CEO, ESO) Augustas Dragūnas (ESO) Ignas Pranskevičius (ESO) Saulius Vaičekauskas (ESO) *Note: Compliance with state's rules on board composition not mandatory because enterprise is an SOE subsidiary*
EPSO-G (Private LLC) *Ministry of Energy*	Two-tier	**Supervisory board:** **Chair:** Viktorija Trimbel (independent) Inga Černiuk (Chancellor, Ministry of Energy) Agnė Amelija Petravičienė (Ministry of Energy) Raimondas Rapkevičius (independent) Audrius Misevičius (Office of the Government of the Republic of Lithuania) **Management board:** **Chair:** Rytis Ambrazevičius (independent) Gediminas Almantas (independent) Valdas Vitkauskas (independent) Rolandas Zukas (CEO, EPSO-G) Algirdas Juozaponis (EPSO-G)	**Supervisory board:** **Chair:** Viktorija Trimbel (independent) Inga Černiuk (Chancellor, MoTC) Agnė Amelija Petravičienė (Chancellor, Ministry of Energy) Raimondas Rapkevičius (independent) **Management board:** **Chair:** Rytis Ambrazevičius (independent) Gediminas Almantas (independent) Valdas Vitkauskas (independent) Rolandas Zukas (CEO, EPSO-G) Algirdas Juozaponis (EPSO-G) *Note: Compliant with state's rules on board composition*

SOE name, legal form and responsible ministry	Board structure and composition		
		December 2016	February 2018
► Litgrid (Public LLC, subsidiary of EPSO-G) *Ministry of Energy*	One-tier management board	**Chair:** Rimvydas Štilinis (EPSO-G) Daivis Virbickas (CEO, Litgrid) Vidmantas Grušas (Litgrid) Nemunas Biknius (EPSO-G) Domas Sidaravičius (independent)	**Chair:** Rimvydas Štilinis (EPSO-G) Daivis Virbickas (CEO, Litgrid) Vidmantas Grušas (Litgrid) Nemunas Biknius (EPSO-G) Domas Sidaravičius (independent) *Note: Compliance with state's rules on board composition not mandatory because enterprise is an SOE subsidiary.*
► Amber Grid (Public LLC, subsidiary of EPSO-G) *Ministry of Energy*	One-tier management board	**Chair:** Nemunas Biknius (EPSO-G) Saulius Bilys (CEO, Amber Grid) Vytautas Ruolia (Amber Grid) Rimvydas Štilinis (EPSO-G) Nerijus Datkūnas (independent)	**Chair:** Nemunas Biknius (EPSO-G) Saulius Bilys (CEO, Amber Grid) Vytautas Ruolia (Amber Grid) Rimvydas Štilinis (EPSO-G) Nerijus Datkūnas (independent) *Note: Compliance with state's rules on board composition not mandatory because enterprise is an SOE subsidiar.*
Klaipėda Oil (Public LLC) *Ministry of Energy*	Two-tier	**Supervisory board:** **Chair:** Agnė Amelija Petravičienė (Ministry of Energy) Romas Švedas (independent) Eimantas Kiudulas (independent) **Management board:** **Chair:** Unassigned Mindaugas Jusius (independent) Mantas Bartuška (CEO, Lithuanian Railways) Dainius Bražiūnas (Ministry of Energy) Giedrius Dusevičius (independent) Bjarke Pålsson (independent)	**Supervisory board:** Unassigned **Management board:** **Chair:** Unassigned Mantas Bartuška (CEO, Lithuanian Railways) Dainius Bražiūnas (Head of Division, Ministry of Energy) Giedrius Dusevičius (independent) Bjarke Pålsson (independent) *Note: Compliant with state's rules on board composition. Supervisory board members were reportedly elected by nomination committee, but not yet nominated by shareholder. The supervisory board will comprise three members (two independent), foreseen for nomination in mid-March.*
Lithuanian Oil Products Agency (State enterprise) *Ministry of Energy*	One-tier management board	**Chair:** Unassigned Karolis Švaikauskas (Ministry of Energy) Rimantas Butkus (independent)	**Chair:** Unassigned Karolis Švaikauskas (Deputy Head of Division, Ministry of Energy) Rimantas Butkus (independent) *Note: Not compliant with state's rules on board composition, undergoing or foreseen to undergo reorganisation (conversion to a public institution).*
Klaipėda State Seaport Authority (State enterprise) *MoTC*	One-tier management board	**Chair:** Unassigned Saulius Kerza (MoTC) Andrius Šniuolis (MoTC) Normantas Marius Dvareckas (independent) Nerijus Udrėnas (independent)	**Chair:** Unassigned Nerijus Udrėnas (independent) Vaidotas Rūkas (independent) Saulius Kerza (Director of Department, MoTC) Kastytis Macijauskas (Director of Department, Klaipėda City Municipality) *Note: Compliant with state's rules on board composition*

SOE name, legal form and responsible ministry		Board structure and composition	
		December 2016	February 2018
Lithuanian Post (Public LLC) *MoTC*	One-tier management board	**Chair:** Unassigned Janina Laskauskienė (MoTC) Irma Kirklytė (MoTC) Jonas Butautis (independent) Algimantas Variakojis (independent)	**Chair:** Nerijus Datkūnas (independent) Gražvydas Jukna (independent) Danielius Merkinas (independent) Žaneta Kovaliova (independent) Darius Kuliešius (Senior Adviser of Department, MoTC) *Note: Compliant with state's rules on board composition*
Lithuanian Airports (State enterprise) *MoTC*	One-tier management board	**Chair:** Arijandas Šliupas (Deputy Vice Minister, MoTC) Vilius Veitas (MoTC) Janina Laskauskienė (MoTC) Tomas Krakauskas (independent) Nerijus Pačėsa (independent)	**Chair:** Tomas Krakauskas (independent) Ramūnas Bagdonas (independent) Waleed Youssef (independent) Andrius Šniuolis (Director of Department, MoTC) Gediminas Almantas (CEO, Lithuanian Airports) *Note: Compliant with state's rules on board composition*
Road Maintenance (State enterprise) *MoTC*	One-tier management board	Not applicable	**Chair:** Vygantas Sliesoraitis (independent) Egidijus Vaišvilas (independent) Saulė Balčiūnienė (independent) Natalija Vaininkevičiūtė (independent) Darius Kuliešius (Senior Adviser of Department, MoTC) *Note: Enterprise established in November 2017 after merger of 11 road maintenance enterprises*
State Forest Enterprise (State enterprise) *Ministry of Environment*	One-tier management board	Not applicable	**Chair:** Gediminas Jasinevičius (independent) Mantas Šukevičius (independent) Alditas Saulius (independent) Agnė Jakštienė (Director of Department, Ministry of Environment) Ina Bikuvienė (State Forest Enterprise) Arūnas Gustainis (State Forest Enterprise) *Note: Enterprise established in January 2018 after merger of 42 regional forestry enterprises and Lithuanian Forest Inventory and Management Institute*

Source: Information provided by the Lithuanian authorities.

Notes: The Table includes all SOEs in the largest size category (category I of the Ownership Guidelines) as well as four listed SOE subsidiaries, all of which individually fulfil the size criteria to fall under category I. The subsidiaries of Lithuanian Railways and Lithuanian Post are not reported on separately in the state's aggregate report, so it was not possible to identify whether any of them would individually meet the criteria to fall under size category I.

Recent or ongoing reforms in the SOE sector

This section of the review synthesises measures undertaken or planned by the Lithuanian authorities to implement recommendations on SOE reform elaborated by the OECD Working Party on State Ownership and Privatisation Practices (WPSOPP). The WPSOPP's recommendations, including those communicated in its 2015 SOE review which preceded Lithuania's accession process, essentially focused on measures in four areas, namely to: (i) strengthen the ownership function; (ii) increase the operational independence of SOE boards of directors; (iii) streamline SOEs' legal and corporate forms; and (iv) ensure that SOEs are subject to high quality accounting and auditing standards. After its first accession discussion on Lithuania held on 24 March 2017, the WPSOPP added a fifth recommendation that Lithuania enact amendments to its Law on Companies to strengthen company board responsibilities, aligning itself with the OECD Corporate Governance Committee's parallel recommendation. The text that follows provides a synthesis of measures taken by the Lithuanian authorities in these five areas, from early 2017 to early 2018.

Strengthening the ownership function

The GCC was transferred in July 2017 from the state-owned SOE the Property Bank (*Turto Bankas*) to the Monitoring and Forecast Agency (*Stebėsenos ir prognozių agentūra*), a public institution under the remit of the Ministry of Economy. The legislative amendments allowing the transfer (to the Law on the Management, Use and Disposal of State Assets and the Law on the Manager of Centrally Managed State Assets) were adopted by the *Seimas* on 20 April 2017 and entered into force on 1 July 2017. The Monitoring and Forecast Agency has a 2018 budget of EUR 354 000. This is approximately double the GCC's 2017 budget of EUR 175 000 and will allow for an increase in the GCC's staff from six to nine analysts, in accordance with a December 2017 decision of the Ministry of Economy.

According to interviews with the staff of the GCC undertaken prior to the transfer, the institutional change would allow the GCC greater autonomy in undertaking its work, since it would no longer report to the CEO of an SOE. They also reported that an increased budget could allow for more extensive analysis of (i) SOEs' special obligations; (ii) SOEs' optimal capital structures; and (iii) the activities and performance of enterprises owned at the municipal level.

An overarching issue identified throughout the review process has been the absence of whole-of-government remedial mechanisms when line ministries or SOEs do not comply with the state's governance and disclosure policies. The transfer of the GCC to a public institution, together with its increased budget and staffing, have the potential to strengthen its capacity to monitor and enforce government policies and regulations bearing on SOEs. This is discussed in greater detail in the Chapter 3.3 assessment section on centralisation of the ownership function.

Increasing the operational independence of SOE boards of directors

On 15 March 2017, amendments to a Government Resolution concerning the SOE board member selection procedure were adopted. The amendments mandate that all SOE boards (where they are in place) consist of a minimum of 1/2 independent directors, an increase from the 1/3 proportion that was previously mandated and only applicable to large SOEs. They prohibit "civil servants of political (personal) confidence" from serving on SOE boards. According to the Lithuanian authorities, this prohibition is interpreted to comprise vice ministers. The amendments also strengthen the selection procedure for SOE board members, notably allowing for (but not requiring) professional recruitment agencies to participate in the process. SOEs had until January 2018 to implement the new requirements, which entered into force on 24 March 2017.

According to the Lithuanian authorities, as of January 2018, no SOE boards include acting politicians. Out of the 43 SOEs that are considered "active" (not foreseen to undergo near-term restructuring), 30 are fully compliant with the requirement to comprise half independent directors, board recruitments are under way in an additional eight SOEs, scheduled to start in the coming months in three SOEs and to be decided in the remaining two SOEs. All of the remaining 23 SOEs are slated for reorganisation, privatisation, liquidation or conversion to another legal form, including the 14 that have no board in place. Of a total of 238 board members, 94 are considered independent according to the latest (January 2018) data provided by the Lithuanian authorities. This constitutes an important change since 2016, when, as shown in Table 2.15, the boards of a number of SOEs – including some of Lithuania's most economically significant SOEs – included politically affiliated individuals such as vice ministers.

Some potential remaining issues with respect to SOE board functioning merit mentioning. Firstly, the Lithuanian authorities apparently only consider 43 SOEs to be "active" and thus under the scope of the board independence requirements. For the remaining SOEs there are no plans to commence independent board member recruitment processes because these SOEs are either "to be privatised, transferred to other public institutions or liquidated". Reporting by the Lithuanian authorities notably referenced seven SOEs in the agricultural sector and four SOEs under the State Property Bank for which independent board recruitments were not planned, due, respectively to foreseen reorganisations and either privatisation or cessation of commercial activities. It would be useful to monitor progress in implementing the foreseen reorganisations and to ensure that any exclusions from the state's rules on board independence are based on objective and transparent criteria. Secondly, external observers interviewed in the context of this review have highlighted some issues with how the state has been implementing the new requirements on board independence. In some cases, the state has reportedly been replacing entire boards (rather than simply adjusting their composition by replacing civil servants with independent directors). When asked for more information on the concerned cases, government officials reported that the board replacements were warranted, for example owing to insufficient competencies on the boards, lack of confidence or trust in their performance or, in some cases, board members' alleged conflicts of interest or involvement in corporate misconduct. The amendments to the Law on Companies concerning board responsibilities and composition (discussed below) are also relevant to SOE board autonomy.

Streamlining SOEs' legal and corporate forms

The Lithuanian authorities have developed a "State Enterprise Reorganisation Plan", which sets out clear plans and timelines for streamlining statutory SOEs' legal and corporate forms. Those plans are as follows: 11 statutory SOEs are to be fully corporatised; ten transformed into public institutions or reorganised; and five will remain statutory SOEs. The 42 forestry enterprises (plus the State Forest Management Institute) and the 11 road maintenance enterprises have been merged, respectively, into two statutory SOEs and the new road maintenance enterprise is planned for conversion to a public LLC in 2018. On 11 July 2017, the Parliament adopted amendments to the Law on Forests, notably removing previous provisions mandating a defined number of forestry SOEs (42) and transferring their ownership from the Directorate General of State Forests to the Ministry of Environment. These amendments entered into force on 1 January 2018 and the final stage of consolidation is expected by end 2018. On 20 June 2017, amendments to the Law on Strategic Enterprises were passed allowing for the merger of road maintenance SOEs into one entity. On 1 November 2017, the merger was completed. A Government Resolution passed on 22 March 2017 also transferred the ownership of road assets from the road maintenance enterprises to the Lithuanian Road Administration.

Also related to SOEs' legal forms, during the February 2018 fact-finding mission, the OECD Secretariat was informed of an additional amendment to the Law on Companies enacted in April 2017 that requires that the CEOs of SOEs be dismissed after five years if they do not fulfil their objectives, and places a two-term limit on their employment. The amendment was apparently introduced by the Office of the President with the intention of inducing a dismissal of underperforming and long-serving CEOs, particularly in the forestry sector. While the legislative reform may have been undertaken with the intention of prompting higher management performance, it is not in line with international standards of corporate governance because (i) it effectively prevents SOE boards from being able to reappoint a well-performing CEO (who has already served two terms or may have failed to achieve certain objectives due to extenuating circumstances) and creates incentives to set less ambitious objectives if they wish to avoid being required to terminate the CEO (limiting their ability to effectively monitor management); (ii) it exacerbates already existing differences in legal treatment between SOEs and private companies; and (iii) it weakens the potential corporate governance gains associated with corporatising commercially-oriented statutory SOEs.

Ensuring that SOEs are subject to high quality accounting and auditing standards

Amendments to the Transparency Guidelines promulgated on 11 August 2016 made their disclosure standards mandatory for all large SOEs. Prior to these amendments, all SOEs – regardless of size or legal form – were only required to implement the provisions of the Transparency Guidelines on a comply-or-explain basis. Mandatory compliance now applies to 13 SOEs, according to the Lithuanian authorities. It does not apply to the subsidiaries of directly-owned SOEs. On 24 May 2017, a Government Resolution "On Requirements for the Audit Committees in State-Owned Enterprises and Municipality-Owned Enterprises" was adopted, notably establishing criteria on the independence of SOE audit committee members (which is required for all large SOEs). To be considered independent, an SOE audit committee member notably cannot have any employment or business relationships with the company. The criteria do not include any requirement for independence from the controlling (state) shareholder.

There is still some scope for improvement – or need to monitor progress – in a few areas related to the applicability and implementation of the state's SOE disclosure standards. Firstly, since the state's disclosure standards for SOEs are applicable to a different group of "large" SOEs than the state's governance standards, it would be useful to clarify and disclose the rationale for this distinction to avoid confusion. Secondly, according to information provided by the Lithuanian authorities, at the time of writing eight out of 13 SOEs were compliant with the disclosure standards' provision requiring large SOEs to keep accounts in accordance with IFRS. The Lithuanian authorities have provided a detailed foreseen timetable for implementation of IFRS in four of the five SOEs that are currently non-compliant, according to which IFRS would be implemented in all four of those SOEs (Road Maintenance, Lithuanian Railways, Klaipėda State Seaport Authority and State Forest Enterprise) by end 2020. For the fifth non-compliant SOE (Ignalina Nuclear Power Plant, which is in the process of being decommissioned and does not undertake any commercial activities), the Ministry of Energy reportedly intends to examine the suitability of adopting IFRS over the course of 2018. For information, at the time of writing, Ignalina Nuclear Power Plant was at the centre of an investigation involving suspected abuses by two former CEOs and four other individuals in a 2014 auction of the plant's assets.

Enacting amendments to the Law on Companies

As outlined in the Chapter 2.5 landscape section on recent legal and regulatory changes, amendments to the Law on Companies were enacted by the Parliament in November 2017 and enter into force in July 2018. New provisions on board functioning and on shareholders' access to information are particularly relevant for (some) SOEs. The amendments notably allow public LLCs, including those that are state-owned, to grant one-tier management boards additional supervisory authorities, including notably monitoring the activities of the CEO and providing related feedback to the AGM. For listed SOEs with one-tier management boards, these provisions are mandatory. Listed SOEs will also be subject to the new provisions of the Law on Companies requiring board approval of related party transactions and a 1/3 minimum proportion of independent members on the board performing supervisory functions. The amendments also strengthen minority shareholders' rights by removing the provision that previously allowed controlling shareholders (the state in the case of SOEs) privileged access to corporate information.

Notes

1. See also: OECD (2016), *OECD Economic Surveys: Lithuania 2016: Economic Assessment*, OECD Publishing, Paris. http://dx.doi.org/10.1787/eco_surveys-ltu-2016-en

2. SMEs are defined here according to the 2008 Law on Small and Medium-Sized Business Development, according to which enterprises are considered SMEs if they have fewer than 250 employees, annual income of less than EUR 40 million and total assets valued below EUR 27 million.

3. The full list of tradable funds on the Baltic Fund list is available at this link: http://www.nasdaqbaltic.com/market/?pg=trfunds&currency=EUR&date=30.12.2015 Units or shares issued by collective investment undertakings, for which admission into the fund list is sought, must meet the requirements of the Law on Collective Investment Undertakings of the Republic of Lithuania and other legal acts. The fund unit trading service is suitable for closed-end and open-end funds that need to ensure liquidity for fund unit holders.

4. The full list of Certified Advisers in all three Baltic countries can be found on the Nasdaq Baltic website at http://www.nasdaqbaltic.com/en/products-services/certified-advisers/list-of-certified-advisers/.

5. This assessment is based primarily on two compilations of companies' compliance with the Code, the first prepared by the Bank of Lithuania in 2010 (available only in Lithuanian, online here: https://old.lb.lt/bendroviu_valdymo_praktikos_apzvalga) and the second prepared by Nasdaq Vilnius based on listed companies' compliance with the Code in 2015 (summarised in Table 2.3).

7. According to data from the Register of Legal Entities, there were as of 2016 121 446 private LLCs and 455 public LLCs in Lithuania.

8. The *Principles* refer to boards of directors as encompassing both single-tier and two-tier board systems. While the *SOE Guidelines* use the terminology "management" and "board of directors" to describe the separate executive and supervisory functions in jurisdictions with two-tier systems, this report applies the term "management board" to the executive management function and the term "supervisory board" to the

supervisory function, in order to be consistent with the terminology applied in English translations of Lithuanian legislation and regulations.

9. The Law on Companies is applicable to financial institutions to the extent that other laws regulating the provision of financial services, the activities of financial institutions, the stability of financial institutions and the system of financial institutions do not establish otherwise.

10. The Lithuanian authorities reported that this change had little impact on listed companies, since they had already established at least one collegial body prior to this amendment. The change was targeted more toward small- to medium-sized public LLCs that previously only had a CEO. The requirements entered into force in July 2015.

11. Art. 2.32 of the Law on Audit defines a "public interest entity" as: "an entity that is of significant public relevance because of the nature of its business, its size or the number of clients. The public interest entity shall be: (1) an undertaking whose securities are traded on the regulated market of the Republic of Lithuania and/or any other Member State; (2) a bank and the Central Credit Union; (3) a credit union, where its assets on the last day of the financial year for at least two consecutive financial years exceed EUR 20 million; (4) a financial brokerage firm; (5) a collective investment undertaking as defined in the Law of the Republic of Lithuania on Collective Investment Undertakings, a pension fund as defined in the Law of the Republic of Lithuania on the Accumulation of Pensions and the Law of the Republic of Lithuania on the Supplementary Voluntary Accumulation of Pensions, an occupational pension fund as defined in the Law of the Republic of Lithuania on the Accumulation of Occupational Pensions; (6) a management company which manages at least one of the entities referred to in point 5 of this paragraph, an association of participants of an occupational pension fund/funds; (7) an insurance undertaking, a reinsurance undertaking; (8) the Central Securities Depository of Lithuania, the operator of the regulated market; (9) a state enterprise, a municipal enterprise, a public limited liability company and a private limited liability company whose shares or a part of shares carrying more than ½ of all the votes at the general meeting of shareholders of these enterprises are held by the right of ownership by the State and/or a municipality and which are considered to be large enterprises under the Law of the Republic of Lithuania on Financial Reporting by Undertakings.

12. The EU Directive on disclosure of non-financial and diversity information is available online here: http://eur-lex.europa.eu/legal-content/EN/TXT/?uri=CELEX:32014L0095.

13. The document specifying how listed companies should report on their compliance with the Nasdaq Vilnius Corporate Governance Code is available online here: http://www.nasdaqbaltic.com/files/vilnius/teisesaktai/Nasdaq%20OMX%20Vilnius%20Corporate%20Governance%20Code%20Reporting%20Form.pdf

14. Information on the EU Market Abuse Regulation and the Markets in Financial Instruments Directive and Regulation is available, respectively, at the following links: https://ec.europa.eu/info/publications/market-abuse-regulation-mar_en and https://ec.europa.eu/info/business-economy-euro/banking-and-finance/financial-markets/securities-markets/investment-services-and-regulated-markets-markets-financial-instruments-directive-mifid_en#mifid-2-and-mifir.

15. The Law on Bondholder Interest Protection is available online in Lithuanian at: https://www.e-tar.lt/portal/en/legalAct/25dc33103c5a11e6bcc5c96b48152012.

16. Technically, the Law on the Management, Use and Disposal of State and Municipal Assets outlines the responsibilities of the Monitoring and Forecast Agency, an entity to which the GCC's functions and staff were transferred in 2017.

17. Given that statutory SOEs are created via special law, their conversion to limited liability companies would require the passage of a relevant law by the Parliament.

18. According to the Law on State and Municipal Enterprises, "the owner of a state enterprise shall be the State. The State shall exercise the rights and duties of the owner of the state enterprise via the Government or a state administration institution authorised by it" (Art. 4).

19. The term "one-tier management board" is adopted regardless of the relative proportion of executive and non-executive directors within.

20. This provision on "other natural persons" is applicable to statutory SOEs for which the value of assets is at least USD 15 million (EUR 14 million) and the net turnover is at least ~USD 6 million (EUR 5.8 million). Other statutory SOEs falling outside of this size category may, according to the Law on State and Municipal Enterprises, also include such persons in their boards.

21. As of the enactment of legislative amendments allowing the GCC's transfer to a public institution, its mandate is outlined in the Law on the Management, Use and Disposal of State Assets.

22. Enterprises of strategic importance to national security are explicitly listed in the "Law of the Republic of Lithuania on Enterprises and Facilities of Strategic Importance to National Security and Other Enterprises of Importance to Ensuring National Security". For information, SOEs in size categories I and II account for 87.43% of all Lithuanian SOEs by asset value as of end-2015.

23. Annex 1 provides a list of all SOEs and identifies those 13 SOEs for which compliance with the state's disclosure standards is mandatory. All SOEs that meet the criteria to be considered large under the Law on Financial Reporting by Enterprises are required to comply with the Transparency Guidelines. The Law defines an enterprise as large when two out of the following three criteria are met: revenues exceeding EUR 40 million; assets exceeding EUR 20 million; and employees exceeding 250.

24. This review has not undertaken to conclusively classify the management boards of Lithuania's largest SOEs as adopting either the Type A (executive) management board model or the Type B (mixed) management board model. To recall, Type A management boards are not accorded any supervisory functions, while Type B management boards are accorded some supervisory authority and include a minimum proportion of outside directors. An analysis of the articles of association of 14 of Lithuania's largest SOEs undertaken in the context of the 2015 SOE review found that the responsibilities of most management boards (where they were explicitly outlined in the articles of association) mainly consisted of hiring and firing the CEO and approving transactions beyond a certain threshold. Given that the management boards of statutory SOEs have very limited supervisory capacity, with most decision-making falling to the state ownership entity, they would most likely be considered similar to the Type A management boards in place for limited liability companies.

However, SOE boards (regardless of legal form) often include outside directors, which could align them more with Type B management boards, at least in terms of their composition.

25. It was reported in August 2017 that the board members of Lithuanian Post had recently resigned, including the Vice Minister of Transportation, who was serving as Chair, and that a process had been initiated to identify new members to replace them.

26. ESO was established on 1 January 2016 by merging Lesto and Lithuanian Gas (Lietuvos Dujos). Elsewhere in the report, Lesto and Lithuanian Gas are reported on separately since the majority of data on SOEs is from end-2015.

References

Bank of Lithuania (2016), "Annual Report of the Bank of Lithuania: 2015", Bank of Lithuania, Vilnius, www.lb.lt/en/publications/annual-report-2015.

EBRD (2017), "Introduction of a Covered Bond and Securitisation Legal and Regulatory Framework in Lithuania: April 2017", European Bank for Reconstruction and Development, London, https://finmin.lrv.lt/uploads/finmin/documents/files/Lithuania%20ABS%20CB%20Final%20Concept%20Paper.pdf

EBRD (2012), "Commercial Laws of Lithuania, December 2012: An Assessment by the EBRD", Office of the General Counsel, European Bank for Reconstruction and Development, London, available at www.ebrd.com/legal-reform/where-we-work/lithuania.html.

European Commission (2016), *Commission Staff Working Document: Country Report Lithuania 2016*, Brussels, European Commission.

Ministry of Finance of the Republic of Lithuania (2018), "Economic Development Scenario for 2018-2021 (March 2018)", http://finmin.lrv.lt/en/actual-financial-data/economic-development-scenario.

Nasdaq Baltic (2015), "*Promoting Baltic Economic Growth Through IPOs: Study and Action Proposals April 2015*", Nasdaq Baltic, http://www.nasdaqbaltic.com/files/baltic/IPO_TF/0816-Q15%20Economic%20growth%20IPO_BALTIC_Eng_FNL.pdf.

Nasdaq Vilnius (2016), "The Listing Rules of AB Nasdaq Vilnius", http://www.nasdaqbaltic.com/files/vilnius/teisesaktai/2016/Listing%20Rules%20of%20Nasdaq%20Vilnius%20(effective%20as%20of%2001_01_2016).pdf.

Nasdaq Vilnius (2009), "The Corporate Governance Code for the Companies Listed on Nasdaq OMX Vilnius", http://www.nasdaqbaltic.com/files/vilnius/teisesaktai/The%20Corporate%20Governance%20Code%20for%20the%20Companies%20Listed%20on%20NASDAQ%20OMX%20Vilnius%20(effective%20as%20of%202010-01-01).pdf.

OECD (forthcoming), *Economic Surveys: Lithuania 2018*, OECD, Paris.

OECD (2017), *The Size and Sectoral Distribution of State-Owned Enterprises*, OECD, Paris, http://dx.doi.org/10.1787/9789264280663-en.

OECD (2016), *OECD Economic Outlook, Volume 2016 Issue 1*, OECD, Paris, http://dx.doi.org/10.1787/eco_outlook-v2016-1-en.

OECD (2015), *OECD Review of the Corporate Governance of State-Owned Enterprises: Lithuania,* OECD, Paris, www.oecd.org/corporate/oecd-review-corporate-governance-soe-lithuania.htm.

Transparency International (2017), *Corruption Perceptions Index 2017*, https://www.transparency.org/news/feature/corruption_perceptions_index_2017.

World Bank (2018), *Doing Business 2018: Reforming to Create Jobs*, International Bank for Reconstruction and Development/The World Bank, Washington DC, http://www.doingbusiness.org/reports/global-reports/doing-business-2018.

World Bank (2017), *Doing Business 2017: Equal Opportunity for All*, International Bank for Reconstruction and Development/The World Bank, Washington DC, http://www.doingbusiness.org/reports/global-reports/doing-business-2017.

World Economic Forum (2017), *The Global Competitiveness Report 2017-2018*, World Economic Forum, Geneva, https://www.weforum.org/reports/the-global-competitiveness-report-2017-2018.

Chapter 3

The Roadmap for Accession: Review against core Corporate Governance Principles

This chapter assesses Lithuanian policies and practices with respect to the five "core" corporate governance principles that are set out in the OECD Corporate Governance Committee's agreed methodology for undertaking corporate governance accession reviews. These principles relate to: (1) ensuring the rights and equitable treatment of shareholders, including minority and foreign shareholders; (2) requiring timely and reliable disclosure of corporate information in line with internationally recognised standards; (3) ensuring effective separation of the government's role as owner and regulator of state-owned enterprises; (4) maintaining a level playing field between state-owned enterprises and their private competitors; and (5) recognising stakeholder rights and the duties, rights and responsibilities of corporate boards of directors.

3.1 Ensuring a consistent regulatory framework that provides for the existence and effective enforcement of shareholder rights and the equitable treatment of shareholders, including minority and foreign shareholders.

As noted in the introduction to this report, Lithuania was reviewed against the recommendations of the *OECD Guidelines on Corporate Governance of State-Owned Enterprises* in 2015, while the Committee's "Concept Paper" – *Concepts to Guide Corporate Governance Accession Reviews* – provides a framework for integrating the elements most relevant to assessing each of the core corporate governance accession principles. Following the Concept Paper structure, this section is divided into five sections: (i) shareholder rights and equitable treatment, including treatment of the market for corporate control (**Principles II.C**, **D**, **E**, **H** and **Principle III.B**), as well as an additional assessment of Lithuania's framework for minority shareholder protection, given the concentrated ownership structure of most listed Lithuanian companies; (ii) related party transactions and conflicts of interest (**Principle II.F 1** and **2**); (iii) institutional investor disclosure, corporate governance policies, conflicts of interest and voting (**Principles III.A** and **C**); and (iv) insider trading and abusive self-dealing (**Principle III.E**). The fifth and final section of the chapter deals with equitable treatment of shareholders among state-owned enterprises (*SOE Guidelines* **IV.A** and **IV.C**).

Shareholder rights and equitable treatment

Effective participation in general meetings (Principle II.C)

Principle II.C states that shareholders should have the opportunity to participate effectively and vote in general shareholder meetings and should be informed of the rules, including voting procedures that govern general shareholder meetings. This includes consideration of six sub-topics dealing with (i) provision of sufficient and timely information regarding general meetings; (ii) processes allowing for equitable treatment of shareholders including so that procedures do not make it unduly difficult or expensive to cast votes; (iii) the opportunity for shareholders to ask questions to the board and to place items on the general meeting agenda; (iv) facilitation of effective participation in key corporate governance decisions such as nomination and election of board members; (v) shareholders' ability to vote in person or in absentia; and (vi) the elimination of impediments to cross-border voting.

Lithuania's Law on Companies generally provides the legislative framework for implementing these recommendations. This includes requirements for the provision of timely information (**Principle II.C.1**) regarding general meetings. Under the Law (Art. 24.1), an annual general meeting (AGM) must be held every year not later than within four months of the end of the financial year. A notice of the AGM must be published not later than 21 days before the AGM. Public limited liability companies must publish the aforementioned notices on their websites. (Listed companies publish these notices in both Lithuanian and English.) The notices include information on the date, location, meeting agenda and draft decisions, among other details (Art. 26^2). If the supervisory board, management board, or manager of the company fails to organise the AGM, the AGM may be convened by a decision of the shareholders whose shares carry more than half of all votes (Art. 23.4). If the AGM is not convened within four months from the end of the financial year, then any shareholder has the right to bring the matter to court. In this case, the AGM shall be convened by court order.

The Law on Companies also provides for processes and protections that make it legally possible for all shareholders to participate in general shareholder meetings, either in person or through a representative via written proxy authorisation, thereby addressing the recommendations of **Principles II.C.2 and II.C.5**. In support of the equitable treatment of shareholders, nominal values and rights granted by all shares of the same class are equal (Art. 40.4). All shareholders have the right to vote at AGMs according to voting rights attached to their shares (Art. 16.1.3). To facilitate shareholders' casting of votes, companies may provide a system for shareholders to vote by means of electronic communications (Art. 21.4). If a shareholder requests, the company must prepare and send general ballot papers no later than 10 days prior to the AGM to the shareholder (Art. 30). The ballot may be completed by the shareholder, or by an authorised person, as shareholders may authorise a natural or legal person to represent her- or himself in maintaining contact with the company (Art. 14.7). Proxy holders enjoy the same rights as the shareholders they represent would in general shareholder meetings, including the right to cast votes either in person or by means of electronic communication (Art. 30^1). Following general shareholder meetings, the minutes must be drawn up and signed not later than within seven days after the meeting, and all shareholders are entitled to have access to the minutes and to submit comments or opinions. Listed companies must post the voting results online for their shareholders no later than seven days after the general shareholder meetings (Art. 29.1, 3 and 4).

Shareholders' rights under the Law on Companies also include the right to submit questions to the company related to issues on the agenda for general shareholder meetings (Arts. 16 and 16^1), which broadly meets the recommendation in **Principle II.C.3**. Amendments to the Law on Companies enacted in November 2017 removed two provisions that were identified as problematic during the review process, because they granted controlling shareholders or groups of shareholders privileged access to information concerning the issues to be discussed at the AGM and to other company documents, in exchange for a pledge of confidentiality. Concerning information on the issues to be discussed at the AGM, companies can still refuse to respond to related requests if they concern commercial secrets, but there is no longer an exemption from this possibility for refusal if the information is requested by a controlling shareholder. Concerning other corporate information, a provision has been removed that previously granted controlling shareholders access to "all company documents" subject to signing a confidentiality pledge. Under the amendments, a shareholder (including a controlling shareholder) can access corporate information relating to commercial secrets only if "necessary for the shareholder to fulfil imperative requirements provided for in other legal acts and the shareholder ensures the confidentiality of such information" (Art. 18).

Prior to these amendments, under Art. 16^1, which sets forth the shareholder's right to submit in advance questions to a company, a company could refuse to answer questions submitted by a shareholder if they related to commercial or industrial secrets or confidential information *unless* the requesting shareholder or group of shareholders held or controlled more than half of the shares. In these cases, the controlling shareholder or shareholders could access this information on the condition that they submit a written pledge not to disclose this information. The same rule was applied under Art. 18, which sets forth shareholders' rights to access other corporate information. Data were not available on how often these provisions under the Law on Companies have been applied by shareholders. The amendments enter into force in July 2018.

Legal provisions are also in place to facilitate effective shareholder participation in key corporate governance decisions, such as the nomination and election of board members (**Principle II.C.4**). Under the Law on Companies (Art. 20.1.3-4), the general meeting of shareholders has the exclusive right to elect and remove members of the supervisory board (where one exists). In companies with a one-tier board, the general meeting of shareholders may elect or remove members of the management board. It is also up to the general meeting of shareholders to decide how to distribute profits allocated for the remuneration of members of the supervisory and management boards and to employees (Art. 20.1.10 and Art. 59.2.11).

Finally, the Law on Companies' provisions on shareholder voting, proxy voting, and proxy voting via electronic means do not appear to impede cross-border voting (**Principle II.C.6**) (Arts. 30, 30^1, 30^2). As noted above (**Principles II.C.2** and **5**), each shareholder has a right to authorise a natural or legal person to represent her or him, and this right equally apples to foreign shareholders. Ballots may be cast via electronic communications. Finally, in some cases and to facilitate cross-border voting, company information may be provided in both Lithuanian and English.

Shareholder consultation and co-ordination in the exercise of their rights (Principle II.D)

Principle II.D states that shareholders, including institutional shareholders, should be allowed to consult with each other on issues concerning their basic shareholder rights as defined in the *Principles*, subject to exceptions to prevent abuse.

The Lithuanian authorities report that there are no restrictions on shareholders' ability to coordinate and consult. Keeping in mind that this challenge presents itself more often in jurisdictions with dispersed shareholders, the Lithuanian authorities add that some shareholders may sign shareholders' agreements in order to coordinate their decisions (Civil Code Art. 2.88). As noted above (**Principle II.C.3**), shareholders may also co-operate in order to request specific information from the company, including commercial or industrial secrets or confidential information.

Equal treatment with respect to different share classes (Principle II.E and III.B)

Principle II.E states that all shareholders of the same series of a class should be treated equally. Capital structures and arrangements that enable certain shareholders to obtain a degree of influence or control disproportionate to their equity ownership should be disclosed.

All shareholders have the right to vote at AGMs according to voting rights attached to their shares (Art. 16.1.3). The principle of "one share, one vote" is generally applied (Art. 17.2) in Lithuania, with some rare exceptions. Under the Law on Companies, companies are allowed to issue three different share classes: ordinary shares (one share, one vote), preference shares (priority to receive dividends but usually without voting rights) and employee shares (ordinary shares with time-limit restrictions up to three years on their disposal), though the Lithuanian authorities report the latter two share classes are rarely employed and only ordinary shares are usually listed. (There has only been one case in which preference shares were listed: in 2006, Bank Snoras—which went bankrupt in 2011—issued ordinary registered shares on the Nasdaq Vilnius main list and preference shares on the secondary list.[1])

Within each series of share class, all shares carry the same nominal value and rights (**Principle II.E.1**) and changes to these rights must be subject to approval by a general shareholder meeting (Law on Companies Art. 40). Ordinary shares cannot be converted into preference shares. However, preference shares may be converted into ordinary shares by a decision of the general meeting of shareholders, if the company's articles of association provide for this possibility. Further, any changes to the rights associated with share classes as stipulated in a company's articles of association must be agreed upon by a decision of a general meeting of shareholders (via a qualified majority vote of not less than 2/3 of votes of shareholders attending the meeting). Finally, the public offering of shares can only be exercised after a company publishes its prospectus, which must include information on the entity's assets and liabilities, financial position, profit and loss, prospects of the company, and the rights granted by issuing shares (Law on Securities, Arts. 5-6).

Principle II.E.2 also requires the disclosure of capital structures and control arrangements, including for example pyramid structures, cross shareholdings, shares with limited or multiple voting rights, shareholder agreements and voting caps. The Lithuanian authorities report that they have "broadly implemented" this recommendation. This includes via the requirement that companies include in their publicly disclosed annual financial statements and report information on capital arrangements, structures and any other information that is not considered a commercial or industrial secret (Law on Financial Reporting by Undertakings Art. 23.3.4-6 and the Law on Consolidated Financial Reporting by Groups of Undertakings Art. 10). Amendments to the Law on Financial Reporting by Undertakings enacted on 21 November 2017 require that public and private LLCs, or any partnerships thereof, disclose in their annual corporate governance reports information on the existence and conditions of any shareholder agreements. The concerned companies must comply with this new requirement in their annual reports for the 2018 financial year. This constitutes a significant change, since under previous legislation, the contents of shareholder agreements could be kept confidential by listed companies. The conditions of these new provisions, which will be implemented in 2018 financial statements, would appear to be broadly in line with **Principle II.E.2**. Earlier versions of this review referenced a Bank of Lithuania Resolution establishing that listed companies must include in their annual reports information on the existence of shareholders' agreements (Resolution of the Board of the Bank of Lithuania on the Approval of the Rules on Preparation and Submission of Periodic and Additional Information No 03-48).[2] This Resolution was since repealed by a 22 August 2017 Bank of Lithuania Board Resolution on the Approval of the Rules on the Disclosure of Information. The repeal came into effect on 1 January 2018.

A last area for consideration of the equal treatment of shareholders is **Principle III.B,** which states that votes should be cast by custodians or nominees in line with the directions of the beneficial owner of the shares. As noted above under **Principle II.C**, each shareholder is entitled to authorise a natural or legal person to represent him or her in maintaining contacts with the company (a proxy holder) and proxy holders must vote at general shareholder meetings according to the instructions given by the shareholder (Law on Companies [Arts. 14.7, 30^1.1-3] and the Civil Code [2.88-2.89]).

The market for corporate control (Principle II.H)

Principle II.H is concerned with ensuring an efficient allocation of resources subject to procedures to ensure that other aspects of the *Principles* related to shareholder rights are protected. Specifically, **Principle II.H.1** recommends that rules and procedures for the acquisition of corporate control should be clearly articulated and disclosed and that transactions pursuant to these rules take place at fair prices and under fair conditions. To this end, the Lithuanian authorities report that a shareholder that has increased or decreased ownership must disclose to the Bank of Lithuania and the company these changes in ownership at specific thresholds (5, 10, 15, 20, 25, 30, 50, 75 and 95% ownership) (Law on Securities Arts. 25 and 27). The minimum ownership threshold above which a shareholder must disclose direct or indirect ownership is 5%. In addition, a shareholder who acquires all of a company's shares must inform the company, the manager of which must then inform the Register of Legal Entities (Law on Securities Art. 25). Furthermore, if a shareholder acquires certain financial instruments, other than a company's shares, which enable him/her to take over the control of the company, then the shareholder must publish a notice.[3]

The buying and selling of shares on Lithuania's capital markets, the Lithuanian authorities report, also take place at fair prices that must reflect prevailing market conditions. In engaging in these transactions, each shareholder within a share class has equal rights and duties. According to the Bank of Lithuania, a previously applicable provision of the Law on Securities requiring that listed companies publish a notice of each material event was repealed. New Bank of Lithuania rules on information disclosure regulate insider trading in accordance with applicable EU rules on market abuse, but do not include any requirements for the disclosure of material events.

There have been a series of notable cases in Lithuanian courts addressing potential violations of the Law on Securities' mandatory takeover bid requirements.4 (Box 3.1 includes illustrative examples provided by the Lithuanian authorities of five such cases.) These cases show that the law with respect to takeover bids is enforceable. While the cases have generally taken many years to resolve (indeed, the first case is still at the Supreme Court level after nine years, while other cases have generally taken at least four years to reach the Supreme Court level), they have upheld minority shareholder claims at Supreme Court level to ensure that they receive mandatory takeover bid offers for their shares at fair prices.

Principle II.H.2 further states that anti-takeover devices should not be used to shield management and the board from accountability. Under the Law on Companies, the management bodies of Lithuanian companies must act in the interest of both the company and its shareholders and must comply with laws and other legal acts, as well as the company's articles of association (Art. 19.8). In taking important decisions, the management board must seek the approval of the company's shareholders, though such approval does not exempt the management board from accountability (Art. 34.5). In principle, this would extend, therefore, to the decision by the general meeting of shareholders to engage in a share buyout offer or related actions. The Lithuanian authorities add that, in cases where the management board is suspected of not acting in the best interest of the company or its shareholders, then a shareholder or a group of shareholders holding at least 1/10 of shares in the company may request the court to appoint experts to investigate (Civil Code Art. 2.125).

Minority shareholder protections (Principle II.G)

Principle II.G states that "minority shareholders should be protected from abusive actions by, or in the interest of, controlling shareholders acting either directly or indirectly, and should have effective means of redress" and that "abusive self-dealing should be prohibited." While **Principle II.G** is not included as part of the "Concept Paper", this report includes an additional assessment of Lithuania's position against this recommendation to protect minority shareholders, given the high concentration of company ownership in Lithuania. As noted in Chapter 2.3, 64% of listed companies (21 out of 33 companies) had a controlling shareholder holding more than 50% of company's shares, as of mid-2015. In 10 of these companies, the controlling shareholder held more than 90% of all shares.

The Lithuanian authorities report that the legal and regulatory framework generally protects minority shareholders in that all shareholders (including minority shareholders) of the same class enjoy the same rights to participate in and vote at the general shareholders' meeting (Law on Companies Art. 3.2, Nasdaq Vilnius Corporate Governance Code Principle VI), and companies' management bodies must act in the interest of the company and its shareholders (Law on Companies Art. 19.8, Nasdaq Vilnius Corporate Governance Code Principle IV.2). Court decisions in Lithuania have also underlined the importance of protecting minority shareholder rights. For example, December 2005 and January 2006 Constitutional Court resolutions held that it is universally acknowledged that a mandatory takeover bid is a measure to protect the ownership rights of minority shareholders, protecting minority shareholder rights is a public interest (protecting the constitutional value of private ownership), and that, if the law provides exemptions to this rule, alternative means for protecting minority shareholders' interests should be available.

Box 3.1 Illustrative examples of cases involving mandatory takeover bids

The following five case summaries were provided by the Lithuanian authorities in order to illustrate examples of instances where minority shareholders have pursued their claims in Lithuanian courts. All of the cases pertain to the refusal of majority shareholders (acting independently or in concert) either to submit a mandatory takeover bid, as per the Law on Securities, or to submit a mandatory takeover bid at a fair share price. In four of the five illustrative cases provided below, the courts decided in favour of the minority shareholders, while the remaining case is still under appeal. In almost all of the cases, however, the minority shareholders' claims were initially rejected by the courts of first instance. These decisions were unanimously reversed by the Supreme Court, citing the 2005 and 2006 constitutional court decisions that enshrined the preservation of minority shareholder protections as being in the public interest. Unfortunately, these cases have taken anywhere from four to nine years of legal processes to resolve and one case (AB Linas) still remains subject to further court deliberations after nine years.

1. AB Linas ("AB Linen")

AB Linas is a textiles manufacturing company listed on the Nasdaq Vilnius secondary list and is part of the AB Linas group of companies. In 2007, the then-regulator, the Securities Commission, discovered that certain parties were secretly acting in concert in order to avoid triggering the Law on Securities' mandatory takeover bid rules. The Commission ordered the AB Linas shareholders to make a mandatory bid. After the controlling shareholders failed to comply, the Commission decided to issue sanctions against the controlling shareholders for concealing that they were acting in concert and for failing to issue a mandatory takeover bid at a fair share price. The shareholders responded by lodging several complaints against the regulator in court.

The results in Lithuanian courts were mixed. The District Court (the court of first instance) dismissed the claim on the grounds that, at the time when the court heard the case, the defendants (the controlling shareholders) no longer held enough shares to meet the mandatory takeover bid threshold in the Law on Securities. (The controlling shareholders had sold their majority stake either before the claim was brought to court or during the litigation process.) This decision was appealed by the claimants, but maintained by the Regional Court.

The case was again appealed and subsequently heard by the Supreme Court, which reversed the decision of the District and Regional courts and sent the case back to the Regional Court (court of appeals) to be re-heard, citing the December 2005 and January 2006 Constitutional Court resolutions holding that mandatory takeover bids are an important tool for the protection of minority shareholders and that preserving this protection is in the public interest. The Regional Court re-examined the case and, finally, decided in favour of the minority shareholders, ordering the shareholders acting in concert to submit the mandatory takeover bid at a fair price. However, the defendants subsequently made a number of appeals and, after a lengthy legal process, the Regional Court in 2016 repealed its revised decision on the grounds that the defendants did not have the financial means to submit and implement the mandatory takeover bid.

Taking into account that the parties allegedly have attempted to hide that they were acting in concert and were taking a series of actions aimed at deteriorating their financial situation in order to avoid the requirement to make a mandatory takeover bid, the Bank of Lithuania has filed the information to the responsible judicial authorities aimed at proving the potential criminal activities of the responsible parties, and submitted a cassation appeal to the Supreme Court.

2. AB Lietuvos elektrinė ("AB Lithuanian Power Plant")

Lietuvos elektrinė was a listed electricity generator that was later acquired in 2010 by Lietuvos Energija, a state-owned enterprise. In this case, minority shareholders submitted an application in 2005 to the Securities Commission to approve their request that the company's majority shareholder—who held 95% of the company's shares at the time—initiate a mandatory takeover bid at a fair price. The Commission approved the application and the minority shareholders' proposed share price. The majority shareholder refused to comply and appealed the Commission's decision to court, arguing that (i) the legal obligation to initiate a mandatory takeover bid did not apply because the shares were acquired prior to the entry into force of these provisions in the Law on Securities, (ii) the proposed buyout share price was unfair, and (iii) at the time the claims were made, the company—Lietuvos elektrinė—no longer existed, as it had been merged into Lietuvos Energija.

The District Court (court of first instance) rejected the claim, stating that the obligation to initiate the mandatory takeover bid for the remaining shareholders of Lietuvos elektrinė applied and that the minority shareholders' application to the Commission pre-dated the Lietuvos elektrinė merger. The claimant appealed the District Court decision to the Regional Court, which upheld the District Court's decision, which was subsequently reaffirmed by the Court of Appeal and the Supreme Court. The latter held that the controlling shareholder was obliged to redeem the minority shareholders' shares despite the fact that the shares were acquired prior to the entry into force of the relevant provisions in the Law on Securities.

In February 2016, Lietuvos energijos gamyba (the relevant subsidiary of Lietuvos Energija) announced it would begin the process of complying with the courts' ruling that it redeem the shares of the minority shareholders in this case. As of May 2016, Lietuvos energijos gamyba announced it had completed 1,144 agreements to purchase nearly 4 million Lietuvos elektrinė shares.

3. AB Spauda ("AB Press")

In 2005, controlling shareholders registered a mandatory takeover bid application to buy up the remaining ordinary shares of the Lithuanian printing company, AB Spauda. Minority shareholders holding preference shares appealed this application to court, arguing that the mandatory takeover bid should apply to both ordinary and preference shares. In October 2007, the Supreme Court decided in favor of the minority shareholders.

The controlling shareholders, however, chose to ignore the ruling of the Supreme Court and failed to submit the takeover bid. As a result, the claimants brought their case again in court. Their claim was supported by a written submission to the court prepared by the Securities Commission. In response, the Regional Court (court of first instance) ruled only partly in the claimants' favor, ordering they be reimbursed the costs of litigation. Upon appeal by the claimants, the Court of Appeal upheld the Regional Court's decision.

The case was again appealed and heard by the Supreme Court, which repealed the decision of the Court of appeal and decided in favor of the claimants (the minority shareholders holding preference shares in 2014. As a result, the controlling shareholders were obligated to redeem the preference shares at a fair price. The decision was consistent with previous Supreme Court rulings on the issue and the aforementioned Constitutional Court resolutions.

4. AB Ukmergės keliai ("Ukmergės roads")

AB Ukmergės keliai is a formerly listed road construction company. In 2003, a minority shareholder went to court in order to require shareholders the minority shareholder believed were acting in concert to initiate a mandatory takeover bid. The claimant indicated that the persons acting in concert held 52.53% of the company's voting rights, which should have triggered the mandatory takeover bid provisions in the Law on Securities.

The District Court (court of first instance) dismissed the claim on the grounds that the defendants' actual combined shareholdings did not meet the Law on Securities' mandatory takeover bid threshold. The District Court also ruled that, since the protection of minority shareholders is a public interest, the claimant did not have the right to individually file a claim in order to protect the public interest.

The Regional Court (appellate instance) repealed the District Court's decision, requiring the defendants to issue a mandatory takeover bid. The Regional Court confirmed that the controlling shareholders held 52.53% of the company's shares, which was confirmed in the shareholders' registration list prepared for the company's AGM in 2003. The Regional Court's decision was supported by the Supreme Court. The Supreme Court further reasoned that any minority shareholder has the right to require a controlling shareholder or shareholders acting in concert to initiate a mandatory takeover bid, if conditions stipulated by the Law on Securities are met. In these circumstances, any minority shareholder can submit a claim to defend her or his rights under the law and that this right applies even if the claimant's claim was not authorized by the remaining minority shareholders.

Following the Supreme Court's ruling in 2007, the majority shareholders acting in concert submitted their application for a mandatory takeover bid for approval to the Securities Commission. The initial application was refused, on the basis that the proposed share buyout price was too low. The price was then increased and the takeover bid was implemented in accordance with the Law on Securities.

5. AB Panevėžio statybos trestas ("AB Panevezys Building Trust")

AB Panevėžio statybos trestas is a former state-owned construction company that is today listed on the Nasdaq Vilnius main list. In 2003, a minority shareholder went to court in order to require shareholders acting in concert to submit a mandatory takeover bid for the remaining shares of the company under the Law on Securities. The claimant indicated that the shareholders acting in concert together held 54.72% of the company's voting shares at the time the claim was filed in court. The Securities Commission provided the court its opinion supporting the minority shareholder.

The District Court (court of first instance) hearing the case initially dismissed the claim, reasoning that the claimant did not sufficiently establish that his or her rights were violated and that the claim was limited to just one course of action—obliging the defendant to submit a mandatory takeover bid. (The other alternative under the Law on Securities, the District Court reasoned, was transfer shares to below the takeover bid threshold.) Upon appeal by the claimant, the Regional Court (appellate instance) repealed the District Court decision, requiring the defendants to initiate a mandatory takeover bid and emphasizing the importance of preserving minority shareholder protections. The Regional Court decision was upheld by the Supreme Court in 2009.

Following the ruling of the Supreme Court, the controlling shareholders who had been acting in concert submitted an application for a mandatory takeover bid for the Securities Commission's approval. As in the case of Ukmergės keliai above, the initial application was refused because the proposed share buyout price was too low. The share price was then increased and the mandatory takeover bid was implemented according to the Law on Securities.

Source : Information provided by the Lithuanian authorities.

As important as the framework for minority shareholder protections is its application in practice. Here, the Lithuanian authorities, private sector and civil society indicate that, while the percentage of minority shareholders in listed companies may be small, there have nevertheless been a series of notable cases in Lithuanian courts addressing potential violations of these protections, as illustrated by the takeover law cases cited in Box 3.1. Private sector representatives indicated that, in general, minority shareholders may bring their claims to court and that Lithuanian courts can effectively deal with these disputes. Such cases are not uncommon, and have been brought by both resident and foreign shareholders. The broader challenge may be, private sector representatives suggested, the capacity of the authorities to ensure effective public enforcement against white collar crimes.

Related party transactions and conflicts of interest (Principle II.F.1 and II.F.2)

Principle II.F states that related party transactions should be approved and conducted in a manner that ensures proper management of conflicts of interest and protects the interest of the company and its shareholders. This Principle also recommends that (i) conflicts of interest inherent in related party transactions should be addressed (**Principle II.F.1**); and (ii) members of the board and key executives should be required to disclose to the board whether they, directly, indirectly or on behalf of third parties, have a material interest in any transaction or matter directly affecting the corporation (**Principle II.F.2**).

Amendments to the Law on Companies and to the Law on Financial Reporting by Undertakings enacted in November 2017 have significantly changed the framework for, respectively, board oversight and disclosure of related party transactions involving Lithuanian listed companies. In order to maintain a distinction between the provisions in force at the time of writing and the provisions that will enter into force in July 2018, the text that follows offers: first, an assessment of the rules in force at the time of writing, which primarily relate to the management of conflicts of interest involving board members and management, since related party transactions as such were not regulated prior to the November 2017 amendments; and, secondly details on the content and implications of the November 2017 amendments. The Chapter 3.2 assessment section on disclosure of related party transactions for publically traded companies offers an assessment of Lithuania against the related **Principle V.A.6**.

Rules regulating related party transactions and conflicts of interest in force at the time of writing

The annotations to the *Principles*' recommendation to address conflicts of interest inherent in related party transactions **(Principle II.F.1)** note that a jurisdiction's legal and regulatory framework for related party transactions should include "broad but precise definitions of what is understood to be a related party" as well as "procedures for approving them in a manner that minimises their negative potential".

The Lithuanian authorities report that, for the purposes of transparency and disclosure of related party transactions (see also Chapter 3.2 assessment section on disclosure of related party transactions), the Lithuanian Business Accounting Standards (BAS) rely on the definition of a related party as provided in International Accounting Standards (IAS), which according to the *Principles* usually serves as a reference for this definition. (For ease of reference, the definition of a related party provided by IAS 24 – "Related Party Disclosures" is included in Box 3.2.)

Box 3.2 Definition of a "related party" as per IAS 24

The Lithuanian authorities report that the legal definition of a "related Party" in Lithuanian law draws from IAS. IAS 24 – "Related Party Disclosures" provides the following definitions:

- **Related party transaction:** A transfer of resources, services or obligations between related parties, regardless of whether a price is charged.
- **Related party:** An entity is defined as a related party if:

  (a) directly, or indirectly through one or more intermediaries, the party:

  - *(i)* controls, is controlled by, or is under common control with, the entity (this includes parents, subsidiaries and fellow subsidiaries);
  - *(ii)* has an interest in the entity that gives it significant influence over the entity; or
  - *(iii)* has joint control over the entity;

  (b) the party is an associate (as defined in IAS 28 Investments in associates) of the entity;

  (c) the party is a joint venture in which the entity is a venturer (see IAS 31 Interests in joint ventures);

  (d) the party is a member of the key management personnel of the entity or its parent;

  (e) the party is a close member of the family of any individual referred to in (a) or (d);

  (f) the party is an entity that is controlled, jointly controlled or significantly influenced by, or for which significant voting power in such entity resides with, directly or indirectly, any individual referred to in (d) or (e); or

  (g) the party is a post-employment benefit plan for the benefit of employees of the entity, or of any entity that is a related party of the entity.

Source : http://www.ifrs.org/IFRSs/Pages/IFRS.aspx

In August 2017, the Resolution of the Bank of Lithuania defining "related persons" was repealed with a new Resolution which entered into force on 1 January 2018.[5] The previous version included a definition of "related persons" that was narrower than the IAS 24 definition. A new Resolution of the Board of the Bank of Lithuania on the Approval of the Rules on Disclosure of Information requires that "notifications on the transactions with the securities of the issuer concluded by its managers and persons closely associated with them shall be prepared and disclosed" in accordance with the EU Market Abuse Regulation.

Principle II.F.1 includes the recommendation that the framework for related party transactions should also include "procedures for approving them in a manner that minimises their negative potential". As noted above, prior to the amendments to the Law on Companies enacted in November 2017, the law did not regulate such transactions and the only explicit rule in place to address procedures for review of related party transactions was the Nasdaq Vilnius Corporate Governance Code Principle IV.5, which recommends that material related party transactions be subject to the approval of the company's collegial body (IV.4.5).

Principle II.F.2 requires that members of the board and key executives disclose to the board potential conflicts of interest when considering any transaction or matter affecting the corporation. In terms of disclosure of conflicts of interest, two laws apply. First, candidates to the office of company manager (CEO) and to positions on the management board and supervisory board (where applicable) are required under Art. 19.9 of the Law on Companies to "inform the electing body where and what position he holds, how his other activities are related to the company and to other legal persons related to the company". Second, sitting members of a company's managing body[6] (defined as either a CEO, a management board member, or shareholder), must according to Art. 2.87 of the Civil Code, "avoid a situation where his personal interests are contrary or may be contrary to the interests of a legal person". Where such conflicts of interest arise, these individuals must notify the other members of the company's managing body and this notification must be included in minutes of the meeting of that body (Art. 2.87[3, 5-6]).

Only members of a company's management board are required under the Law on Companies to abstain from voting on decisions regarding transactions or other matters where they have a material interest: Art. 35.6 of the Law on Companies requires a member of the management board to remove him or herself in these situations (specifically, situations where the matter under consideration relates to the board members' work or the issue of his or her responsibility), but no similar provision applies to members of supervisory boards (Art. 32), where such bodies have been established. The Law on Companies allows the management board to decide whether an individual board member should withdraw from voting on a specific issue, once the board member has given notification of a conflict of interest. It appears that no parallel or complementary provisions apply to specifically to the collegial bodies of listed companies, for example in the Civil Code, the Law on Securities, nor in the Law on Markets in Financial Instruments.[7] The November 2017 amendments to the Law on Companies stipulate that a related party (i) cannot vote on decisions regarding the transactions for which they are considered a related party and (ii) cannot participate in the drafting of the board's opinion on the transaction.

The Nasdaq Vilnius Corporate Governance Code complements the legal framework with non-binding recommendations on the issue of identifying and disclosing conflicts of interest. NASDAQ Code Principle III.2 recommends that candidates to be members of a company's collegial bodies (management or supervisory boards) disclose possible conflicts of interest prior to their nomination. Further, Principle VII on "the avoidance of conflicts of interest and their disclosure" calls on listed companies to establish a "corporate governance framework [that] should encourage members of the corporate bodies to avoid conflicts of interest and assure transparent and effective mechanisms for disclosure of conflicts of interest regarding members of the corporate bodies", including reporting such transactions when they are concluded (Principle VII.3) and abstaining from voting when decisions concerning such transactions are voted on (Principle VII.4). Finally, Principle X.1 recommends that companies disclose the conclusion of related party transactions.

In practice, the Lithuanian authorities report that some listed companies have included rules regarding the approval and conduct of related party transactions, including the management of potential conflicts of interest, in their articles of association or other governing documents (although this could not be verified). These companies include Lietuvos energijos gamyba (Lithuanian Energy Production), LITGRID, Klaipėdos nafta (Klaipėda Oil), Gubernija, Amber Grid, and City Service. Lithuania's recent legislative reforms (discussed below) for the approval, conduct and disclosure of related party transactions were undertaken in part to align with the provisions of the EU Shareholder Rights Directive, which was adopted on 3 April 2017.

Rules regulating related party transactions that enter into force in July 2018

As mentioned in the beginning of this section, amendments to the Law on Companies enacted in November 2017 introduce new criteria for the definition, approval and scrutiny of related party transactions. The amendments notably introduce a number of additional rules regarding the process for approving and disclosing related party transactions involving listed companies. The amendments introduce language specifying that a related party can be defined in accordance with the accounting standards adopted by the company in question (i.e. either international or national accounting standards). According to the Lithuanian authorities, the definitions of related parties and related party transactions in Lithuania's national Business Accounting Standards have the same meaning as those established in IAS. The amendments establish that a related party must inform the manager of a listed company of the reasons for which it could be considered "related", following which the manager must obtain the approval of the supervisory board (or the management board if tasked with supervisory functions) prior to entering into a transaction with the concerned party, if the transaction (i) is concluded outside of ordinary market conditions; (ii) is not undertaken in the course of the ordinary economic activities of the company; or (iii) has a significant influence on the company, its finances, assets and liabilities (with "significant influence" to be defined in the company's articles of association). The amendments furthermore require that the audit committee undertake an assessment of any related party transaction (that fulfil the aforementioned criteria) submitted for approval by the company manager, notably concerning whether it is entered into under market conditions and whether it is "fair and justified" with respect to the company and its shareholders. This assessment must be communicated to the company within 20 days of receiving the related information from the company manager, who is then required to immediately inform shareholders, the board(s) and the related party of the assessment. These stakeholders must then be given access to the audit committee's opinion at the registered office of the company. Finally, the amendments also require that listed companies publish information on related party transactions (that fulfil the aforementioned criteria) on their web site no later than the date of undertaking the transaction. These amendments are complemented with amendments to the Law on Financial Reporting by Undertakings, also enacted in November 2017, which require that listed companies report on related party transactions in their annual corporate governance reports (see also Chapter 3.2 assessment section on the disclosure of related party transactions for publicly traded companies).

Once they enter into force, these reforms establish a framework for strengthened oversight and independent scrutiny of related party transactions in Lithuanian listed companies, thus helping to address many of the issues outlined earlier in this section. Furthermore, many of the concerns highlighted during the corporate governance accession review process – which were based on draft legislation under consideration in Parliament over the course of 2017 – appear to have been largely addressed in the legislation that was ultimately enacted. Perhaps most importantly, the fundamental concern that listed companies could be excluded from the provisions on review of related party transactions if operating under single-tier management boards appears to have been addressed with concurrent amendments requiring that all such management boards be accorded supervisory functions. It will therefore no longer be possible that responsibility for approving related party transactions falls only to the AGM, addressing a significant corporate governance vulnerability highlighted during the corporate governance accession review process. Other concerns that appear to have been largely addressed, or that are in the process of being addressed, include the following: (i) draft amendments that would have allowed for related party transactions to be excluded from the oversight provisions if entered into with the company founder were not ultimately enacted; (ii) a previously narrow proposed definition of related party transactions subject to review, based only on transactional value, has been replaced with a broader definition including references to "significant influence on the company, its finances, assets and liabilities" (i.e. materiality); and (iii) the Bank of Lithuania amended its rules on audit committee composition to eliminate an exemption from independence requirements in cases where the audit committee is entirely composed of supervisory board members. The elimination of this exemption strengthens audit committees' independence from controlling shareholders.

Institutional investor disclosure, corporate governance policies, conflicts of interest and voting (Principles III.A and III.C)

Principle III.A states that "Institutional investors acting in a fiduciary capacity should disclose their corporate governance and voting policies with respect to their investments, including the procedures that they have in place for deciding on the use of their voting rights."

As noted in Chapter 2.3, institutional investors—such as mutual funds, pension funds, insurance companies and hedge funds—do not play a major role in Lithuanian capital markets. Nevertheless, Lithuanian legislation does provide for institutional investors to disclose investment and voting policies. These requirements generally fall under the Law on Companies and the Law on Collective Investment Undertakings. Under this framework, a shareholder who has acquired shares in his own name, but on behalf of other persons, must disclose to the issuer before voting at a general meeting of shareholders: the identity of the final customer, the number of shares that are put to vote and the content of the voting instructions submitted for the voting shares or any other explanation regarding the customer's agreed participation and their agreement to vote at the general shareholders' meeting (Law on Companies, Art. 30^3). Institutional investors must also disclose to clients "sufficient information related and necessary", they must publish their investment policies and other relevant information as requested by clients and they must invest in the best interest of their clients (Law on Collective Investment Undertakings, Art. 11).

In addition, Lithuania's Law on the Accumulation of Occupational Pensions, which regulates pension funds, requires pension funds' management boards to include in their pension fund rules information on the fund's investment policy (Art. 15.3.9), which can be accessed at any time by participants in the fund (Art. 15.7). The investment policy must include at least the following aspects: (1) the procedure for the investment of pension assets and the fields of investment; (2) risk assessment methods; (3) the applied risk management procedures and methods; and (4) strategic distribution of pension assets (Art. 46.2).

Principle III.C states that institutional investors acting in a fiduciary capacity should disclose how they manage material conflicts of interest that may affect the exercise of key ownership rights regarding their investments. The Law on Collective Investment Undertakings requires such undertakings to establish an organisational structure that prevents conflicts of interest (Arts. 11.1.7 and 11.2). While these provisions of the law do not explicitly require disclosure of institutional investors' means for preventing material conflicts of interest, they do—as noted above under **Principle III.A**—require that these entities disclose to clients "sufficient information related and necessary", though the law does not define what information is "sufficient" and "related and necessary".

For pension funds, the Law on the Accumulation of Occupational Pensions requires pension funds to "try to avoid conflicts of interests and, in the case it is not possible to avoid them, ensure fair treatment of the participants", while always acting "fairly in the interests of its members and market credibility" (Art. 7.1 and 5). In addition, members of pension fund management boards should avoid conflicts of interest and act with proper care (Art. 13.3).

Insider trading and abusive self-dealing (Principle III.E)

Principle III.E states that insider trading and market manipulation should be prohibited and the applicable rules enforced. In Lithuania, insider trading and abusive self-dealing are prohibited under the Law on Markets in Financial Instruments Art. 62 ("Prohibition of the Use of Inside Information when Trading in Financial Instruments) and Art. 63 ("Prohibition of Market Manipulation"). Further, sections 23.6-8 of the Nasdaq Vilnius Listing Rules prohibit disclosing information that could have an impact on the price of listed financial instruments until the information is made public through official means via Nasdaq Vilnius.

Sanctions and other punishments for violating rules against insider trading and abusive self-dealing are provided for in the Law on Markets in Financial Instruments, the Code of Administrative Offences, the Criminal Code and the Nasdaq Vilnius Listing Rules. Applicable fines were updated in July 2016 to align Lithuania's framework with EU regulations and increase sanctioning authority.[8] The government agency primarily responsible for enforcing rules against insider trading and abusive self-dealing is the Bank of Lithuania, which co-operates where necessary with Lithuanian police and government prosecutors (particularly where possible criminal violations are concerned). Administrative offences may be tried in court. The Bank of Lithuania reported on one recent case of imposing administrative penalties for insider trading, though the case is currently under appeal (see Box 3.3). However, the Bank of Lithuania has expressed a preference for a softer approach involving the issuance of verbal and written warnings as more efficient and effective in influencing the market. The Chapter 2.6 section on consistency with the rule of law, transparency and enforcement outlines the more extensive activity undertaken by the Bank to review suspicious trading activity, which has led to 36 verbal and written warnings issued to companies between 2013 and 2015 related to potential cases of market manipulation and insider trading.

Box 3.3 Case study: Insider trading ahead of the Agrowill - Baltic Champs merger

In 2014, the Bank of Lithuania initiated an investigation into possible insider trading in advance of the still-undisclosed merger between agricultural investment group Agrowill Group AB and mushroom cultivator Baltic Champs UAB.[1] The investigation was opened after the Bank noticed messages posted in an online investors' forum indicating one forum user ("the user") had obtained information about the pending merger before it had been publicly disclosed. (At the time, the two companies had informed the Bank of Lithuania of the pending merger, which was considered inside information until the merger was signed and publicly announced.)

After identifying the identity of the user, the Bank of Lithuania applied to the courts for authorisation to obtain information from the user's computer. With access granted, the Bank of Lithuania confirmed that the user had access to inside information on the prospective Agrowill/Baltic Champs merger and that the information had been shared with the user by the employee of a financial brokerage firm. The investigation further proved that the user and the financial brokerage firm employee were aware that their actions violated the Law on Markets in Financial Instruments' rules against insider trading and abusive self-dealing. Finally, the Bank's investigation was able to prove that the user applied this inside information for his own private interests by retaining his shares in Agrowill Group and waiting for the post-merger share price increase.

The Bank of Lithuania summarised the results of its investigation and prepared reports on the administrative violations performed by the two natural persons in the case—the user and the financial brokerage firm employee—and submitted the reports to the district court. The district court found both natural persons to have violated the Law on Markets in Financial Instruments and imposed penalties of EUR1 600 and EUR1 500. The rulings were appealed to the Supreme Court, which upheld the district court decisions. The Bank of Lithuania also imposed a penalty of EUR 20 000 on the financial brokerage firm for violating the Law on Markets in Financial Instruments prohibition to either directly or indirectly forward inside information to another person. The decision has been appealed and a final decision was pending as of the time of writing (mid-2016).

1. See online here for the merger announcement: http://www.agrowill.lt/en/agromedia/baltic-champs-merges-with-agrowill-group

Source : Information provided by the Lithuanian authorities

Equitable treatment of shareholders among state-owned enterprises

Shareholder protections (Guideline IV.A)

Guideline IV.A provides that the state should strive toward full implementation of the *G20/OECD Principles of Corporate Governance* when it is not the sole owner of SOEs and of all relevant sections when it is the sole owner of SOEs. Concerning shareholder protection this includes the following recommendations: (i) The state and SOEs should ensure that all shareholders are treated equitably; (ii) SOEs should observe a high degree of transparency, including as a general rule equal and simultaneous disclosure of information, towards all shareholders; (iii) SOEs should develop an active policy of communication and consultation with all shareholders; (iv) The participation of minority shareholders in shareholder meetings should be facilitated so they can take part in fundamental corporate decisions, such as board election; and (v) Transactions between the state and SOEs, and between SOEs, should take place on market consistent terms.

Ensuring equitable treatment (Guideline IV.A.1)

Concerning the general legal framework for shareholder rights, fully corporatised SOEs are subject to the relevant provisions of the Law on Companies, including notably Article 3 which stipulates that "Under identical circumstances all holders of shares of the same class shall have equal rights and duties". Listed SOEs are also included in the scope of applicability of the Law on Securities, including notably its provisions (i) requiring mandatory takeover bids where a shareholder acquires 1/3 of voting rights and (ii) allowing for a controlling shareholder to purchase minority shareholdings once it reaches the threshold of 95% of voting shares, provided that the shares are purchased at a fair price.

That being said, in certain SOEs, exceptions to equitable treatment of shareholders are provided for by law. The Law on Enterprises and Facilities of Strategic Importance to National Security notably identifies eight strategically important SOEs in which "the capital may be held by private national and foreign persons conforming to the national security interests, provided the power of decision is retained by the State" (Art. 4.1). Article 7 of the Law provides that any investor seeking to acquire 5% or more of the votes in strategically important SOEs must be screened by a commission set up by the Government. Such a transaction can only take place if the commission concludes that the concerned investor meets criteria in line with national security interests.

Transparency toward all shareholders (Guideline IV.A.2)

Amendments to the Law on Companies enacted in November 2017 removed provisions that explicitly granted controlling shareholders (in the case of SOEs, the state) privileged access to corporate information and thus constituted a fundamental limitation to SOE shareholders' equal access to information. Prior to these amendments, simultaneous disclosure of information to all shareholders (including minority shareholders) was not fully provided for by law, given the fact that controlling shareholders were accorded the right to access any and all company documents upon request, subject to a written confidentiality pledge. While the confidentiality pledge did provide a measure of protection, it did not guard minority investors against the risk of privileged use of corporate information by the controlling state shareholder.

Communication and consultation with shareholders (Guideline IV.A.3)

SOE boards in Lithuania are not required to maintain a list of non-state shareholders, as recommended in the SOE Guidelines. However, SOEs are subject to provisions of the Law on Companies requiring that a list of shareholders be provided upon any individual shareholder's request.

In the context of the 2015 SOE review, representatives of the management of Lithuanian Energy offered a recent example of measures taken to promote active consultation with minority shareholders (OECD 2015). Prior to the company's recent restructuring, the company reportedly made efforts to actively engage with minority shareholders and the investor community to communicate details on the foreseen restructuring and governance changes. This included presentations made to market participants outlining plans prior to their formal approval via shareholder meetings.

Minority shareholders' participation (Guideline IV.A.4)

SOEs are subject to provisions of the Law on Companies pertaining to minority shareholders' participation in corporate decision-making. This includes notably provisions requiring a qualified majority (2/3 of votes) for certain corporate decisions (which, importantly, do not include board elections) and provisions allowing all shareholders to vote *in absentia*. Listed SOEs do not allow electronic voting, although this is apparently the case for all listed companies in Lithuania. The provisions pertaining to qualified majority votes have little relevance for SOEs, since most listed SOEs have less than 5% non-state ownership.

According to corporate practitioners interviewed in the context of the 2015 SOE review, in practice minority shareholders in SOEs are generally not very active in shareholder meetings or corporate decision-making (OECD, 2015). This probably reflects in part the low and/or dispersed minority ownership of SOEs. Minority shareholders' involvement in key corporate decisions would possibly increase if SOEs augmented their free float on the stock exchange.

Transactions between the state and SOEs and between SOEs (Guideline IV.A.5):

There are no special rules or procedures regarding the market consistency of transactions between the state and SOEs. However, as a member of the European Union, Lithuania is obliged to follow the European State Aid regulations which place relatively strict restrictions on the amount of public money that can be granted to companies for purposes other than compensating for services in the general economic interest.

There is evidence to suggest that, at least in some cases, the relationship between SOEs is not based on purely commercial grounds. In a recent example, Lithuanian Shipping Company was on the verge of entering insolvency procedures in August 2015 following the sequester of several of its ships in foreign ports as collateral for unpaid debts. Lithuanian Shipping Company received a EUR 3 million loan from Lithuanian Railways and a EUR 500 000 loan from Smiltynė Ferry Terminal, both state-owned and under the purview of the Ministry of Transport and Communications. Given that three banks had reportedly refused to finance the distressed SOE, the loans provided by other SOEs were arguably not market consistent. Lithuanian Shipping Company has since been transformed into a subsidiary of Lithuanian Railways, which recuperated only part of its original loan through the sale of the shipping company's assets.

Disclosure of public policy objectives (Guideline IV.C)

Guideline IV.C states that, where SOEs are required to pursue public policy objectives, adequate information about these should be available to non-state shareholders at all times. There are no explicit provisions in place to ensure that the nature and scope of SOEs' public policy objectives are available to non-state shareholders at all times. However, public policy objectives are reported annually to the GCC and disclosed to the public as of 2014, in accordance with requirements set forth in the Transparency Guidelines. Therefore in principle, non-state shareholders would also have access to this information, but only after the carrying out of the public policy activities.

3.2 Requiring timely and reliable disclosure of corporate information in accordance with internationally recognised standards of accounting, auditing and non-financial reporting.

The Concept Paper, in its guidance for assessing Lithuania's corporate governance framework relative to this *Roadmap* principle, suggests three main areas of focus. A first key issue is the application of accounting and auditing standards and practices (**Principles V.B** and **C** and **Guidelines VI.A**, **B**, and **C**). A second key emphasis is the importance of disclosing information on two aspects of corporate information: enterprise governance, ownership and voting structures (**Principles II.E.2**, **V.A.3** and **V.A.9** and **Guideline VI.A.3**); and disclosure of related party transactions (**Principle V.A.6** and **Guideline VI.A.8**). This section, therefore, begins with a brief introduction to the overall framework for the disclosure of company information in Lithuania, and then is broken down into three substantive sections: accounting and auditing standards; disclosure of governance, ownership, and voting structures; and disclosure of related party transactions.

Framework for the disclosure of company information

The framework for the disclosure of company information applicable to all Lithuanian companies consists of the following laws: the Civil Code, the Law on Companies, the Law on Financial Reporting by Undertakings and, for parent companies in a group situation, the Law on Consolidated Financial Reporting by Groups of Undertakings. For listed companies, the Law on Securities also applies. At the most basic level, all documents concerning significant company matters must be easily accessible by actual and potential investors and other interested persons, as per the Civil Code, which requires legal entities to register with and deposit all relevant information as required by law in the publicly accessible national Register of Legal Entities (Civil Code Arts. 2.66, 2.71[1], and 2.72[3-5]). Together, these laws set forth minimum requirements for the preparation by all companies of annual reports and financial statements, as well as additional requirements for other periodic disclosures by listed companies, for example of auditors' reports, to the regulator and to the public. The content of companies' disclosure is discussed in more detail below.

Private sector representatives indicated during the Secretariat's May 2016 fact-finding visit that most companies do not go beyond the legal disclosure minimum. Among issues on which there tends to be low levels of disclosure include financial information on activities abroad, information on internal corporate governance structures, codes of ethics, or executive remuneration. (See also the Chapter 3.2 assessment on disclosure of ownership, voting structures and governance structures for more on disclosures of compliance with the Nasdaq Vilnius Corporate Governance Code.)

Concerns were also raised in relation to the functioning of the Lithuanian Register of Legal Entities, a state-owned enterprise under the responsibility of the Ministry of Justice, which is responsible for registering the existence of all companies and providing access to company information. As noted in the Chapter 2.3 section on the institutional framework for corporate governance, the government decides what information is collected by the Register and is available to users for free and what information must be paid for by users, but the Register lacks any enforcement powers. Both government entities – which must also pay for access to certain kinds of information in the Register, and the private sector and civil society – expressed concerns that the Register is not effectively fulfilling its responsibility for collecting and ensuring public access to company information in

Lithuania. Some critics say that this problem is so serious that it could negatively impact public procurement procedures in Lithuania and the enforcement of Lithuania's framework for supervising and disclosing related party transactions.

Accounting and auditing standards

Accounting standards for listed companies (Principle V.B)

Principle V.B recommends that listed companies' information be prepared and disclosed in accordance with high quality standards of accounting and financial and non-financial reporting. In Lithuania, accounting standards applicable to listed companies are set forth in the Law on Accounting and, for parent companies with subsidiaries (i.e. companies in a so-called group situation), the Law on Consolidated Financial Reporting by Groups of Undertakings.[9] (See the Chapter 3.2 assessment section on the framework for disclosure of company information for an overview of accounting standards applicable to SOEs.)

Under the Law on Accounting (Art. 3.2), listed companies may apply either International Accounting Standards (IAS) or the national standard, the Business Accounting Standards (BAS) to individual accounts, and they must apply IAS to consolidated annual accounts (where applicable).

Companies were given the choice to apply either IAS or BAS to individual accounts as of 1 January 2016, after the Law on Accounting was amended (at the initiative of the Bank of Lithuania). Prior to this date, listed companies were required to apply IAS to both individual and consolidated accounts. The Lithuanian authorities report that the change was made in order to facilitate entry to capital markets by reducing the administrative burden imposed by IAS. They argue that this change is in compliance with Regulation (EC) No. 1606/2002, which makes it optional for member states to require listed companies to prepare their individual financial statements according to IAS. The Lithuanian authorities add that BAS are 97% aligned with international standards. However, a number of differences between BAS and IFRS were identified by the Lithuanian authorities—building on previous critical assessments of the BAS made by the World Bank—and are listed in Box 3.4 (World Bank 2007 and World Bank, 2002). These differences could be significant, depending on a company's operations and circumstances.

A 2007 World Bank assessment found that many of the complex areas dealt with by IFRS are not relevant to most Lithuanian companies, given the simplicity of their operations, but that this could change as companies' operations, remuneration schemes and funding arrangements evolve (World Bank, 2007). The same World Bank assessment also found that for companies reporting according to national accounting standards, a key area of non-compliance with those standards concerned the disclosure of related party transactions. Together these factors point to some issues of concern regarding the quality of financial statements in Lithuania, although the Lithuania authorities report that significant improvements in accounting practices have taken place over the past decade. As of end-2014, all listed companies prepared and disclosed their annual financial reports using IAS, according to the Lithuanian authorities (although two issuers received warnings from the Bank of Lithuania in 2015 because their financial statements were not in accordance with certain IFRS requirements). The Lithuanian authorities further specify that as of mid-2015, the Lithuanian Business Accounting Standard on "Explanatory Notes" specifically stipulates that the legal definition of "related parties" has the same meaning as that provided in International Accounting Standards (IAS 24). Finally, at the time of writing in early 2018, the Ministry of Finance of Lithuania informed the Secretariat that revisions to national accounting standards were under way in the two areas where differences between IAS and BAS were considered the most material, namely concerning the treatment of inventories and the treatment of financial assets and liabilities.

Box 3.4 Key differences between IFRS and Lithuanian BAS

According to the Lithuanian authorities, the national accounting standards (BAS) are generally based on IFRS, with the following differences. Revisions to national accounting standards were under way in early 2018 to better align with IFRS in the two areas considered by the Lithuanian authorities to be the most material, namely concerning the treatment of inventories and the treatment of financial assets and liabilities.

- Under IFRS goodwill must be capitalised and tested for impairment on an annual basis. Under BAS goodwill must be capitalised and amortised. According to the Lithuanian authorities, the Directive 2013/34/EU on the annual financial statements, consolidated financial statements and related reports of certain types of undertakings, amending Directive 2006/43/EC of the European Parliament and of the Council and repealing Council Directives 78/660/EEC and 83/349/EE) establishes amortisation of goodwill. The appropriate provisions are implemented in national law. Different provisions than those of the Accounting Directive cannot be established.
- BAS does not require a statement of other comprehensive income. The Lithuanian authorities report that under BAS, if other comprehensive income is significant, then it would need to be explained in the Explanatory Notes to the Statement of Changes in Equity.
- IFRS does not permit the "last in, first out" formula (LIFO) as the basis for inventory valuation. BAS permits LIFO, but only in very rare cases. Draft amendments are reportedly under consideration to prohibit listed companies from using LIFO.
- Where an entity undertakes a sale and leaseback transaction where the sale is not at fair value, companies are not required to defer any element of the gain or loss and amortise over the period of expected use of the asset. Under IFRS certain elements of the gain or loss must be deferred and amortised. According to the Lithuanian authorities, this difference will be considered when discussing the BAS amendment in accordance with the 16 IFRS "Lease" approved by the EU.
- BAS requires recognising some types of non-current assets in state enterprises by specific rules that are not dealt with by IFRS. According to the Lithuanian authorities, this difference is no longer relevant, since the Transparency Guidelines require (large) SOEs to keep accounts in accordance with international accounting standards.
- Under BAS, for the purpose of measuring, financial assets are classified into three categories: held-for-sale; held-to-maturity; originated loans and amounts receivable. The gains and loss on a financial asset must be recognised in profit or loss. Under IFRS financial assets are classified in an additional available-for-sale category, where gains and loss must be recognised in other comprehensive income.
- Under IFRS at initial recognition a financial asset or financial liability arising from a financial instrument shall be recorded at its fair value. Under BAS it shall be recorded at its acquisition cost. According to the Lithuanian authorities, this difference will be considered while discussing the amendment to BAS following the 9 IRFS "Financial Instruments" approved by the EU.
- The goodwill and non-controlling interest may be measured differently under IFRS and under BAS due to the IFRS permitting the acquirer to measure a non-controlling interest at its fair value at the acquisition date, which is not permitted under BAS. According to the Lithuanian authorities this difference is no longer relevant, because measurement of non-controlling interest is relevant in drawing up consolidated financial statements. Consolidated financial statements of the listed companies are drawn up under the IFRS.
- Under IFRS biological assets shall be measured on initial recognition and at the end of each reporting period at its fair value less cost to sell, except for the case when the fair value cannot be measured reliably. Under BAS, biological assets shall be measured applying one of these methods: at the fair value less cost to sale or at the acquisition (production) costs. Draft amendments are reportedly under consideration to require listed companies to measure biological assets at fair value less cost to sell.

Source: Information provided by the Lithuanian authorities.

The main institution responsible for the development of the Lithuanian accounting framework is the Ministry of Finance. This includes the laws and standards described above, including BAS.[10] Ensuring implementation and enforcement of this framework for unlisted companies rests with the newly established Authority of Audit, Accounting, Property Valuation and Insolvency Management, which was created under the amended new Law on Accounting and replaces the former Authority of Audit and Accounting as of 1 January 2016. The so-called "Authority" is under the Ministry of Finance. Enforcement of the accounting framework for listed companies rests with the Bank of Lithuania. Finally, under the Law on Securities, the Bank of Lithuania may inspect whether issuers' individual and/or consolidated financial statements have been drawn up in accordance with the relevant requirements.

Audit standards (Principle V.C)

Principle V.C recommends that an annual audit should be conducted by an independent, competent and qualified auditor, in accordance with high-quality auditing standards in order to provide an external and objective assurance to the board and shareholders that the financial statements fairly represent the financial position and performance of the company in all material respects.

The audit framework for companies is set forth in the Law on Audit, including requirements for external auditors, for how audits are carried out, as well as for supervising and overseeing the audit profession. Under the law, external audit must be carried out by an independent and qualified auditor (Art. 4 and 5). The companies subject to external audit are outlined in the Law on Financial Reporting by Undertakings, which requires all public limited liability companies to be subject to external audit (Art. 24.1). The Law on Audit was amended on 15 December 2016, with its new provisions entering into force on 1 March 2017, to ensure compliance with EU Directive 2014/56/EU on the audit of financial statements. According to the Lithuanian authorities, the amendments notably establish more stringent requirements for independence, objectivity and professional ethics of the auditors and audit firms that undertake audits of financial statements. The amendments also establish new requirements for the composition, formation and functions of audit committees. The additional functions assigned to audit committees notably include playing a stronger role in selecting the auditor or audit firm, as well as monitoring related remuneration.

Amendments to the Law on Audit are complemented by a 24 January 2017 Resolution of the Bank of Lithuania pertaining to the independence of audit committees for listed companies. The Resolution notably requires that the majority of audit committee members, including the committee chair, be independent, an increase over the previous requirement that at least one member be independent. The Resolution furthermore outlines criteria for independence, which is defined not only relation to company management, but also in relation to controlling shareholder(s).

As mentioned in the section on related party transactions and conflicts of interest, the Resolution was revised by the Bank of Lithuania in early 2018 to remove an exemption from the aforementioned independence requirements in situations where the audit committee was composed entirely of supervisory board members. The elimination of this exemption supports audit committee's enhanced independence from controlling shareholders.

Audit rules applicable to companies

The Law on Audit requires all public interest companies to be subject to external audit according to International Audit Standards (Art. 27). The external auditor or audit firm is elected or removed from their position by the general meeting of shareholders, taking into account the proposal of the management body or the supervisory body (Law on Companies, Art. 20.1.5 and Law on Audit Art. 52.4).

The Law on Audit also requires every public interest company to establish an audit committee to monitor the effectiveness of the enterprise's internal audit function and to ensure the independence and objectivity of the external auditor or audit firm, which reports to the audit committee (Art. 52). The requirements for audit committees (applicable to listed companies) were established by the Resolution of the Securities Commission as of 21 August 2008 No 1K-18. It establishes the main rules and procedures to be followed while forming the audit committee (e.g. it shall be composed of non-executive staff members and (or) the members of supervisory board and (or) persons appointed by the general meeting, at least one member of the audit committee shall be independent and the criteria to be used to assess whether the member of the committee shall be regarded as independent. These requirements are complemented by Nasdaq Vilnius Corporate Governance Code Principle IV.14, which recommends the establishment of a specialised audit committee along with other measures regarding their role, composition and responsibilities; 22 out of 28 listed companies fully complied with this recommendation in 2015.

In discussions with representatives from the private sector during the Secretariat's fact-finding mission to Vilnius in May 2016, there appeared to be some confusion over the composition and responsibilities of audit committees, required of all large companies, as well as their relationship to the management board or the supervisory board (where one exists). There may be some risk that the audit committee functions at too great a distance from the management and/or supervisory board, since its composition may be entirely separate from that of the management or supervisory board. While the Nasdaq Vilnius Corporate Governance Code recommends that specialised committees regularly report back to the management and/or supervisory board, there is scope for clarification and further elaboration regarding requirements or good practices for audit committees. The amendments to the Law on Audit adopted on 15 December 2016 (which entered into force on 1 March 2017) introduce greater clarity regarding the composition, formation, activities and functions of audit committees.

Additionally, the Bank of Lithuania recently established requirements applicable to audit committees to complement the Law on Audit of Financial Statements' provision, which entered into force on 1 March, 2017. The Bank of Lithuania reported that the revised requirements are aimed at increasing the effectiveness of the process of preparing the financial statements and carrying out of the statutory audit thereof, increasing the efficiency of systems on internal control, risk management and internal audit, strengthening the supervision of the adherence to the principles of independence and fairness of the statutory auditor. They set out the procedure for the formation of the audit committee, the requirements applicable to audit committee members, the main principles on the procedures of the audit committee and additional duties of the audit committee regarding the recommendations provided to the supervisory body on the appointment of the statutory auditor, supervision of the independence and fairness of the statutory auditor and the efficiency of the statutory audit.

The requirements apply to listed companies, banks, central credit unions, insurance companies, reinsurance companies, the national stock exchange and the CSD. The Bank of Lithuania reported that in order to spread good practice and to provide some insights on how the requirements stipulated in the legal acts shall be applied, the revised requirements will be complemented by guidelines on audit committees prepared and adopted by the Supervisory Service of the Bank of Lithuania. (For more on the Law on Audit's requirements applicable to companies, see the Chapter 2.5 section on the legal and regulatory framework for corporate governance. For more on boards' specialised committees, see the Chapter 3.5 assessment section on the rights, duties and responsibilities of boards.)

Audit rules applicable to auditors and audit firms

The Law on Audit specifies the minimum requirements for qualifying to serve as a certified auditor in Lithuania. Under the Law on Audit, certified auditors must: (1) hold a university degree; (2) be of good repute; (3) have work experience; (4) have passed qualification examinations; and (5) have been sworn in as an auditor (Art. 8). In terms of audit firm requirements, the head of the firm must be an external auditor and at least three-quarters of the firm's members must be auditors (Art. 18.1-2). All auditors must comply with the provisions of the International Federation of Accountants' (IFAC) Code of Ethics for Professional Accountants.[11]

The Law on Audit includes provisions securing the independence of external auditors and audit firms (Section 2). These provisions were strengthened from mid-2016, when Regulation (EU) No 537/2014 of the European Parliament and of the Council was applied to public interest entities and their auditors (see the Chapter 2.5 section on the legal and regulatory framework for corporate governance). The Regulation establishes strict requirements for auditor's independence and avoidance of conflicts of interest. It also strengthens existing rules for the selection of external auditors and audit firms and other matters (i.e. auditor duties to prepare audit report, report to the audit committee, report to supervisors of public interest entities and transparency report).

Prior to the adoption and entry into force of the aforementioned amendments to the Law on Audit, public oversight of the audit profession (quality assurance, investigations and sanctions) was the responsibility of the Authority of Audit, Accounting, Property Valuation and Insolvency Management, with the Chamber of Auditors sharing responsibility for the quality assurance of audits. Following a quality review, sanctions could be imposed only with the approval of the Authority. As of the entry into force of the amendments, the Authority oversees (undertakes inspections and investigations) the auditors and audit firms of "public interest entities" (a category which includes listed companies and large SOEs). For other entities, reviews of the quality of audits performed by auditors and audit firms are undertaken by the Chamber of Auditors, which also provides continuing education, oversees auditors' and audit firms' compliance with ethics requirements and holds qualification examinations. (The amendments transferred the inspection of audits of public interest entities from the Chamber of Auditors to the Authority. Quality assurance of audits for non-public-interest entities is undertaken by the Chamber of Auditors.) The Authority has ultimate responsibility for the oversight of all auditors and audit firms and is answerable to the Ministry of Finance, as the ministry responsible for the development of the Law on Audit. The amended Law on Audit delegates some functions (e.g. reviews) to the Chamber of Auditors.

The amended Law on Audit also establishes rules for how the Authority carries out quality controls of auditors and audit firms (of public interest entities), as per Regulation [EU] No 537/2014. Where review, inspection or investigation weaknesses are identified, the Authority may impose disciplinary penalties with compulsory recommendations for improvement. Disciplinary penalties may include a warning and the suspension or withdrawal of an auditor's license. (See Tables 3.1 and 3.2 for the results of similar controls carried out by the Chamber of Auditors under the Law on Audit in force as of mid-2016.) In 2015, sanctions were applied after investigating the audit of a state-owned enterprise and, in 2014, sanctions were applied against two audit firms and two auditors after investigations of audits of listed companies.

Table 3.1. Inspections of auditors and audit firms undertaken by the Chamber of Auditors, 2013-2016

	Sanctions/decisions applied after Chamber of Auditors inspections			
Year	No. of audit firms & auditors inspected by the Chamber of Auditors	Instruction by the Chamber of Auditors for the audit firm/auditor to rectify deficiencies	Instruction from the Chamber of Auditors for the auditor to develop professional qualification(s)	Decision taken by the Authority to perform an additional audit investigation[0]
2013	85	2	4	1
2014	62	2	6	
2015	78	3	7	1
2016	92	5	9	1

1. According to the Law on Audit in force as of end-2015, the Authority on Audit and Accounting could decide not to approve the decisions proposed by the Chamber of Auditors after performing inspections and to perform the investigation itself. Such decisions could be taken in cases where material deficiencies are identified during the Chamber of Audit inspection. Only after the performance of investigations by the Authority could maximum sanctions (for example, withdrawal of the auditor's licence) be applied.

Source: Authority of Audit, Accounting, Property Valuation and Insolvency Management and Ministry of Finance

Table 3.2. Disciplinary penalties imposed against auditors and audit firms, 2013-2016

	Sanctions/decisions applied by the Authority on Audit and Accounting after performing investigations						
Year	No. of investigations[0]	Instruction to rectify deficiencies	Warning to audit firm	Warning to auditor	Withdrawal of auditor's license	Suspension of auditor's license	Suspension of audit firm license
2013	2	1		1			
2014	4	2	1		4		
2015	2	1				1	1
2016	3	2		1			

1. The basis for opening an investigation against an audit or audit firm is outlined in the Law on Audit.

Source: Authority of Audit, Accounting, Property Valuation and Insolvency Management and Ministry of Finance. Note: In 2016, there were also two instructions given for the auditor to develop professional qualification(s).

Accounting, audit and disclosure standards for SOEs and aggregate reporting (Guidelines VI. A, B and C)

The Transparency Guidelines detail the accounting, audit and disclosure standards applicable to SOEs and also outline the process for aggregate reporting. Before examining the content of their individual provisions (detailed in the following sections), some general observations on their nature, scope of applicability and degree of implementation by SOEs merit mention.

- Compliance with the Transparency Guidelines became mandatory for 85 large and "public interest" SOEs, through amendments passed in August 2016. Mandatory compliance was later restricted to only 13 "large" SOEs, based on information provided by the Lithuanian authorities during the Secretariat's February 2018 fact-finding visit. Prior to August 2016, their provisions were to be implemented on a comply-or-explain basis, which remains the case for other SOEs. In case of non-compliance with any provisions, no explicit standards for the quality of SOEs' explanations have been established.

- More time is needed to meaningfully assess compliance with the Transparency Guidelines by SOEs for which they have become mandatory. A non-trivial number of SOEs are not in compliance with a number of their provisions, pointing to persistent issues with the quality and credibility of SOEs' corporate disclosure. According to the state's 2015 aggregate report, for the majority of SOEs, significant improvements are necessary in order to bring disclosure practices in line with the Transparency Guidelines (State-Owned Enterprises Governance Coordination Centre, 2016). Concerning the provision requiring IFRS implementation, eight out of 13 large SOEs were in compliance as of early 2018. For the remaining five SOEs, the Lithuanian authorities provided a timetable by the end of 2020 for IFRS implementation in four and reported that for the fifth SOE, Ignalina Nuclear Power Plant, the ownership entity was going to review the appropriateness of implementing IFRS since the SOE does not undertake any commercial activities.

- By national definitions, only SOEs under direct state ownership (and not their subsidiaries) are explicitly within the Transparency Guidelines' scope of applicability. While parent companies would be required to include consolidated financial information on their subsidiaries in their financial statements, subsidiaries arguably face less stringent disclosure standards concerning their non-financial performance.

- In addition to the disclosure standards detailed in the Transparency Guidelines, all SOEs are called upon to disclose on a comply or explain basis how they address the provisions of the national corporate governance code related to information disclosure (Principle X of the code and other provisions throughout the code that relate to information disclosure).

- The frequency of required reporting is higher for large SOEs. Annual reports and financial statements are required of all SOEs, while large SOEs (the 24 SOEs in categories I and II) must also produce quarterly reports and financial statements.[12]

- All reports and financial statements must be made available on SOEs' websites, or in the absence of one, on the website of the relevant ownership entity.

Accounting standards for SOEs (Guideline VI.A).

Guideline VI.A recommends that all SOEs report material financial and non-financial information in line with high quality internationally recognised standards of corporate disclosure. Article 16 of the Transparency Guidelines (again, mandatory for 13 large SOEs) outlines that SOEs should keep their accounts in accordance with international accounting standards. As noted above, eight of 13 large SOEs currently follow IFRS while four are transitioning to their implementation. According to government representatives and professional auditors interviewed in the context of the 2015 SOE review, the national standards are in line with EU directives and broadly reflect IFRS (OECD, 2015).

The 2015 SOE review pointed to some exceptional instances in which the application of national standards apparently differed materially from IFRS, primarily to remain consistent with other laws regulating the ownership of strategic state assets. This concerned notably: (i) the state-owned forestry enterprises, which were not required to include the value of forests in their financial statements as per the Law on Forestry, even though the enterprises derive economic benefit thereof; and (ii) the state-owned road maintenance enterprises, which must, according to Business Accounting Standard Principle 12, include the value of roads in their balance sheets as non-current tangible assets, even though they do not generate revenue for the enterprises. The National Audit Office recommended in 2010 that the state forest enterprises change their accounting practices to reflect the value of state forests in their balance sheets.[13] Recent consolidations of the multiple state-owned forestry and road maintenance enterprises have made the new enterprises large enough to trigger mandatory compliance with the Transparency Guidelines. Prior to consolidation, five of the 11 road maintenance enterprises fell under their scope of applicability owing to their size, but their transition to IFRS was not planned until after consolidation in the sector. As of early 2018, the Lithuanian authorities reported that both the new State Forest Enterprise and the new Road Maintenance SOE would prepare their 2019 financial statements in accordance with IFRS, to be published in 2020. It would appear that accounting practices for state roads will no longer present an issue, because the ownership of state roads was legally transferred from individual enterprises to the Lithuanian Road Administration by Government Resolution in March 2017. Similarly, the Ministry of Environment plans to transfer forestry assets to the new State Forest Enterprise, which together with the implementation of IFRS by the new SOE would largely address the related accounting issue. Representatives of some of the ownership ministries responsible for the four large SOEs with plans to implement IFRS in the near future indicated that it would take longer than initially planned, given that full IFRS implementation requires that financial accounts for the preceding two years be prepared in accordance with IFRS. This concerns the State Forest Enterprise, Klaipėda State Seaport Authority, Lithuanian Railways and Road Maintenance. Klaipėda State Seaport Authority is foreseen to implement IFRS for its 2017 financial statements, while the others are foreseen to do so for their 2019 financial statements.

SOEs' disclosure of material financial and non-financial information

Guideline VI.A addresses more specifically standards for disclosing material financial and non-financial information, including areas of significant concern for the state as an owner and the general public. Specific areas of disclosure under **Guideline VI.A** are detailed below. Each section discusses the relevant requirements outlined in the Transparency Guidelines applicable to SOEs, which are mandatory for 13 large SOEs and recommended on a comply-or-explain basis for others. Each section also highlights disclosure practices by individual SOEs. Information on disclosure practices draws on an examination of the annual reports of 14 of Lithuania's largest SOEs undertaken in the context of the 2015 SOE review, as well as analysis by the GCC published in the 2015 state aggregate report (OECD, 2015 and State-Owned Enterprises Governance Coordination Centre, 2016).

Company objectives and their fulfilment (Guideline VI.A.1): Under the SOE Guidelines, SOEs should disclose a clear statement to the public of enterprise objectives and their fulfilment. The Transparency Guidelines mandate that for all SOEs, the annual reports include "information on their operational strategy and objectives (financial and non-financial)" and the extent to which they have achieved those objectives. Those SOEs are also explicitly required by the Transparency Guidelines to publicly disclose the "objectives and tasks set by the authority representing the state" (i.e. the ownership entity).

According to information obtained in the context of the 2015 SOE review, all SOEs in practice disclose their financial and non-financial objectives in their annual management reports or activity reports. Furthermore, the examination of the annual reports of Lithuania's 14 largest SOEs (mentioned above) found that all of those SOEs have published comprehensive statements on their objectives and implementation.

Financial and operating results (Guideline VI.A.2)

Guideline VI.A.2 recommends the disclosure of enterprise financial and operating results, including where relevant the costs and funding arrangements pertaining to public policy objectives. All SOEs are required by the Transparency Guidelines to disclose their "main financial indicators characterising performance (profitability, liquidity, efficiency of asset utilisation)" and changes during the preceding three years. All SOEs are also required to disclose information on the nature and costs related to their public policy objectives, in accordance with the definitions and methodology provided in a related ministerial resolution (Minister of Economy Decree of 20 December 2013 "On the Approval of Recommendations on Identifying and Providing Information on SOEs' Special Obligations").[14] In practice, all SOEs do disclose information on their financial and operating results. Furthermore, an assessment of SOEs' annual reports undertaken by the GCC in 2015 found SOEs' disclosure of financial performance to be of a high standard. The GCC also conferred a positive evaluation on SOEs' practices related to accounting and disclosure of public policy objectives.

Remuneration (Guideline VI.A.4)

Guideline VI.A.4 recommends the disclosure of remuneration levels for board members and key executives as well as the policies that underpin them. SOEs in Lithuania are required to disclose information on the remuneration of board members and the CEO in accordance with relevant information disclosure provisions of the national corporate governance code. Those provisions call for *inter alia*, public disclosure of the total remuneration paid to the CEO and to individual members of the supervisory and/or management boards, as well as information on the company's remuneration policy.[15] The Transparency Guidelines also require that all SOEs provide state ownership entities with information on senior executive remuneration for the previous year and on the performance indicators used to establish the agreed variable component of senior executive remuneration. According to the Lithuanian authorities, this requirement only applies to the CEO, not to other key executives.

According to the examination of the annual reports of 14 large SOEs undertaken in the context of the 2015 SOE review, disclosure by SOEs of remuneration levels is generally limited to the average salary of SOE employees and the average salary of all executives (OECD, 2015). Out of the SOEs examined, only Klaipėda Oil disclosed its remuneration policy in its most recent annual management report. However, this last issue is not specific to SOEs: according to a report by the Bank of Lithuania, among listed SOEs, the disclosure of remuneration policy is the least respected principle of the corporate governance code (Bank of Lithuania, 2010). Related to this, amendments to the Law on Financial Reporting by Undertakings enacted on 21 November 2017 require that public and private LLCs disclose information on the remuneration of individual board members, applicable to financial statements drawn up from January 2018 onwards.

Although disclosure by individual SOEs is apparently lacking in this regard, the state does publish in its aggregate report the provisions of the most recently applicable regulation concerning SOE executive remuneration levels, which were mandatory for statutory SOEs and recommended to fully corporatised SOEs for the duration of 2015.[16] In this sense, the disclosure of policies underpinning SOE executive remuneration levels can be considered relatively sound, at least at the level of the state and concerning statutory SOEs (since the regulation is not mandatory for fully corporatised SOEs). The aggregate report also includes extensive information on the average salaries of SOE key executives, including a breakdown according to job category, corporate form and sector of operation, as well as information on the proportion of fixed versus variable remuneration.

Board member qualifications, selection and independence (Guideline VI.A.5)

Guideline VI.A.5 recommends full transparency regarding board member qualifications, selection process and whether individual board members are considered independent. The new rules outlining SOE board nomination procedures (enacted in March 2017) establish that SOEs are required to publish information on available board positions, including the criteria that candidates must fulfil and information on the selection process. Concerning transparency about the board members that are ultimately elected, SOEs in Lithuania are not explicitly required to publicly disclose information on board member qualifications, selection process, roles on other company boards or whether they are considered as independent. The Transparency Guidelines require all SOEs to disclose information on their governance organs, but do not provide details on what type of information should be disclosed. The corporate governance code's principles on information disclosure (mandatory for 13 large SOEs) recommend disclosure of information on the professional background, qualifications and potential conflicts of interest of board members and CEOs.

In practice, most SOEs disclose only the names and positions of board members. However, while not required, the GCC discloses information on the board composition of the majority of SOEs on its website: http://www.vkc.sipa.lt/en/company. If no board is in place, disclosure consists of the names of the CEO and the chief accountant. As of end-2016, the GCC's related online disclosure specifies, for each SOE, the following information: the public institutions represented on the board; the company affiliations of any non-governmental representatives; and which board members are considered independent.

Material foreseeable risk factors (Guideline VI.A.6): **Guideline VI.A.6** recommends that SOEs report on material foreseeable risk factors as well as measures taken to manage risks, e.g. political, operational, or exchange rate risks. SOEs are explicitly required to disclose information on "material foreseeable risk factors", as per the information disclosure standards of the corporate governance code. According to the Lithuanian authorities, in practice SOE management boards typically include information on their risk management measures in the annual strategic plans that are submitted to the GCC for review.

According to the 2015 aggregate report, SOEs' disclosure on material risk factors is generally insufficient: 85 SOEs did not disclose information on key risks in their latest annual reports. An earlier aggregate report identified this as an issue of particular relevance for the state-owned forestry enterprises, whose annual reports apparently contained the least robust information on risk factors.

Financial assistance and commitments made on behalf of SOEs (Guideline VI.A.7)

Guideline VI.A.7 recommends that SOEs disclose information on any financial assistance, including guarantees, received from the state and commitments made on behalf of the SOE, including contractual commitments and liabilities arising from public-private partnerships. The national Business Accounting Standards, which as mentioned previously are used by the majority of SOEs, require the disclosure of grants and subsidies in the balance sheet. They also require that the explanatory notes to the financial statements contain detailed information on: the nature and amount of grants and subsidies; a description of off-balance sheet assets and liabilities related to grants and subsidies and their possible impact for company; and information on any other financial assistance provided by the state.

SOEs do not as a rule benefit from (explicit) state guarantees on their commercial debt and as such there are no related disclosure requirements. According the Lithuanian authorities, SOEs do not engage in public-private partnerships and as such there are no specific requirements for the disclosure of related contractual commitments and liabilities. The examination of the annual reports of the 14 largest Lithuanian SOEs found that all of those examined disclosed information on financial assistance received from the state.

Issues relating to employees and other stakeholders (Guideline VI.A.9)

Guideline VI.A.9 recommends that SOEs disclose information on any relevant issues relating to employees and other stakeholders, for example those that might materially affect SOEs' financial and non-financial performance or significantly impact stakeholders. All SOEs are required to report on "material issues regarding employees and other stakeholders", as per the information disclosure standards of the corporate governance code for listed companies.

The examination of the annual reports of 14 large SOEs found that in practice, only two did not disclose any relevant issues related to employees and other stakeholders in their most recent annual reports. Eight of the SOEs examined published detailed information on their corporate social responsibility policies, with three SOEs (Lithuanian Post, Lesto and Lithuanian Energy Production) publishing separate corporate social responsibility reports.

Independent external audit of SOEs

Guideline VI.B recommends that SOEs' financial statements be subject to an independent external audit based on high-quality standards. The Guideline also specifies that specific state control procedures do not substitute for an independent external audit. SOEs' annual financial statements are required by the Transparency Guidelines to undergo an independent audit, to be published online along with the annual report and financial statements. Independent audits must be conducted in accordance with international auditing standards. For fully corporatised SOEs, as per the Law on

Companies, the external auditor is selected by the general meeting. For statutory SOEs, as per the Law on State and Municipal Enterprises, the external auditor is selected by the state ownership entity.

While the requirements concerning external audit applicable to SOEs appear to be in line with good practice standards, in practice questions have been raised concerning the quality and credibility of SOEs' disclosure. According to interviews with stakeholders conducted in the context of this review, the financial statements of some of Lithuania's largest SOEs are audited by small audit firms, which may not have the ability to credibly and reliably assess the soundness of SOEs' financial statements. Furthermore, SOEs are not all explicitly required to establish an internal control function, and in many cases do not do so, a practice which is not consistent with the *SOE Guidelines*.[17] The professionalism of SOEs' external auditors was called into question by the GCC when two important banks in Lithuania (Bank Snoras and Ūkio Bankas) went bankrupt in 2011-12. This led to significant losses for a number of SOEs with deposits in those banks, which were purportedly not adequately accounted for in their annual financial statements. That being said, the GCC evaluated SOEs' independent audit practices as generally sound in the 2015 aggregate report, noting that the majority of SOEs "regularly change their independent auditors and receive unconditional opinions in audit findings". According to the 2015 aggregate report, only four SOEs had not changed their external auditor in the last six years and 16 SOEs had changed their external auditor only once during that period.

Aggregate annual reporting on SOEs

Guideline VI.C recommends that government ownership entities develop consistent reporting on SOEs and publish annually an aggregate report on SOEs. Aggregate reports on the SOE sector have been published annually since 2009. The first report gave an overview of the performance of the SOE sector from 2007 to 2009. The reports are readily accessible on the GCC website and also available in English: http://www.vkc.sipa.lt/en. Starting with its 2013 report, the GCC includes information on the estimated costs related to the implementation of SOEs' public policy objectives. The GCC website also serves as a central repository for the main legal acts and other documents applicable to SOEs in Lithuania. In addition to annual aggregate reports, quarterly aggregate reports have been published regularly since 2011. The website also includes information on SOE governance reforms, standardised financial results of individual SOEs, as well as the names of CEOs and board members of SOEs.

The Transparency Guidelines establish the process and schedule leading up to the publication of the aggregate reports, including the respective roles of SOEs, state ownership entities and the GCC. SOEs are notably required to submit their annual and quarterly reports and financial statements to the relevant state ownership entities according to a pre-determined timeline. Ownership entities then must submit the information to the GCC, within three working days of the deadline for receiving the information from SOEs. The GCC is then mandated to draft and publish on its website annual and quarterly summary reports on SOEs, including information on SOEs' compliance with the provisions of the Transparency Guidelines. The annual aggregate report must include information on the nature and estimated cost of SOEs' public policy objectives.

Disclosure of ownership, voting structures, and governance structures and policies for publicly traded companies (Principles II.E.2, V.A.3 and V.A.9)

Principle II.E.2 recommends requiring the disclosure of capital structures and control arrangements. **Principle V.A.3** similarly recommends requiring the disclosure of material information on major share ownership, including beneficial owners, and voting rights, and **Principle V.A.9** recommends requiring the disclosure of governance structures and policies, including the content of any corporate governance code or policy and the process by which it is implemented.

The disclosure of share ownership is regulated under the Law on Securities. Under this framework, companies' annual reports must disclose shareholders' ownership once ownership meets 5% or more of total voting shares (Law on Securities, Art. 2). As noted above (see discussion of **Principle II.H.1** in the Chapter 3.1 sub-section dealing with the market for corporate control), a shareholder that has increased or decreased ownership must disclose to the Bank of Lithuania and the company changes in ownership at specific thresholds (5, 10, 15, 20, 25, 30, 50, 75 and 95% ownership) (Law on Securities Arts. 25.1 and 27.1). A notice of the change in ownership must also be posted to the Nasdaq CSD Lithuania branch.

The disclosure of share ownership must be made at least annually, according to the Law on Financial Reporting by Undertakings. This information should include data on major blocks of shares owned either director or indirectly (by beneficial owners), shareholders holding special control rights, all existing restrictions on voting rights, the number of all the shares acquired by the entity and the entity's own shares, the number of the entity's own shares acquired and transferred during the reporting period, and other information. These requirements are complemented by Art. 10 of the Law on Consolidated Financial Reporting by Groups of Undertakings, applicable to parent companies with subsidiaries, which outlines what should be included in a consolidated annual report. (See also the discussion above of **Principle II.E.2** in the Chapter 3.1 assessment section on shareholder rights and equitable treatment, as well as Box 3.5 for the full text of these disclosure requirements). Further, Nasdaq Vilnius Corporate Governance Code Principle X.1 recommends that companies listed on Nasdaq Vilnius disclose information on share ownership.

Under the Law on Financial Reporting by Undertakings and the Law on Securities (Art. 22), listed companies are also required to disclose at least annually information on the corporate governance code applied by the company and a report on the company's compliance with the Code, including explanations for non-compliance where applicable (see also Chapter 2.2). The annotations to **Principle V.A.9** also recommend that, beyond disclosing which corporate governance code the company applies and how the code is put into practice, companies also be required to describe the structure and division of authority between shareholders, management and board members. The Law on Financial Reporting by Undertakings largely includes these elements, as well, in the annual report requirements for listed companies, provided in Box 3.5. Amendments to the Law on Financial Reporting by Undertakings enacted in November 2017 expand listed companies' related disclosure requirements, notably obliging companies to disclose the conditions of any shareholder agreements in their annual corporate governance reports.

Box 3.5 Legal requirements for the disclosure of ownership, voting structures, and governance structures and policies for listed companies

Disclosure requirements relating to share ownership

Law on Securities

Article 23. Obligation to Inform about Acquisition or Disposal of a Holding

1. A person who has acquired 5, 10, 15, 20, 25, 30, 50, 75 and 95 per cent of votes at the general meeting of shareholders of an issuer must, not later than within four trading days, inform the supervisory institution and the issuer about the total amount of votes. This obligation shall also be binding where the specified limits are exceeded in the descending or the ascending order. (...)

Article 25. Obligation of the Issuer to Notify an Acquisition or Disposal of Own Shares and Publish Additional Information

1. The issuer, himself or via another person acting in his own name but on the issuer's behalf, having acquired or transferred 5 or 10 per cent of own shares shall not later than within four trading days announce in the manner described in Article 28 of this Law and post into the Central Storage Facility, and notify the supervisory institution of the relative number of the shares held thereby. This obligation shall also be binding where the specified limits are exceeded in the descending or the ascending order. The relative number of shares shall be calculated having regard to the total number of shares to which the voting rights attach.

Law on Consolidated Financial Reporting by Groups of Undertakings

Article 10. Consolidated Annual Report

1. In addition to annual consolidated financial statements, undertakings must draw up the consolidated annual report.

2. The consolidated annual report must include:

(...)

7) the number and par value of the shares of the parent undertaking belonging to the undertaking itself, subsidiary undertakings thereof or the persons acting under the authorisation thereof, but on their own behalf;

Disclosure requirements related to control arrangements, voting structures, and governance structures and policies

Law on Financial Reporting by Undertakings

Article 23. Annual Report

(...)

3. Companies whose securities are admitted to trading on a regulated market, in addition to the information set out in paragraph 2 of this article, must include a corporate governance report in the annual report.

Article 23^1. Corporate Governance Report

1. The Corporate Governance Report must include:

1) reference to the applied code (codes) of corporate governance and the medium of its (their) publication and/or reference to the entire required information published about the undertaking's governance practice;

2) in the event of derogation from provisions of the applied code (codes) of corporate governance and/or a failure to comply therewith, those provisions and the reasons for derogating from and/or not complying with them shall be indicated;

3) information about the scope of risk and management thereof – management of various types of risk, measures of reduction thereof and the internal control system of the undertaking shall be described;

4) information about the major shareholding interests held directly or indirectly;

5) information on transactions with related parties as stipulated in Article 37^2 of the Law on Companies

(...)

6) information about the shareholders holding special control rights and a description of those rights;

7) information about all existing restrictions of voting rights, such as restrictions of the voting rights of the persons holding a certain percentage or number of votes, the time limits until the expiry whereof the voting rights may be exercised or the systems according to which the property rights as granted by securities are separated from the holding of the securities;

8) information about the rules regulating election and replacement of members of the board, also amendments to the undertaking's articles of association;

9) information about powers of members of the board;

10) information about the competence of the general meeting of shareholders, rights of shareholders and exercise thereof, unless this information has been provided for by laws;

11) information about the composition of management and supervisory bodies and committees thereof, their fields of activities and those of the head of the undertaking.

(...)

14) information on all agreements between shareholders (their substance, conditions)

Source: Information provided by the Lithuanian authorities and the legal and regulatory texts cited here, including official translations of amendments to the Law on Financial Reporting by Undertakings provided by the Lithuanian authorities.

In practice, and as noted in Chapter 2.2, all listed companies broadly comply with the requirement to include in their annual reports a report on compliance with the Nasdaq Vilnius Corporate Governance Code. This assessment is based on a review of two compilations of companies' corporate governance disclosures, one performed by the Bank of Lithuania in 2010 and one performed by Nasdaq Vilnius in 2015. However, these disclosures tend to be superficial in many cases. According to these reports and to opinions expressed by the private sector and civil society, many companies do not adequately explain instances of non-compliance with the Code. More specifically, overall compliance with the Code in the following areas remains weak: disclosures related to practices for the composition and responsibilities of the supervisory and management boards; the application of director independence rules; and disclosure of executive remuneration policies. Relative to this last area of disclosure, amendments to the Law on Financial Reporting by Undertakings enacted in November 2017 notably expand listed companies' disclosure requirements to include reporting on individual supervisory and management board members' remuneration.

SOE disclosure of ownership and voting structures

Guideline VI.A.3 recommends disclosure of SOEs' ownership and voting structures, including the content of any corporate governance code or policy and its implementation processes. SOEs are not explicitly required to publicly disclose information on their governance, ownership and voting structures. However, the information disclosure standards of the national corporate governance code, which 13 large SOEs are mandated to implement, state that companies should disclose "information on governance structures and strategy". Fully corporatised SOEs are furthermore, as per the Law on Companies, required to disclose in their articles of association information on the number of shares, share classes and governance structure (i.e. board structure). Listed SOEs are required as per the Listing Rules (Art. 24.10.2) to disclose information about major shareholders who directly or indirectly hold more than 5% of the outstanding shares and are subject to the new provisions in the Law on Financial Reporting by Undertakings requiring annual reporting on the conditions of any shareholders' agreements.

The analysis of SOE disclosure practices undertaken in the context of the 2015 SOE review found that, among the 14 large SOEs examined, most did include information on their governance, ownership and voting structures. Furthermore, at the level of the state, the GCC website provides information on the degree of state ownership in all SOEs and, as mentioned earlier, details on the board structure and composition.

Disclosure of related party transactions for publicly traded companies (Principle V.A.6)

Principle V.A.6 recommends requiring the disclosure of material information on related party transactions and the terms of such transactions to the market individually. As mentioned in the Chapter 3.1 section on related party transactions, amendments to the Law on Companies enacted in November 2017 introduce new procedures for their review and disclosure, which entered into force in July 2018. Concerning related disclosure to the market, the Law on Companies amendments require that listed companies publish on their websites details on material related party transactions no later than undertaking the transactions. The published details must identify the related party, describe why it is considered as such, report the date and value of the transaction and provide other information "required to assess whether the transaction is fair and justified with regard to the public limited liability company and its shareholders who are not parties to the transaction".[18] These Law on Companies amendments are complemented by additional amendments to the Law on Financial Reporting by Undertakings (also enacted in November 2017) requiring that listed companies include in their annual corporate governance reports information about related party transactions, notably indicating "the parties to the transaction [...] and the transaction value".

Other disclosure requirements applicable to related party transactions undertaken by listed companies are established by a Resolution of the Board of the Bank of Lithuania.[19] The Resolution notably establishes that notifications regarding "transactions with the securities of the issuer concluded by its managers and persons closely associated with them" shall be prepared and disclosed in accordance with the EU Regulation on Market Abuse. Complementing this framework is the Nasdaq Vilnius Corporate Governance Code recommendation (Principle X.1) that a company should disclose information on "transactions between the company and connected persons, as well as transactions concluded outside the course of the company's regular operations".

For the purposes of disclosure, and as described in the Chapter 3.1 assessment section on related party transactions, the definition of a "related party" draws upon IAS definitions.[20] The Lithuanian authorities further assert that the definitions of related parties and related party transactions established in IAS, which have the same meaning in Lithuania's local BAS, are sufficiently broad to capture a real risk of potential abuse.

In practice, the Lithuanian authorities report that, based on an analysis of companies' financial reports and the annual reports as of the year 2014, all companies have disclosed information on related party transactions. Many companies include a separate segment detailing the conditions of the transactions, while some companies only include information in their financial reports and do not give additional facts about the related party transactions. The Lithuanian authorities and representatives of the Nasdaq Vilnius exchange stated during the May 2016 Secretariat fact-finding mission to Vilnius that it would be difficult for listed companies to hide major related party transactions, given that Lithuania's active media and investors' associations pay close attention to this issue.

SOE disclosure of material transactions with the state and other related entities (Guideline VI.A.8)

Guideline VI.A.8 recommends that SOEs disclose information on any material transactions between SOEs and the state or other related entities. The information disclosure standards of the corporate governance code, which 13 large SOEs, as mentioned earlier, are required by the Transparency Guidelines to implement, call for disclosure of information on "Transactions between the company and connected persons, as well as transactions concluded outside the course of the company's regular operations" (Principle X.1). SOEs are not subject to the provisions of the code which explicitly recommend board approval of related party transactions, defined as "transactions concluded between the company and its shareholders, members of the supervisory or managing bodies or other natural or legal persons that evert or may exert influence on the company's management" (Principle IV.5).

It would appear that SOE practices differ significantly with respect to how transactions between SOEs, the state and other SOEs are disclosed in financial statements. As an illustrative example, Klaipėda Oil notes in its annual report that "parties are considered related when one party has a possibility to control the other one or has significant influence over the other party in making financial and operating decisions" (Klaipėdos Nafta, 2015). In the Explanatory Notes to the Financial Statements it discloses all transactions with state-controlled entities including SOEs and governmental agencies, such as the State Tax Inspectorate. By contrast, Lithuanian Energy and its subsidiaries disclose transactions with all SOEs, but, as stated in its annual report, "For the purposes of disclosure of related parties, the Republic of Lithuania excludes central and local government authorities" (Lithuanian Energy, 2015). Litgrid, on the other hand, limits its disclosure of related party transactions to those directly related to its parent company EPSO-G (Litgrid, 2015).

3.3 Establishing effective separation of the government's role as an owner of state-owned companies and the government's role as regulator, particularly with regard to market regulation

The Concept Paper and 2015 *SOE Guidelines* include a stronger focus on the overall responsibilities of the state ownership entity and, in assigning and implementing these responsibilities, ensuring that there is a clear separation between the government's role as an owner of state-owned companies and its role as regulator. Relevant recommendations under the *SOE Guidelines* in this regard include Guidelines III.A (separation of functions); I.B (ownership policy); I.D (SOE ownership rationale and objective-setting); II.A (simplifying and standardising SOE legal forms); II.B (SOE operational autonomy); II.D (exercise of state ownership rights); and II.F.2 (board nomination processes).

Separation of functions (Guideline III.A)

Guideline III.A calls for a clear separation between the state's ownership function and other state functions that may influence the conditions for state-owned enterprises, particularly with regard to market regulation. Under the current institutional arrangements, there is no clear overall separation between the state's ownership function and other functions that can influence conditions for Lithuanian SOEs. In many cases, ministries that are responsible for sectoral policy and/or regulation also exercise ownership in SOEs that operate in the relevant markets. Some degree of functional separation occurs in markets where there is an independent sectoral regulator, but most regulation bearing on SOEs is the responsibility of ministries and their subordinate institutions.

At the level of SOE boards of directors, the issue of civil servants serving simultaneously a sectoral policy and an ownership function has been the subject of monitoring by the GCC. According to the state's 2015 aggregate report, the boards of about half of all SOEs included civil servants who also served a policy function in the relevant sector (State-Owned Enterprises Governance Coordination Centre, 2016). In many cases those individuals constituted a majority of the board members. In addition, SOE boards have in a number of cases included vice ministers from the state ownership entity. The new rules for SOE board composition enacted in March 2017, when fully implemented, will help address these concerns. In addition to requiring that at least half of SOE board members be independent and barring politicians from serving on SOE boards, the rules also establish that persons responsible for policy making cannot serve on the boards of SOEs operating in the relevant market.

Ownership policy (Guideline I.B)

Guideline I.B recommends development of an ownership policy defining the overall rationales for state ownership, the state's role in SOE governance and the responsibilities of government offices involved in its implementation.[21] The Lithuanian authorities have developed an ownership policy in the form of the 2012 Ownership Guidelines (described in the Chapter 2.8 section on ownership policy and related SOE regulations). The Ownership Guidelines outline the respective roles and responsibilities of the main entities responsible for their implementation, notably placing responsibility for their implementation on state ownership entities (ministries and other public authorities) and responsibility for monitoring implementation on the entity carrying out the function of the GCC.

While the Ownership Guidelines represent a definite improvement, some concerns remain regarding the degree to which they are implemented in practice. The development of the ownership policy occurred during a reform process during which a centralisation of SOE ownership was reportedly strongly resisted by a number of line ministries. This has given rise to questions about the degree to which the agreed policy is widely accepted and implemented on a whole-of-government basis. This review does not attempt to definitively assess implementation of all relevant aspects of the Ownership Guidelines. However, implementation has been identified as lacking in at least some areas. For example, a previously applicable provision of the Ownership Guidelines requiring that board nominations involve an inter-ministerial selection committee was reported in 2015 to be only implemented in two of the six fully corporatised SOEs to which it was applicable. As of early 2018, it would appear that most of the more recent SOE board nominations (undertaken to implement new independence requirements adopted in March 2017, for which compliance was mandatory by January 2018) have undergone the state's agreed inter-ministerial selection process, indicating an overall improvement in ministries' compliance with the state's SOE rules. However, SOE board nominations are still ongoing in some eight SOEs, pointing to some remaining issues with timely compliance. Another issue related to the implementation of the ownership policy is the fact that the state's rules and regulations on SOE governance and disclosure do not always use the same criteria – notably size criteria – for determining their mandatory applicability to SOEs. For example, both the Ownership Guidelines and the Transparency Guidelines are mandatory for "large" SOEs, but each according to different criteria for determining which enterprises are considered "large". At a minimum, there should be a clear and transparent rationale for why different guidelines use different criteria for determining which SOEs must follow them.

SOE ownership rationale and objective-setting (Guideline I.D)

Guideline 1.D recommends that the state define the rationales for owning individual SOEs and subject these to recurrent review. **Guideline I.D** also recommends that any public policy objectives assigned to an individual SOE or group of SOEs be clearly mandated and disclosed. Lithuania goes some way towards disclosing the rationales for owning individual SOEs through its categorisation of SOEs according to their overarching objectives (described in the Chapter 2.8 section on ownership policy and related SOE regulations). In brief, the categorisation identifies those SOEs that are primarily expected to engage in profit-seeking activities (Group 1A), those that are expected to also fulfil social or public policy objectives (Group 1B) and those that are expected to primarily fulfil social or public policy objectives (Group 2). For the latter two categories, the rationale for state ownership is effectively defined as the fulfilment of social or public policy objectives. However, for the SOEs in Group 1A, their rationales for state ownership are perhaps less evident. For those SOEs, the state expects primarily a growth in business value and a yield from dividends (or profit contributions for statutory SOEs), but does not communicate why they should remain in state ownership. The state has also identified a number of enterprises which must be owned by the state, as per the Law on State Enterprises and Facilities of Strategic Importance to National Security and Other Enterprises of Importance to Ensuring National Security. While the rationale for maintaining those enterprises under state ownership is implicitly established, i.e. to protect national security, this remains relatively broad and not enterprise-specific.

There is no formal mechanism in place for the recurrent review of SOE objectives. The classification of SOEs according to their objectives is based on reporting by state ownership entities, which may have an incentive to place some SOEs in Group 2 to avoid subsequent performance or governance requirements applicable solely to Group 1A and/or 1B enterprises. In practice, the review of SOEs' objectives does take place. For example, in June 2014 nine of the SOEs under the purview of the Ministry of Agriculture were reclassified, by Government resolution, from Groups 1A and 1B to Group 2. The reclassification of SOEs requires a Government resolution, but it is undertaken upon proposal from the line ministry. The Lithuanian authorities in early 2018 issued a "State Enterprise Reorganisation Plan", proposing changes in SOEs' legal forms according to their objectives, for example by converting public policy SOEs into public institutions and incorporating commercially-oriented statutory SOEs into limited liability companies. The plan builds on previous work undertaken by a working group established by the Ministry of Economy to review the objectives of SOEs and propose changes to their legal forms accordingly. These efforts constitute instances of recurrent review of SOE objectives, in line with **Guideline I.D**. They are discussed in more detail in the section that follows on simplifying and standardising SOE legal forms.

SOEs' public policy objectives, or "special obligations" by national nomenclature, are in principle mandated by law. The nature and cost of special obligations must be disclosed by SOEs according to a 2013 amendment to the Transparency Guidelines. The accompanying Recommendation of the Ministry of Economy (Minister of Economy Decree of 20 December 2013) "On the Approval of the Recommendations on Identifying and Providing Information on SOEs' Special Obligations" defines special obligations as "functions performed by the SOEs, which the SOEs are obligated to carry out by law or another legal act, in order to ensure the implementation of specific social, strategic and political goals of the state".

The criteria contained in the Recommendation for determining whether an SOE is carrying out a special obligation preclude a number of "informal" obligations that SOEs may be expected to fulfil (for example related to employment levels or local political or community causes), some of which could, for the purpose of the SOE Guidelines, be considered public policy objectives. Insofar as these informal obligations go unreported by individual SOEs and/or their ownership ministries, it cannot be concluded that SOEs' public policy objectives are unequivocally mandated by law and disclosed.

Simplifying and standardising SOE legal forms (Guideline II.A)

Guideline II.A recommends that governments simplify and standardise the legal forms under which SOEs operate and that SOEs' operational practices follow commonly accepted corporate norms. Overall, no explicit specificities in SOEs' legal status protect them from insolvency or bankruptcy procedures, or provide for differences of treatment of employees as compared to private enterprises (e.g. concerning remuneration, pension rights and job protection). However, the different legal forms under which SOEs operate do have important implications on their corporate governance arrangements. The 49 SOEs incorporated as public or private limited liability companies are obliged to operate under the same laws applicable to private companies, notably the Law on Companies. The 79 statutory SOEs (or 27, following the 2017 mergers in the forestry and road maintenance sectors) are not incorporated according to ordinary company law. Their legal form can be considered partially standardised since all statutory SOEs operate under one unified law, the Law on State and Municipal Enterprises. However, a number of legal provisions in the Law on State and Municipal Enterprises (discussed in more detail below) effectively weaken the decision-making powers and operational autonomy of statutory SOEs' boards of directors, thus creating non-trivial shortcomings in their corporate governance arrangements. Importantly, April 2017 amendments to the Law on Companies and parallel amendments to the Law on State and Municipal Enterprises introduced maximum term limits and reappointment criteria applicable only to the CEOs of SOEs (outlined in the Chapter 2.8 section on recent or ongoing reforms in the SOE sector). These new provisions exacerbate already existing differences in legal treatment between SOEs and private companies and constitute a significant departure from international corporate governance standards.

Key differences in the legal framework applicable to statutory SOEs

The legal framework for statutory SOEs differs from that of fully corporatised SOEs in a few important respects related to corporate governance:

- Since statutory SOEs manage state assets on behalf of the state, and are not legally the owners of those assets, creditors' ability to initiate insolvency procedures against those SOEs, and access collateral, is arguably quite limited.

- Statutory SOEs may only establish one-tier management boards, while public and private limited liability companies can establish one- or two-tier boards.

- For statutory SOEs, the power to hire, remove and decide on the remuneration of the CEO/manager is explicitly under the remit of the state ownership entity. This function is the responsibility of boards for limited liability companies (or the general meeting if neither a supervisory nor a management board is formed).

- The boards of statutory SOEs may include the CEO. For fully corporatised SOEs with one-tier management boards, the Law on Companies explicitly prohibits the CEO from serving on the board if the articles of association have accorded the board, among others, the function of supervising the CEO's activities.

- The responsibility for approving the enterprise's strategy falls to the state ownership entity for statutory SOEs, whereas this is the function of the management boards in limited liability companies (or the CEO if a management board is not formed).

For those statutory SOEs that perform primarily commercial functions, and especially those in competition with private enterprises, the fact that they are not fully corporatised is not consistent with the recommendations of the SOE Guidelines. Corporatising statutory SOEs engaged in economic activities would strengthen the operational autonomy of their boards, since (as discussed above) the legal framework applicable to statutory SOEs significantly limits boards' power of decision *vis-à-vis* the state. It also has the potential of according those statutory SOEs greater commercial autonomy, e.g. the ability to participate in joint ventures, which, as highlighted in interviews with independent board members, is currently prohibited by the Law on State and Municipal Enterprises.

The plans to convert 11 statutory SOEs into limited liability companies (set forth in the "State Enterprise Reorganisation Plan" outlined in the Chapter 2.8 section recent or ongoing reforms in the SOE sector) would, once implemented, constitute significant steps forward in addressing some of these concerns. Under the plan, only five statutory SOEs will remain under this separate legal form. Once the priority corporatisations have been implemented, the Lithuanian authorities may wish to consider whether there is scope for corporatising remaining statutory SOEs engaged in economic activities. For the corporatisation of statutory SOEs to be effective, the Lithuanian authorities should ensure that the criteria for selecting enterprises for conversion are clearly defined and that all statutory SOEs are objectively assessed based on those criteria.

Rationalising sectors with multiple SOEs

A "simplification" of the legal forms of SOEs may also be taken to imply that there should not be a larger number of SOEs than what is needed for efficient operation. In this context, the recent consolidation of the 42 separate state-owned forestry enterprises (plus one Forest Management Institute) and the 11 road maintenance enterprises into single SOEs (summarised earlier in the Chapter 2.8 section on recent or ongoing reforms in the SOE sector) appear to pave the way for significant efficiency gains and governance improvements. Their consolidation has made both enterprises large enough to trigger mandatory compliance with the state's governance and transparency rules, notably the requirement to establish boards and to implement IFRS. Efficiency gains are foreseen in the state-owned forestry sector, notably through a consolidation of the 42 regional units into 26 units, a reduction in the number of employees (including lay-offs of 42 CEOs), a centralisation of administrative services and an optimisation of operational assets (machines). This so-called "optimisation" phase is foreseen to occur over the course of 2018. Similarly, efficiency gains of EUR 8.5 million are foreseen in the state-owned road maintenance sector. The Ministry of Transport and Communications has reportedly communicated this target to the new enterprise's board in its latest shareholder expectations letter, applicable to returns in 2019 compared with 2016. (The estimated savings is based on an expectation that the new Road Maintenance SOE can maintain the roads at a cost not exceeding that of the median performant enterprise under the previous structure.) According to information obtained during the Secretariat's February 2018 fact-finding visit, a new board of directors was established in December 2017 to oversee the State Forest Enterprise and its composition included four independent directors out of seven, in line with the state's rules for large enterprises. Similarly, independent directors were selected in October 2017 to serve on the board of the new Road Maintenance SOE. Full implementation of IFRS requires that two years of comparable accounts be prepared. Given that both enterprises commenced their activities recently, full implementation of IFRS is unlikely before 2020, but the authorities plan to prepare the required two years of comparable accounts for the 2018 and 2019 financial years.

For background, the previous structure of 11 road maintenance enterprises was formally motivated by the country's regional structure (10 regions plus one state road network) but contrasted with most OECD countries which tend to have only one such firm, if (as is not always the case) the state acts as an enterprise owner in this sector. The large number of state-owned forestry enterprises (compared with just one SOE in this sector in neighbouring Latvia [OECD, 2014]) reflected historical traditions and development but the structure was apparently kept alive by ongoing political considerations, including at the local or sub-national level.

SOE operational autonomy (Guideline II.B)

Guideline II.B recommends that governments allow SOEs full operational autonomy to achieve their defined objectives and refrain from intervening in SOE management. The annotations clarify that governments may still act as active owners, but that direction given by the state to the SOE or its board should be limited to strategic issues and public policy objectives.

Prior to examining in some detail the legal framework affecting SOEs' operational autonomy, three points regarding the potential for political intervention in SOEs merit mention. First, the boards of some of Lithuania's most economically important SOEs have in the recent past been predominantly composed of representatives of the ownership ministry, and in some of the largest SOEs, have included politically connected officials such as vice ministers. At the time of writing, this was changing with the ongoing implementation of the state's new rules requiring a proportion of ½ independent directors on SOE boards and barring politicians from serving on SOE boards. Secondly, for SOEs with one-tier management boards, the ownership entities are effectively given the explicit legal right to remove any and all board members prior to the expiry of their term of office. This issue is in principle somewhat mitigated by the state's inter-ministerial board member nomination committee, which has introduced some degree of structure and transparency to the process. While the process had previously only been implemented in two large SOEs (as reported in the state's 2015 aggregate report), the latest 30 board nominations undertaken to implement the new board composition rules have reportedly undergone the process, with an additional eight SOE boards in the process of doing so, with delays.

Thirdly, according to interviews with stakeholders, the use of verbal or written "instructions" from ministers to board members representing the state is not an uncommon practice. While insufficient information was available for the Secretariat to determine the extent to which shareholding ministries provide voting instructions to board members in practice, either in written or oral form, the anecdotal evidence suggests that at least in some cases such instructions have been given, effectively weakening the power of boards to make collegial decisions in the interest of the enterprise. The practice of instructions is not consistent with the *SOE Guidelines*, which clearly call for any direction given by the state to be limited to strategic issues and public policy objectives.

Lithuania's accession review process highlighted the need to clarify the formal (or legal) basis for such instructions in order to determine what measures would be needed to abolish the system, both formally and in practice. A provision of the Law on Civil Service, which requires that civil servants obtain an authorisation from their responsible minister in order to be nominated and selected as an SOE board member, was identified as potentially relevant in this regard. The Lithuanian authorities have since clarified that the content of such authorisations only concerns the right to serve on SOE boards and does not include any instructions for how to exercise board duties or how to vote. The Law on Civil Service was undergoing review at the time of writing and the Parliament was considering a draft amendment, foreseen for enactment in the first half of 2018, which would eliminate this written authorisation requirement. Concerning other potential sources of formal justification for written instructions, a preliminary review by the OECD Secretariat of the articles of association of some of Lithuania's largest SOEs found therein provisions stating that decisions by ownership ministries "must be executed in writing". The OECD Secretariat was unable to verify whether this refers to the instructions system within boards of directors or whether related practices differ between fully corporatised and statutory SOEs (the reviewed articles of association were both in statutory SOEs, for which the law in any event accords boards weak powers compared to the state).[22]

On a separate but related topic, during interviews conducted in the context of this review, insufficient competencies and/or qualifications of SOE board members was highlighted as a potential issue limiting board effectiveness, including by independent board members. The issue of insufficient remuneration of SOE board members was also underlined in this respect, including by the National Audit Office, which found in its ongoing performance audit that SOE executives (a category which includes board members) receive on average 20% to 25% lower remuneration than executives in the private sector. They suggested that it remains possible to attract sufficiently qualified board members, since some are motivated to contribute their services for the benefit of the public interest. However, independent board members suggested that there remain problematic cases where remuneration is insufficient to attract good candidates. The introduction of a bonus system for the board members of statutory SOEs has, according to some independent board members, paved the way for reducing the gap in remuneration in some cases. As corporatised SOEs do not have the same bonus system, further investigation would be necessary to determine whether additional remedies would be necessary for them. Stakeholders have also highlighted issues with SOE board members being paid on an hourly basis subject to hourly activity reports, leading to both insufficient remuneration and a perception of excessive control by the state over board operations.

(i) Fully corporatised SOEs

For fully corporatised SOEs, the legal powers of the state, and the extent to which it can intervene in day-to-day management, vary according to the board structure and composition. As mentioned, the majority of fully corporatised SOEs have one-tier management boards. For these SOEs, the Law on Companies requires management boards to "consider and approve: […] the business strategy of the company […] the management structure of the company and its employees", in addition to electing and removing from office the CEO (Art. 34.1 and 34.2). The Law also lists a number of explicit domains in which the management board is competent to take decisions (Art. 34).

Of note, the Law on Companies allows for a company's articles of association to require the approval of the general meeting for certain transactions (e.g. those outlined in Article 20, including increases or reductions in capital and distribution of dividends). This could in principle convey on the ownership entity a high degree of control over SOEs' operational autonomy. A study of the CEOs in Lithuanian SOEs found some, albeit not overwhelming, evidence of political affiliations and links with the electoral cycle in the top management of a number of companies (Baltic Institute of Corporate Governance, 2013).

(ii) Statutory SOEs

Concerning statutory SOEs, the Law on State and Municipal Enterprises accords state ownership entities the explicit right to approve enterprise strategy, appoint and remove the CEO and management board members (if formed) and select the auditor or audit firm (Article 4.4.8). Given that statutory SOEs can only have one-tier management boards, which must include civil servants, the legal framework evidently allows for non-trivial state intervention in the day-to-day management of SOEs.

Centralisation of the ownership function (Guideline II.D)

Guideline II.D recommends that the exercise of state ownership rights be clearly identified within the state administration and centralised in a single ownership entity or carried out by a co-ordinating body. This "ownership entity", the Guideline further recommends, should have the capacity and the competencies to effectively carry out its duties. Lithuania has not established a centralised ownership entity to exercise state ownership, relying instead on a co-ordinating body, the GCC, to provide some centralised functions and to support a decentralised ownership model consisting of 12 ministries or ministerial departments and seven other public institutions that exercise ownership rights in SOEs. With some exceptions, the state ownership function tends to be exercised by the governmental bodies that also regulate the relevant markets.

In the absence of a centralised ownership entity, the GCC as well as the Ministry of Economy effectively serve a policy coordination function. As per the Transparency Guidelines, the Ministry of Economy is responsible for coordinating policies and guidelines related to SOE governance. As per the Ownership Guidelines, the GCC is responsible for monitoring compliance with those policies and guidelines and preparing the state's aggregate report on SOEs. The GCC also exercises some level of policy coordination, for example through its mandate to provide technical advice, as requested, to individual ownership entities on such areas as the board self-evaluation process and working methods. In practice, ownership entities do sometimes request the GCC's technical advice, for example on the content of line ministries' shareholder expectations letters (which outline financial and non-financial targets, usually applicable to several year periods), but this is undertaken on an *ad hoc* basis and on the initiative of line ministries. By early 2018, the Ministry of Economy was considering a proposal to make it mandatory for line ministries to seek feedback from the GCC on shareholder expectations letters. The GCC's mandate is reproduced in Box 2.3 in the Chapter 2.8 section on ownership policy and related SOE regulations.

Important questions arise in connection with the resourcing of the coordinating function(s) as well as the relative effective influence of the government institutions involved in SOE ownership. At the time of the 2015 SOE review, the staffing of the GCC was five full-time employees, whereas (as mentioned elsewhere) the line ministries are expected to allocate one official to the oversight of each SOE in their portfolio. This is very low in international comparison. Concerns have in the past been raised first about whether the GCC can effectively fulfil the multiple roles assigned to it by the Ownership Guidelines; secondly, given the regulatory roles of the line ministries, about the separation of ownership and regulation. The doubling of the GCC's budget in 2018 could help mitigate this issue, since it will allow for an increase its staff.

Additional questions relate to the ability of the GCC to ensure implementation of relevant government decisions. Its main leverage (apart from raising issues via its aggregate reporting) consists of notifying the Ministry of Economy of its concerns about the conduct of SOEs or line ministries. Whether the Ministry takes corrective action may in practice depend both on political considerations and its administrative capacities. In practice, the Ownership Guidelines, which have been approved by the whole of Government, have been only partly implemented in a number of cases, giving rise to concerns in this respect.

As mentioned in the Chapter 2.8 section on recent or ongoing reforms in the SOE sector, the GCC was transferred in July 2017 from the state-owned SOE the Property Bank (*Turto Bankas*) to the Monitoring and Forecast Agency (*Stebėsenos ir prognozių agentūra*), a public institution under the remit of the Ministry of Economy. Its annual budget has also been increased from EUR 175 000 in 2017 to EUR 354 000 for 2018. The transfer of the GCC to a public institution addresses a concern raised during Lithuania's corporate governance accession review process, namely that the GCC should not be housed within an SOE that it is notionally tasked with monitoring. The budget increase could help the GCC more effectively fulfil its functions – and improve compliance with the state's SOE rules – once the GCC hires additional staff and assuming it devotes more resources to its SOE monitoring and shareholder advisory functions. According to the Lithuanian authorities, the new budget will allow for an increase in the GCC's staff from six to nine analysts, in accordance with a December 2017 decision of the Ministry of Economy, but the new staff have yet to be recruited. A head of the GCC (or, more specifically, of the Monitoring and Forecast Agency) was nominated end 2017 but was not ultimately confirmed in the position and the search for a new head is ongoing.

According to interviews with the staff of the GCC undertaken prior to the transfer, the institutional change would allow the GCC greater autonomy in undertaking its work, since it would no longer report to the CEO of an SOE. They also reported that an increased budget could allow for more extensive analysis of (i) SOEs' special obligations; (ii) SOEs' optimal capital structures; and (iii) the activities and performance of enterprises owned at the municipal level. Even following the GCC's transfer and budget increase, the absence of whole-of-government remedial mechanisms when line ministries or SOEs do not comply with the state's governance and disclosure policies remains an overarching issue which the Lithuanian authorities should take steps to address in the years to come.

Board nomination processes (Guideline II.F.2)

Guideline II.F.2 recommends that the state, in exercising its rights as an informed and active owner, establish well-structured, merit-based and transparent board nomination processes in full- or majority-owned SOEs, actively participate in the nomination of all SOEs' boards and contribute to board diversity. In March 2017, the Lithuanian authorities amended a Government Resolution on SOE board nominations, notably harmonising SOE board nomination practices across legal forms, strengthening the foreseen selection procedure for SOE board members and allowing for professional recruitment agencies to participate in the process. The selection of SOE boards according to this new process is currently under way, with a view to implementing Lithuania's new rules (established by the same Government Resolution) that mandate at least half of board positions be filled by independent directors and prohibit politicians from serving on SOE boards. Annex 2 provides a status update of board appointment processes in Lithuanian SOEs, as of February 2018. Prior to the adoption of these amendments, SOE board nomination procedures differed for fully corporatised and statutory SOEs. The foreseen process, as laid out in the Government Resolution, appears to be well-structured, merit-based and transparent. It notably describes the selection process in detail; establishes minimum criteria for SOE board candidates (e.g. concerning educational level, professional competencies and experience); and requires state shareholding institutions to publish the announcement of available board positions online. As of early 2018, the process had reportedly been implemented in 30 SOE boards and was under way (albeit with delay) in an additional eight SOE boards. According to the Lithuanian authorities, there are no plans to implement the board nomination process in SOEs that are undergoing, or foreseen to undergo, restructurings such as conversions to public institutions or privatisations. Interviews conducted in the context of the February 2018 fact-finding mission pointed to some scope for making the nomination process more time efficient, for example by (i) relying more extensively on selection agencies to identify a preliminary pool of qualified applicants; and (ii) providing greater flexibility on the number of candidates to be interviewed by the selection committee (currently at least one-third must be interviewed, regardless of the number of applicants).

3.4 Ensuring a level playing field in markets where state-owned enterprises and private sector companies compete in order to avoid market distortions.

To ensure a level playing field and fair competition in the marketplace when SOEs undertake economic activities, the Concept Paper calls for consideration of Chapter III.B-G of the SOE Guidelines. (*SOE Guidelines* Chapter III.A is addressed in section 3.3 above.)

Stakeholders' access to redress (Guideline III.B)

Guideline III.B recommends that SOEs' stakeholders and other interested parties, including creditors and competitors, have access to efficient redress through unbiased legal or arbitration processes when they consider that their rights have been violated. SOEs' stakeholders have, in principle, access to the same legal and arbitration processes as those available to the stakeholders of private companies in Lithuania. Commercial disputes between SOEs are to be resolved through the court system and without special arbitration procedures. That being said, the fact that statutory SOEs do not legally own the state assets under their management could in practice limit the ability of lenders to access collateral in the case of non-payment.

Transparency and disclosure of public policy objectives and related costs (Guidelines III.C & D)

Guidelines III.C and **III.D** recommend that state ownership entities and SOEs maintain transparency and disclose costs and revenue structures in cases where SOEs combine economic activities and public policy objectives. Costs related to public objectives should be clearly identified, disclosed and adequately compensated by the state on the basis of specific legal provisions and/or through contractual mechanisms. The nature, scope and cost of SOEs' public policy objectives are not always well defined in Lithuania. Many SOEs are simultaneously engaged in commercial activities while also filling a public policy function, and usually the two types of activities are not subject to separate accounting. However, a 2013 amendment to the Transparency Guidelines and an accompanying Decree by the Ministry of Economy (Minister of Economy Decree of 20 December 2013 "On the Approval of the Recommendations on Identifying and Providing Information on SOEs' Special Obligations") requires SOEs to identify and disclose the costs related to existing public service obligations ("special obligations" by national nomenclature).

The scope and cost estimations for SOEs' special obligations have been included in state aggregate reports since 2014. Overall, Lithuania's practices toward identifying (and in some cases covering through budgetary allocations) the costs of public policy obligations go beyond, and are superior to, what is seen in most OECD countries. However, the strong element of self-reporting does create a level of uncertainty about the accuracy of the information – except for the cases where actual subsidies have been the subject of audits by the state auditors. Also, the relatively low rates of return in the SOE sector may contribute to an impression that certain "informal obligations" (e.g. in terms of staffing, contributions to politically favoured causes, etc.) continue to exist and largely go unreported.

Practices for funding the costs of public policy objectives vary and include the following:

- Some SOEs receive yearly funding to contribute to the delivery of their public policy activities. The amount of funding is partially linked to the foreseen scope or cost of public policy activities (e.g. road maintenance SOEs receive funding in accordance with foreseen works needed to deliver a certain level of service provision). If costs exceed funding amount, the remainder is funded by cross-subsidisation from commercial activities. This applies, for example, to the road maintenance SOEs.

- Some SOEs are compensated for their public policy activities based on the actual cost of activities undertaken. This applies notably to Smiltynė Ferry Terminal and Lithuanian Post. For Lithuanian Post, the related costs are evaluated by an independent regulatory authority.

- Some SOEs are only partially compensated for their public policy activities and the remainder is funded by cross-subsidisation from their commercial activities. This applies to Lithuanian Railways, for which the nature and scope of public policy activities are agreed in advance via a contract with the state.

- Some SOEs are not compensated for their public policy activities, which are funded entirely by cross-subsidisation from commercial activities. This applies notably to the state-owned forestry enterprises. (According to the 2014 aggregate report, forestry enterprises did receive grants from the state, but they only represented about 3% of the cost of public policy objectives, meaning the large majority of public policy objectives were financed by commercial activities.)

In these respects Lithuania does not appear to differ materially from most OECD countries. For example, a large number of countries rely on regulation and legislation to ensure universal coverage and affordability in the utilities sector. This effectively implies a redistribution within these companies' client base rather than (as recommended by the *SOE Guidelines*) a transparent monetary compensation by the state for these obligations. However, it should be noted that the definition of public policy objectives employed by the Lithuanian authorities excludes a number of other potential sources of competitive distortion related to objectives other than profit maximisation, for instance maintaining SOE employment at levels that a private company could not viably pursue.

Application of general laws, tax codes and regulations (Guideline III.E)

Guideline III.E recommends that SOEs undertaking economic activities should not be exempt from the application of general laws, tax codes and regulations, that laws and regulations should not unduly discriminate between SOEs and their market competitors, and that SOEs' legal form(s) should allow creditors to press their claims to initiate insolvency procedures. Lithuanian SOEs are not formally exempt from the application of general laws, tax codes and regulations. However, OECD experience indicates that statutory SOEs, in particular, may in practice benefit from some advantages arising from their less complete state of corporatisation. In the case of Lithuania, the generally weaker corporate governance-related requirements that are placed on statutory SOEs could be a source of competitive advantage. On the other hand, their legal framework may also be a source of competitive disadvantage: Lithuanian statutory SOEs, with some exceptions, are required by the Law on State and Municipal Enterprises to distribute 50% of profits to the state budget, an obligation that is not placed on fully corporatised SOEs. In addition, the April 2017 amendment prohibiting corporatised SOEs from re-appointing CEOs to more than two five-year terms or in the event that they have not met all performance objectives puts SOEs at a disadvantage in comparison to private sector companies (as discussed above under **Guideline II.A** on "Standardising and simplifying SOE legal forms").

Access to debt and equity finance (Guideline III.F)

Guideline III.F recommends that SOEs' economic activities face market consistent conditions regarding access to debt and equity finance. In particular, the Guideline recommends the following: (i) SOEs' relations with all financial institutions, as well as non-financial SOEs, should be based on purely commercial grounds; (ii) SOEs' economic activities should not benefit from any indirect financial supportthat confers an advantage over private competitors; and (iii) SOEs' economic activities should be required to earn rates of return that are, taking into account their operational conditions, consistent with those obtained by competing private enterprises.[23]

SOEs' relations with financial institutions (Guideline III.F.1)

Concerning the conditions for private debt financing, SOEs do not as a rule benefit from state guarantees that could motivate preferential rates by commercial lenders. The Law on State Debt explicitly identifies the types of loans for which state guarantees can be issued, which notably include: (i) loans that are used to finance state investment projects; and (ii) loans that are used to refinance existing state-guaranteed loans (Article 4). As a recent example, the Lithuanian Parliament granted a twenty-year state guarantee to Nordic Investment Bank for its commercial loan to Klaipėda Oil, in support of implementation of the Liquefied Natural Gas (LNG) terminal project.[24]

Furthermore, concerning the conditions for public debt financing, Lithuania as a general rule does not have state-owned financial institutions (beyond a few entities with a very narrowly-defined commercial focus) that would provide loans to SOEs. That said, large or systemically important SOEs will, like in most other countries, be perceived by commercial lenders as being backed by an "implicit guarantee" from their government owners. The Lithuanian authorities have taken no measures to eliminate the commercial advantages that SOEs may derive from this source of concessionary funding. There is furthermore evidence to suggest that, at least in some cases, the relationship between SOEs is not based on purely commercial grounds. The recent case of loans provided to Lithuanian Shipping Company by two other SOEs, mentioned in the Chapter 3.1 assessment section on equitable treatment of shareholders among state-owned enterprises, provides an illustrative example.

Indirect financial support (Guideline III.F.2)

Most SOEs face the same tax treatment as private enterprises, according to the Lithuanian authorities. All SOEs notably fall under the purview of the Law on Corporate Income Tax, which applies a 15% tax rate on income (Article 5). However, statutory SOEs are subject to additional financial obligations which in practice can confer a competitive disadvantage compared to private companies. They are notably required by the Law on State and Municipal Enterprises to distribute 50% of profits to the state budget (with exceptions possible, e.g. if the enterprise is implementing a strategic project for the state) (Article 15). While this could be considered a dividend payment, the fact that, unlike dividends, the rate is non-negotiable makes it the functional equivalent of a tax rate that is higher than the 15% tax on income provided for by the Law on Corporate Income Tax. Other laws applicable to specific categories of statutory SOEs impose additional tax obligations. For example, according to the Law on Forestry, state-owned forestry enterprises must pay to the state budget an additional 10% turnover tax on income from the sale of round wood. This tax is not applicable to private forestry enterprises. According to information provided to the OECD Secretariat, payment arrears among non-financial SOEs in Lithuania do not commonly occur and/or do not exceed what would be permitted for a private firm.

SOE rates of return (Guideline III.F.3)

SOEs with primarily commercial or mixed objectives (categories 1A and 1B) were required to earn rates of return on equity of 5% for the period 2013-15. They are not, as a rule, required to benchmark their rate-of-return targets against the returns obtained by competing private enterprises. In practice, SOEs in categories 1A and 1B performed somewhat below this target, obtaining an average annual return on equity of 4.6% over the defined period. State-owned forestry enterprises were notably excluded from the 5% rate-of-return obligation and over the period 2013-2015 were instead required to achieve a minimum aggregate average net profit. The SOE sector as a whole achieved a rate of return on equity of 2.5% in 2015, up from a negative rate of -4.4% the previous year. While average returns on equity increased, this was primarily due to results in the energy sector, where returns went from -13.2% to 4.6%. Most other sectors reported slight reductions in average returns on equity in 2015. The below figure provides an overview of SOEs' rates of return on equity by sector in 2014 and 2015. More recently, the average rate of return for the SOE portfolio was 4.8% in 2016.

Figure 3.1. Return on equity of SOEs by sector (2014-15)

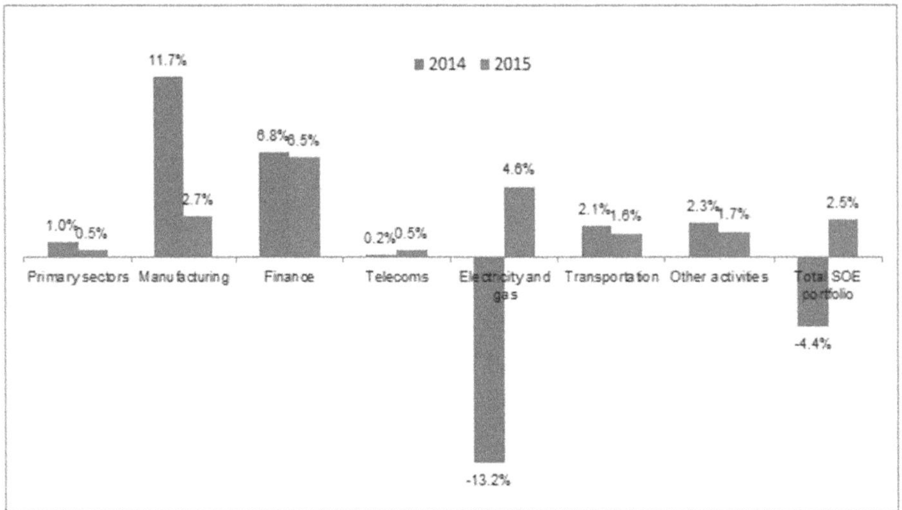

Source: Information provided by the Lithuanian authorities.

The state's dividend expectations for SOEs are well defined but not explicitly linked to those placed on comparable privately-owned enterprises. Fully corporatised SOEs are required to pay dividends of at least 7% of equity capital but not exceeding 80% of company net profits, according to Government Resolution No. 20 "On the Dividends of Company Shares Held by the State […] and Profit Contributions from State Enterprises". Requiring SOEs to achieve a return on equity of 5% and then distribute 7% in dividends raises questions regarding the rationale behind those dual financial targets, and notably whether the state is attempting withdraw excess capital from SOEs. (However, in most cases this is of theoretical interest because the SOEs do not reach levels of profitability sufficient to make the 7% rule apply.) Statutory SOEs are required to pay 50% of annual profits in the form of "profit contributions", according to the Law on State and Municipal Enterprises (Art. 15.6). Together, these documents outline a number of situations wherein a state ownership entity can propose a lower dividend (or "profit contribution") expectation than those outlined above, or wherein statutory SOEs can be exempt from the payment of a profit contribution. These include notably instances where:

- The statutory SOE is implementing a project of strategic national importance that is recognised as such by Government resolution or other legal act.
- The SOE is identified as an enterprise of strategic importance to national security (applying to all enterprises listed in Table 2.13).
- The prices or tariffs of goods or services sold by the SOE are regulated by law. This is effectively a means by which the state can finance public policy objectives via foregone dividend revenues.
- The resultant dividend levels would be so high as to cause the SOE's equity capital to fall below the authorised capital or mandatory reserve.

SOEs' engagement in public procurement (Guideline III.G)

Guideline III.G recommends that, when SOEs engage in public procurement, procedures applied should be competitive, non-discriminatory and safeguarded by appropriate standards of transparency. SOEs acting in a capacity as procuring entity or supplier for public procurement contracts are included in the scope of the Law on Public Procurement, which requires that public procurement procedures respect minimum standards of non-discrimination and transparency. As is the case with state aid, in this area the Lithuanian authorities are also subject to EU legislation imposing standardised rules aimed at safeguarding a level playing field in public procurement. A new version of the Law on Public Procurement, transposing EU procurement directives into national law, was adopted on 2 May 2017 and entered into force on 1 July 2017.

In practice, SOEs that act as prospective suppliers for public procurement can benefit from exemptions to the Law which could arguably jeopardise fair competition and transparent procedures. First, if an SOE procures goods or services from a subsidiary company that derives most of its commercial activity from the parent company, then the contract in question does not have to go through the standard procurement process. The provisions of the Law relative to prospective suppliers for public procurement contracts notably exclude from their application any controlled subsidiary entity with a separate legal status that derives at least 80% of its turnover from the contracting authority. This would in principle apply to subsidiaries of SOEs that meet those requirements (Article 10.1). This could potentially lead to competitive distortions if SOE subsidiaries operate in competition with private enterprises (e.g. in the railway sector). Furthermore, since the SOE subsidiaries meeting those criteria are not themselves subject to public procurement rules, they can obtain goods and services from other companies according to their own rules. This has the potential to create inefficiencies in the procurement of goods to SOE parent companies, or, in the worst of cases, to facilitate the use of kick-backs in exchange for contracts. Secondly, if the public procurement contract in question is below a certain value threshold, then it does not have to go through the standard procurement process. This provision is not in itself a cause for concern, but one implication is that small statutory enterprises, e.g. in the forestry and road maintenance sectors prior to their recent consolidation, are not required to publish tenders. The Lithuanian authorities report that a number of these issues have been addressed through the May 2017 amendments to the Law on Public Procurement. For example, the Lithuanian authorities report that new provisions in the law (i) restrict the use of in-house transactions to situations where outside procurement would jeopardise the continuity, accessibility or quality of public services and (ii) prohibit SOEs from concluding in-house transactions.

3.5 Recognising stakeholder rights as established by law or through mutual agreements and the duties, rights and responsibilities of corporate supervisory boards

This *Roadmap* core principle relates mainly to Chapters IV and VI of the *Principles* and Chapters V and VII of the *SOE Guidelines* on stakeholders and boards. The Concept Paper notes that a full assessment of these chapters could potentially call for quite detailed information about actual board practices (including in relation to stakeholders). It therefore recommends focusing on some of the key framework conditions, such as the legal framework defining the duties of board members, and the enforcement mechanisms and the legal rights of stakeholders. It suggests focusing particularly on: (i) stakeholder rights (**Principles IV.A, B** and **E**); (ii) the rights, duties and responsibilities of supervisory boards (**Principle VI.A**); and (iii) SOE recognition of stakeholder rights and SOE supervisory boards (**Guidelines V.A, B, C** and **VII.C**).

This section includes three additional Principles not included in the Concept Paper. First, given that Lithuania's insolvency framework has been highlighted in the past by external observers and the private sector as an area of possible concern, and given that this framework has been the subject of a number of recent reforms, this section will also include consideration of Lithuania's position against **Principle IV.F**, which recommends an effective and efficient insolvency framework and effective enforcement of creditor rights. For similar reasons, this section also includes an assessment of Lithuania's position against two additional board-related recommendations: **Principle VI.E.1**, which recommends that boards are empowered to exercise objective independent judgment, given the number of experts who highlighted director independence as a corporate governance challenge that should be addressed; and **Principle VI.E.2**, which recommends considering setting up specialised committees to support the full board in performing its functions, given the aforementioned confusion over audit committees and the general low level of compliance with these recommendations in the Nasdaq Vilnius Corporate Governance Code.

Stakeholder rights

Respect for stakeholder rights (Principle IV.A)

Principle IV.A recommends that the rights of stakeholders that are established by law or through mutual agreements should be respected. Under Lithuanian law, citizens' rights are ultimately protected under the Constitution, then by the Civil Code. Particular stakeholder groups' rights are further protected under specific laws, such as employees, who are protected under the Labour Code (which was under Parliamentary review as of mid-2016).[25] Disputes between employers and employees under the Labour Code may be settled via labour dispute commissions under the State Labour Inspectorate; decisions of these commissions may be contested in court. Other protections include, for example, consumer protections enshrined in the Law on Consumer Protection (and enforced by the State Consumer Protection Authority) and environmental protections afforded under a series of separate legal acts and implemented by the Environmental Protection Agency.

Stakeholders' access to redress (Principle IV.B)

Principle IV.B recommends that, where stakeholder interests are protected by law, stakeholders should have the opportunity to obtain effective redress for violation of their rights. Under Lithuanian law (and primarily under the Civil Code[26]), a legal contract that is entered into between two parties has the force of law and the party that breaches the contract is liable in court. This applies equally to commercial disputes: any shareholder, creditor, manager, or member of a supervisory or management board may address the court if they believe that certain decisions made by the company's bodies are invalid.

Specific protections are stipulated in the Law on Companies, which protect the rights of shareholders and creditors.[27] Most of these describe conditions under which stakeholders may bring a claim to court. Lithuanian authorities further report enactment in June 2016 of a new Law on Bondholder Interest Protection that entered into force on 1 November 2016. The new law regulates bondholders' trustee rights, companies' duties to bondholders, as well as bondholders' rights and obligations.

Communicating concerns about illegal or unethical practices (Principle IV.E)

Principle IV.E recommends that stakeholders, including individual employees and their representative bodies, be able to freely communicate their concerns about illegal or unethical practices to the board and to the competent public authorities and that their rights should not be compromised for doing this.

On 28 November 2017, the Lithuanian Parliament enacted a new Law on the Protection of Whistle-blowers, which provides for the protection of both public and private sector whistle-blowers (OECD, 2017). Prior to the enactment of this new legislation, some government agencies were already undertaking practices to promote whistle-blowing. For example, the State Labour Inspectorate had established a "trust phone line" to facilitate anonymous reports on "illegal work" and the State Tax Inspectorate could receive anonymous reports on possible tax violations.[28] The Law on Markets in Financial Instruments and the Law on Banks also require that banking and financial services institutions establish effective mechanisms for enabling the reporting of potential or actual infringements of the law, as required by recent EU legislation.[29] Some private sector companies (such as TEO LT), have also been proactively implementing whistle-blower channels and protections as part of broader efforts to comply with international anti-corruption standards, which they see as a means to attract business partners (who may be subject to cross-border anti-bribery legislation) and investors outside Lithuania.

Insolvency framework and enforcement of creditor rights (Principle IV.F)

As noted above, external observers and the private sector have in the past highlighted Lithuania's insolvency framework as an area of potential concern.[30] The framework has also been recently amended and further amendments are currently under review, warranting consideration here against **Principle IV.F**.

Creditor rights are protected under the Civil Code, the Enterprise Bankruptcy Law and the Law on Restructuring of Enterprises. The legal framework applies to all enterprises registered in Lithuania, with some exceptions.[31] The Ministry of Finance is responsible for the overall oversight of the insolvency legal framework. These laws set forth creditors' rights and the procedure for satisfying creditors' claims in the course of insolvency proceedings.

In recent years, this framework has been amended numerous times in order to strengthen the legal framework for undertaking insolvency and restructuring procedures and for appointing and remunerating insolvency and restructuring administrators. On 13 May 2016, the Lithuanian Parliament returned drafts of the Enterprise Bankruptcy Law and the Law on Restructuring of Enterprises to the Government with a view to ultimately consolidating the insolvency legislation into one unified law. The new law is reportedly planned for submission to the Parliament in the second quarter of 2018. (Box 10 provides an overview of the amendments that were previously being considered by the Parliament to strengthen the requirements and controls applicable to insolvency practitioners in Lithuania.) Data on Restructuring and Bankruptcy Proceedings, as of end-2015, are included in Table 3.3. Because an assessment of the effectiveness of the insolvency framework would be quite complex, and data provided in Table 3.3 do not provide a conclusive picture of overall trends and impacts of recent legislation, it was not possible for the OECD Secretariat to develop a clear assessment with respect to this Principles' recommendation. Additional interviews with experts and stakeholders would be necessary to develop a more informed judgement.

Box 3.6 Proposed amendments to the Enterprise Bankruptcy Act and the Law on Restructuring of Enterprises

The main proposals foreseen in amendments to the Enterprise Bankruptcy Law and the Law on Restructuring of Enterprises are summarised below. At the time of writing, the proposal to consolidate both laws into one unified law – taking into account the proposed amendments to the individual laws – was expected to be submitted to Parliament in the second quarter of 2018.

- Petitions for initiation of bankruptcy and restructuring should be examined together, in order to make a comprehensive analysis and a proper decision regarding the perspective of insolvency proceedings;
- Creditors' right to initiate restructuring proceedings is established;
- The term for filing the restructuring plan with the court is reduced to 4 months (instead of 6);
- Classes of creditors are established (i.e. secured creditors, public institutions and the other creditors);
- The right to vote on a restructuring plan would be assigned to the affected creditors;
- The administrator in the course of restructuring will not be compulsory;
- The commencement criteria for bankruptcy proceedings are changed: An insolvency of an enterprise would be specified as a state of an enterprise when the overdue liabilities of the enterprise are in excess of half of the value of the assets entered in the enterprise's balance and (or) the enterprise fails or will fail to discharge its obligations;
- A possibility for an enterprise in the course of bankruptcy to terminate bankruptcy proceedings and convert to restructuring proceedings is established;
- Provisions related to the sale of assets are improved, such as principles and order of assets sale, including a possibility for secured creditors to take pledged assets before auction, as well as legal certainty is ensured in the scope of sale as a going concern in bankruptcy proceedings.

Source: Information provided by the Lithuanian authorities.

Table 3.3. Data on restructuring and bankruptcy proceedings, as of end-2015

Process and indicators	Totals per period					
Enterprise restructuring	**2001-2015**	**2011**	**2012**	**2013**	**2014**	**2015**
INSTITUTED RESTRUCTURING PROCESSES	392	58	44	48	31	39
COMPLETED RESTRUCTURING PROCESSES, of them:	272	39	30	46	41	43
Terminated restructuring proceedings (according to the date of termination)	251	37	30	45	39	32
Duration of terminated processes, in years (on average per one company)	1.7	0.9	1.2	2.2	2.5	2.4
Completed restructuring processes (plan implemented)	21	2	0	1	2	11
Duration of successfully completed processes, in years (on average per one company)	4.5	6.1	0.0	4.1	3.5	4.7
Satisfaction of creditors' claims in completed processes (%)	82.6	100	-	44.0	57.0	85.6
Enterprise bankruptcy	**1993 -2015**	**2011**	**2012**	**2013**	**2014**	**2015**
INSTITUTED BANKRUPTCY PROCESSES	18 208	1 274	1 401	1 553	1 685	1 985
COMPLETED BANKRUPTCY PROCESSES, of them:	13 952	1 004	1 382	1 449	1 606	1 853
Terminated the bankruptcy proceedings (according to the date of termination)	376	32	32	43	55	36
Duration of terminated processes , in years (on average per one company)	1.3	1.9	0.6	1.3	1.1	1.0
Satisfaction of creditors' claims in terminated processes (%)	37.2	14.2	30.3	29.6	37.8	32.8
Completed bankruptcy processes (by the date of deregistration)	13 576	972	1 350	1 406	1 551	1 817
Duration of completed processes in years (on average per one company)	2.1	2.1	2.3	2.5	2.5	2.4
Satisfaction of creditors' claims in completed processes (%)	9.7	10.5	10.6	11.1	8.6	8.1
Personal bankruptcy	**2013 -2015**			**2013**	**2014**	**2015**
INSTITUTED BANKRUPTCY PROCESSES	918			118	367	433
COMPLETED BANKRUPTCY PROCESSES, of them:	75				18	57
Terminated bankruptcy proceedings (according to the date of termination)	54				14	40
Duration of terminated processes, in years (on average per one company)	0.7				0.6	0.8
Completed bankruptcy processes (plan implemented)	21				4	17
Duration of completed processes, in years (on average per one company)	1.3				0.9	1.6
Satisfaction of creditors' claims in completed processes (%)	4.9				0.2	9.7

Source: Lithuanian Ministry of Finance

The rights, duties and responsibilities of boards

Principle VI.A recommends that board members should act on a fully informed basis, in good faith, with due diligence and care and in the best interests of the company and its shareholders.

The flexibility for Lithuanian companies to establish either two-tier boards or different forms of single-tier boards are described in detail in Chapter 2.4, together with the recent related legislative changes applicable to listed companies. The fiduciary duty of members of supervisory boards (where they exist) and management boards is set forth in the Law on Companies and the Civil Code. The Law on Companies (Art. 19.8) requires that management boards act in the interest of the company and its shareholders, to comply with laws and other legal acts and to be governed by the articles of association of the company. There is no parallel requirement for members of supervisory boards.[32] Furthermore, Art. 2.87 of the Civil Code states that a "member of a legal person's body shall have to act in good faith and in a reasonable manner in respect of the legal person and members of other legal person's bodies". Finally, the Nasdaq Vilnius Corporate Governance Code Principle IV.2 recommends that members of a company's collegial body "act in good faith, with care and responsibility for the benefit and in the interests of the company and its shareholders with due regard to the interests of employees and public welfare".

Regarding directors' liability for breach of their fiduciary duty, the Lithuanian authorities report that members of a managing body may be held liable for damages incurred by the legal person, except as otherwise provided by law, incorporation documents, or an agreement. Specifically, the Civil Code provides for four conditions under which director liability may be applied (see provisions in Box 3.7). The Lithuanian authorities cited one court case in particular in which fiduciary duty liability was enforced (albeit only against the CEO). The case was brought by a creditor against the CEO and directors of the company UAB GlaxoSmithKline Lietuva. In rulings issued in 2013 and 2015, the Supreme Court found in favour of redress for violation of fiduciary duties. The Supreme Court stated that lower courts did not make a proper investigation and fact-finding and returned the case to the Court of Appeal for a second hearing. The Court of Appeal decided to award EUR 2.5 million in damages in favour of the claimant, more specifically in relation to the CEO, due to illegal transactions. The Court ruled that the management board was not liable due to the fact that it had not yet been formed at the time of the transaction.

Box 3.7 Conditions under which director liability may be applied

The Lithuanian Civil Code establishes four conditions under which director liability may be applied for damages incurred by a legal person. These conditions are as follows:

Article 6.246. *Unlawful actions*

1. Civil liability shall arise from non-performance of a duty established by laws or a contract (unlawful refrainment from acting), or from performance of actions that are prohibited by laws or a contract (unlawful acting), or from violation of the general duty to behave with care.

2. It may be established by laws that a person shall be bound to compensate damage he has not caused himself but is responsible for the actions of another person who inflicted the damage (indirect civil liability).

3. Damage caused by lawful actions must be compensated only in cases expressly specified by laws.

Article 6.247. *Causation*

Only those damages can be compensable which are related to actions (acting or refrainment from acting) giving rise to civil liability of the debtor in such a manner that the damages, taking into account their nature and that of the civil liability, can be imputed to the debtor as a result of his actions (acting or refrainment from acting).

Article 6.248. *Fault as a condition for civil liability*

1. Civil liability shall arise only upon the existence of the fault of the obligated person, except in the cases established by laws or a contract when civil liability arises without fault. The fault of a debtor shall be presumed, except in the cases established by laws.

2. Fault may be expressed by intention or negligence.

3. A person shall be deemed to have committed fault where taking into account the essence of the obligation and other circumstances he failed to behave with the care and caution necessary in the corresponding conditions.

4. Where damage has also been caused through the fault of the creditor himself, the repairable damages shall be

diminished in proportion to the degree of gravity of the creditor's fault committed, or the debtor can be released from civil liability.

Article 6.249. *Damage and damages*

1. Damage shall include the amount of the loss or damage of property sustained by a person and the expenses incurred (direct damages) as well as the incomes of which he has been deprived, i.e. the incomes he would have received if unlawful actions had not been committed. Damage expressed in monetary terms shall constitute damages. Where the amount of damages cannot be proved by the party with precision, it shall be assessed by a court.

2. If the person who is liable towards another has derived profit from his unlawful actions, upon the demand of the creditor the profit received may be attributed to damages.

3. The court may postpone the evaluation of damage which has not yet occurred or may evaluate future damage upon assessment of its real probability. In such cases, the court may adjudge either to pay a lump sum or to make instalment payments, or it may obligate the debtor to furnish security upon compensation for damage.

4. In addition to the direct damages and the incomes of which a creditor has been deprived, damages shall comprise:

1) reasonable costs to prevent or mitigate damage;

2) reasonable costs incurred in assessing civil liability and damage;

3) reasonable costs incurred in the process of recovering damages within extrajudicial procedure.

5. Damage shall be assessed according to the prices valid on the day when the court judgement was passed unless the law or the nature of the obligation requires the application of prices that were valid on the day the damage arose or on the day when the action was brought.

6. In the event where one and the same action has created both damage and benefit for the aggrieved person, the benefit received may, to the extent that this does not contradict to the criteria of reasonableness, good faith and justice, be computed into damages to be repaired.

Source : Lithuanian Civil Code Articles 6.246 - 6.249

Lithuanian law does not differentiate between *de jure* and *de facto* directors in relation to their fiduciary duties.[33] For the purpose of this review, *de jure* directors are those who have been appointed to their roles according to the Law on Companies and the company's articles of association, while *de facto* directors are those that effectively undertake a supervisory role on a company with a "Type A" (executive) management board, even though that management board has not been assigned supervisory functions (see Chapter 2.4 section on governance responsibilities). It is unclear how directors performing in a *de facto* capacity could be held individually legally liable under Lithuanian law for any supervisory responsibilities in relation to their *de facto* supervisory role. The possible lack of legal liability for board members acting in a *de facto* supervisory role within Type A management boards could continue to be a concern for non-listed companies. However, recent Company Law amendments prohibiting use of Type A boards for listed companies would appear, once implemented, to mitigate this concern with respect to listed companies. Listed companies opting for a single tier board will only have the possibility to adopt a Type B management board with legally designated *de jure* supervisory functions.

Another area of concern, but which the Lithuanian authorities appear to be in the process of addressing, relates to the legal liabilities of civil servants who are also board members of SOEs. According to information obtained during the Secretariat's August 2017 fact-finding mission, the Law on Civil Service prohibits civil servants from acting "individually" (i.e. they must act on behalf of the state). This potentially conflicts with the provisions of the Law on Companies requiring management boards to act in the interests of the company and its shareholders. The Lithuanian authorities assert that civil servants are subject to the same legal duties as other board members – notably to act in the interest of the company and its shareholders – and can also be held individually liable for damages incurred in relation to their board duties. The text of the Law on Public Service stipulates that (i) a public servant may only serve on an SOE board subject to authorisation from the shareholding ministry or institution and (ii) any board fees received by a public servant serving on an SOE board must be transferred to the state budget. Although these provisions do not concern individual liability *per se*, they could create a perception (including among civil servants) that they are expected to act on behalf of the state. At the time of writing, the Law on Civil Service was reportedly undergoing review. The draft proposed amendments shared with the Secretariat notably establish that public servants cannot engage in any activities that present a conflict of interest and remove the requirement that public servants must receive a written authorisation in order to serve on SOE boards. The amendments to the Law on Civil Service were foreseen for enactment in the first half of 2018.

Regarding Lithuanian companies' application of these rules in practice, the Lithuanian authorities report that, based on an analysis of 33 company financial and annual reports as of 2014, 25 companies declared that board members act in the best interest of the company and shareholders, though not all companies provided explanations of how this is achieved.

Finally, external observers have noted that, until recently, there has been little to no case law (which is considered a secondary law source in Lithuania) on directors' duties. Court proceedings applying these provisions have increased in recent years, due in part to the post-crisis increase in corporate insolvencies, which led insolvency administrators in some cases to initiate proceedings against former directors based on alleged breaches of director duties.[34]

Board exercise of objective independent judgment (Principle VI.E)

The limited presence and roles of independent directors on Lithuanian listed companies' boards has been identified as a corporate governance challenge. The annotations to **Principle VI.E** note that, in ensuring that company boards are able to exercise objective judgment, many jurisdictions either require in law or recommend in codes that a certain number of board members be independent, defined in various ways and via various means (i.e. via independence criteria or "negative" criteria and either in law, corporate governance codes, or listing requirements). This is further emphasised in **Principle VI.E.1**, which recommends "assigning a sufficient number of non-executive members capable of exercising independent judgment to tasks where there is a potential for conflict of interest."

As outlined in Chapter 2.4 and the Chapter 2.5 section on recent legal and regulatory changes, amendments to the Law on Companies enacted in November 2017 introduce new requirements for listed companies' boards of directors, notably that they must include at least 1/3 independent directors and that one-tier management boards must be assigned supervisory functions. Prior to this, the legal independence requirements for Lithuanian listed companies were (i) only applicable to supervisory boards or to management boards assigned supervisory functions (and therefore not applicable to the most commonly used one-tier executive management board) and (ii) only defined independence in relation to the company (i.e. a director could be considered independent if he or she had no employment relationships with the company). Furthermore, listed companies could be overseen by one-tier management boards with purely executive functions. Also of relevance to board independence, other amendments to the Law on Companies, together with recent revisions to Bank of Lithuania rules on listed companies' audit committee composition, require that related party transactions be assessed by an audit committee comprising at least 1/2 directors that are independent, including from the controlling shareholder. Because the new requirements on board composition enter into force in July 2018, the text that follows focuses mainly on the situation at the time of writing in early 2018, but with reference as relevant to the foreseen impact of the amendments once they enter into force and are implemented within Lithuanian listed companies.

Lithuania's legal and regulatory corporate governance framework (again, in force at the time of writing, in early 2018) provides some rules and regulations that are consistent with **Principle VI.E**'s overall recommendations for ensuring boards' exercise of objective independent judgment. First, under the Law on Companies (Art. 31.6 and Art. 33.6), a member of the management board cannot simultaneously serve on the supervisory board (where one exists), and vice versa. Under these same provisions, the company manager (CEO) cannot serve on the supervisory board (where one exists) or on the management board, if the AGM has assigned the management board supervisory functions, thereby separating the roles of CEO and chairperson. Companies are obligated to disclose information on the composition of their boards in their annual reports (Civil Code Art. 2.47 Part 1[6] and Art. 2.66 Part 1[6] and the Law on Financial Reporting by Undertakings Articles 23[8] and [10]). Further, the Law on Companies stipulates that more than half of the members of a supervisory board (where one exists) (Art. 31.7) and more than half of management boards with supervisory functions (Art. 33.7) must be non-executive (or, more precisely, must not have any employment relationships with the company). Finally, Principle III.6 of the Nasdaq Vilnius Corporate Governance Code recommends that a "sufficient number" (undefined[35]) of members of a company's collegial body should be independent, and Principle III.7 provides an explicit list of independence criteria (see Box 3.9).

However, it is important to recall that more than half of Lithuanian listed companies have Type A executive management boards without supervisory functions. Prior to the amendments enacted to the Law on Companies in November 2017, there were no legal requirements for independent or non-executive board members on these boards. (The amendments enter into force in July 2018. The boards in place prior this date may serve until the expiry of their terms, but the Bank of Lithuania has indicated that it does not foresee any major obstacles to a timely compliance by listed companies with the new provisions.) One-tier executive boards have a clear conflict of interest in supervising the CEO (even if the CEO does not necessarily serve on the board), since at the same time they work for and may be hired or fired by the CEO. A practical example of how the Type A executive board structure may be problematic from a corporate governance perspective can be found in the 2016 experience of AB Rokiskio suris (RSU), a listed Lithuanian dairy products company recently involved in a dispute between controlling and minority shareholders. The company's dispute with the shareholder East Capital has received considerable press coverage, highlighting a number of corporate governance concerns (See Box 3.8). While it is not claimed that RSU is representative of all Lithuanian listed companies, its example does point to risks or weaknesses in the previous Lithuanian legal framework with respect to boards of directors' responsibilities and capacities to carry them out with objective and independent judgement.

Box 3.8 RSU: An illustration of single-tier boards in practice and related corporate governance concerns

AB Rokiskio suris (RSU) is a leading dairy products company in Lithuania producing processed milk and cheese products. Founded in 1925, RSU was first listed on the Lithuania secondary market in 1995, and has traded on the main list since 1997, with market capitalisation valued at approximately EUR 10.4 million as of 4 August, 2016. As of the end of 2015, three related shareholders (UAB "Pieno pramones investiciju valdymas" (30%), SIA "RSU Holding" (26.6%) and Antanas Trumpa (21%)), linked through shareholder agreements, maintained a combined 77.5% of shares. Another 7.2% were held by the company itself. These shareholders further maintain control of the company through Antanas Trumpa's role as RSU's CEO, and placement of his son, Dalius Trumpa, as Chairman of the board and CEO of two RSU subsidiaries. The only publicly disclosed minority shareholder in 2015 was SEB SA Omnibus, with 5.3%. All other shareholders (including East Capital, a Swedish-based investment fund that has filed a lawsuit against RSU in January 2016), hold less than 5%, and thus their shareholding percentages are not publicly disclosed.

RSU's board of directors has undergone considerable evolution over the last 10 years, according to press releases issued on the Nasdaq Vilnius web site reporting on material events. While RSU has maintained a one-tier management board during this period, they reported to have one non-executive board member in 2006-2007, before the board moved to a 9-person management board in 2008 with all executive members. However, one investor made it onto the board in April 2012, after which the shareholders called an extraordinary meeting and decided to reduce the size of the board to five, and to allocate one seat to minority shareholders. However, the fifth seat was left empty, resulting in a four-person executive board. The Investors' Association of Lithuania has complained that the reduction in board seats was undertaken in order to make it harder for minority shareholders to elect a board member, because it would have required 20% of shareholder votes. Since that time, the board has remained a fully executive board composed of members of management (but not the CEO).

As a Type A management (executive) board, the RSU board of directors is not deemed to have supervisory responsibilities, which are assigned to the AGM. Nevertheless, the Type A management board does have responsibility for deciding on company strategy, for appointing the CEO (who in this case is the father of the management board chairman), and for approving material transactions (including those that may be related party transactions), which are not approved by the AGM. Related party transactions are disclosed in the company's annual reports, which must be approved by the shareholders, but these disclosures do not provide much detail regarding the nature, character and value of the transactions (e.g. "purchase of inventory, 7.4 million euros"). While the audit committee is required to have a majority of independent members, they do not have a legal responsibility to review or provide opinions on related party transactions, nor does the external auditor. Moreover, RSU has not established a separate remuneration committee and does not disclose its remuneration policies.

In filing a lawsuit against RSU in January, 2016, East Capital claimed that Antanas Trumpa breached company law by providing unlawful financial support from the company to the shareholder in buying up shares of the company. The lawsuit estimated damage of EUR 11.5 million. RSU has countered by requesting that Bank of Lithuania investigate actions by East Capital that they allege to involve potential market manipulation. With the court case pending, this review does not attempt to evaluate the merits of the lawsuit or counter charges, which have been reported in the Lithuanian press. But from a corporate governance perspective, it is clear that the legal framework allows for the establishment of board structures that lack checks and balances on management, particularly when controlling shareholders and management are tightly linked, as they are in this case. The case also points to weaknesses within the framework for ensuring objective and independent judgement by the board in reviewing related party transactions and other sensitive matters.

Source : Case study information provided by Paulius Martinkus, commissioned by OECD based on public information and interviews with representatives of Bank of Lithuania, Nasdaq Vilnius, the Investors' Association of Lithuania and other relevant stakeholders.

The application of legal requirements and Code recommendations for independence in practice appears to remain a challenge for listed Lithuanian companies. This challenge was highlighted by representatives from the private sector and civil society in meetings with the Secretariat during the May 2016 fact-finding mission to Vilnius. Similar views were expressed by representatives from the Nasdaq Vilnius Exchange, who identified the lack of independent directors as "issue number one" in terms of areas where Lithuanian companies could improve their corporate governance practices. Confirming these views are the data available on listed companies' low compliance with the Nasdaq Vilnius

Corporate Governance Code recommendations on this issue. The Bank of Lithuania's 2010 review of 35 listed companies' compliance with the Code found that only 10 companies (29%) had independent members on either their management board or the supervisory board (where one existed). The situation was slightly worse in 2015, according to Nasdaq Vilnius data, with only 7 out of 28 reporting companies (25%) fully complying with Nasdaq Vilnius Corporate Governance Code Principle III.6. Moreover, in a review by Nasdaq Baltic of corporate governance practices across the Baltic region, Lithuania ranked last out of the three Baltic countries for its compliance with the recommendation to include independent members on listed companies' collegial bodies (Nasdaq Baltic, 2015). Finally, of the listed Lithuanian companies that have independent directors, only a third disclose the names of independent members in their reports or on their company's website. This particular issue can be expected to change as of next year, owing notably to November 2017 amendments to the Law on Financial Reporting by Undertakings which make the requirements for disclosure of board composition more explicit, requiring that companies identify individual supervisory and management board members in annual reports and disclose information on their (other) places of employment. This requirement applies to annual reports drawn up for the 2018 financial year onward.

Reasons cited for non-compliance with the Code's provisions on independence vary and include: difficulty finding qualified independent directors; that trading of company shares is not active and that there are not active minority shareholders with an interest to elect independent directors; that the general meeting of shareholders has decided to elect board members that they believe will best serve their interest; or that board members act independently even while not meeting the formal Code definition of independence.

On this issue of director independence, it should be noted that representatives from the private sector, civil society and the Nasdaq Exchange pointed to certain large SOEs as positive examples for their private sector counterparts. Specifically mentioned in this regard was Lithuanian Energy, which is unlisted but which has two subsidiaries with listed shares (94.98%-owned ESO and 96.74%-owned Lietuvos Energijos Gamyba, as of 1 January 2016). Lithuanian Energy's seven-member supervisory board includes three independent directors, one of whom serves as Chair.[36]

A number of the corporate governance vulnerabilities stemming from limited board independence can be expected to change once the November 2017 amendments to the Law on Companies enter into force in July 2018. As detailed in Chapters 2.4 and 2.5, the amendments notably require that the boards of all listed companies comprise at least one third independent directors. To be considered independent, directors must not have any "family, kinship marriage or partnership relations" with the company, its controlling shareholder or the members of its supervisory or management boards. Independent members must also not have had any business relations with the company in the year preceding their board appointment, either directly or as a shareholder, board member or CEO. As mentioned previously, while these independence requirements enter into force in July 2018, the boards in place prior to that date can serve until the expiry of their terms. This may cause potential delays in attaining the required portion of independent board members in all listed companies and therefore may justify further follow up in the future.

Box 3.9 Nasdaq Vilnius Corporate Governance Code - Independence Criteria

Principle III.7 provides explicit independence criteria for independent members of listed companies' collegial bodies. This Principle recommends the following:

3.7. A member of the collegial body should be considered to be independent only if he is free of any business, family or other relationship with the company, its controlling shareholder or the management of either, that creates a conflict of interest such as to impair his judgment. Since all cases when member of the collegial body is likely to become dependent are impossible to list, moreover, relationships and circumstances associated with the determination of independence may vary amongst companies and the best practices of solving this problem are yet to evolve in the course of time, assessment of independence of a member of the collegial body should be based on the contents of the relationship and circumstances rather than their form. The key criteria for identifying whether a member of the collegial body can be considered to be independent are the following:

1. He/she is not an executive director or member of the board (if a collegial body elected by the general shareholders' meeting is the supervisory board) of the company or any associated company and has not been such during the last five years;
2. He/she is not an employee of the company or some any related company and has not been such during the last three years, except for cases when a member of the collegial body does not belong to the senior management and was elected to the collegial body as a representative of the employees;
3. He/she is not receiving or has been not receiving significant additional remuneration from the company or associated company other than remuneration for the office in the collegial body. Such additional remuneration includes participation in share options or some other performance-based pay systems; it does not include compensation payments for the previous office in the company (provided that such payment is no way related with later position) as per pension plans (inclusive of deferred compensations);
4. He/she is not a controlling shareholder or representative of such shareholder (control as defined in the Council Directive 83/349/EEC Article 1 Part 1);
5. He/she does not have and did not have any material business relations with the company or associated company within the past year directly or as a partner, shareholder, director or superior employee of the subject having such relationship. A subject is considered to have business relations when it is a major supplier or service provider (inclusive of financial, legal, counseling and consulting services), major client or organization receiving significant payments from the company or its group;
6. He/she is not and has not been, during the last three years, partner or employee of the current or former external audit company of the company or associated company;
7. He/she is not an executive director or member of the board in some other company where executive director of the company or member of the board (if a collegial body elected by the general shareholders' meeting is the supervisory board) is non-executive director or member of the supervisory board, he/she may not also have any other material relationships with executive directors of the company that arise from their participation in activities of other companies or bodies;
8. He/she has not been in the position of a member of the collegial body for over than 12 years;
9. He/she is not a close relative to an executive director or member of the board (if a collegial body elected by the general shareholders' meeting is the supervisory board) or to any person listed in above items 1 to8. Close relative is considered to be a spouse (common-law spouse), children and parents.

Source : Corporate Governance Code for the Companies Listed on NASDAQ OMX Vilnius

Specialised board committees

Principle VI.E.2 calls on boards to "consider setting up specialised committees to support the full board in performing its functions, particularly in respect to audit, and, depending upon the company's size and risk profile, also in respect to risk management and remuneration." **Principle VI.E.2** is included in this review, given the aforementioned confusion related to audit committee requirements and the low level of listed companies' compliance with Nasdaq Vilnius Corporate Governance Code recommendations on specialised committees.

As described in the Chapter 3.2 assessment section on accounting and auditing standards, the Law on Audit requires all public interest entities to set up audit committees. The amendments to the Law on Audit which entered into force on 1 March 2017, together with the complementary Bank of Lithuania Resolution on the composition of listed companies' audit committees, should help address concerns raised during the review process regarding the apparent confusion over the composition, role, and responsibilities of audit committees *vis-à-vis* companies' management boards and/or supervisory boards (where they exist). Together, these two legal instruments strengthen the role of audit committees, including requirements pertaining to their composition, formation, activities and functions. The new requirements (established by the Bank of Lithuania Resolution) assign responsibility for deciding upon the audit committee composition to the supervisory body (subject to applicable rules), i.e. to whichever board is assigned supervisory functions, or, in the absence of such a board, the AGM. Of note, the new requirements stipulate that an audit committee must comprise at least three members, the majority of which must be independent (including from the company's management and its shareholders). One of the independent members must have at least three years of experience in accounting or in the audit of financial statements. The chair of the audit committee must be independent.

Other than an audit committee, Lithuanian companies are not legally required to establish specialised committees. However, the Nasdaq Vilnius Corporate Governance Code does recommend the establishment of specialised committees (Principle IV.8), specifically nomination (Principle IV.4.12) and remuneration committees (Principle IV.13). (Audit committees, which are legally required of listed companies, are also recommended, under Principle IV.14.) According to the Nasdaq Vilnius Corporate Governance Code (Principle IV.9), specialised committees should normally be composed of at least three members, with some exceptions. (Smaller companies may exceptionally establish two-member specialised committees.) This Principle further recommends that the majority of committee members should be independent and, in companies with a one-tier management board, that "the remuneration and audit committees should be entirely comprised of non-executive directors." Many listed companies do not comply with these recommendations. The average compliance for Principle IV.4.9 dealing with the composition of these committees is 39%. (See also Table 2.3 in Chapter 2.2.) Figures on compliance with the relevant recommendations described in this paragraph are provided in Table 3.4.

Table 3.4. Average compliance with the Nasdaq Vilnius Corporate Governance Code Principle IV, 2015

Principle	Fully comply	Partially comply	Do not comply	Not applicable
PRINCIPLE IV. THE DUTIES AND LIABILITIES OF A COLLEGIAL BODY ELECTED BY THE GENERAL SHAREHOLDERS' MEETING The corporate governance framework should ensure proper and effective functioning of the collegial body elected by the general shareholders' meeting, and the powers granted to the collegial body should ensure effective monitoring of the company's management bodies and protection of interests of all the company's shareholders.	Overall: 53%	Overall: 12%	Overall:31%	Overall: 5%
4.8. The key objective of the committees is to increase efficiency of the activities of the collegial body by ensuring that decisions are based on due consideration, and to help organize its work with a view to ensuring that the decisions it takes are free of material conflicts of interest. Committees should exercise independent judgement and integrity when exercising its functions as well as present the collegial body with recommendations concerning the decisions of the collegial body. Nevertheless the final decision shall be adopted by the collegial body. The recommendation on creation of committees is not intended, in principle, to constrict the competence of the collegial body or to remove the matters considered from the purview of the collegial body itself, which remains fully responsible for the decisions taken in its field of competence.	32%	25%	50%	4%
4.9. Committees established by the collegial body should normally be composed of at least three members. In companies with small number of members of the collegial body, they could exceptionally be composed of two members. Majority of the members of each committee should be constituted from independent members of the collegial body. In cases when the company chooses not to set up a supervisory board, remuneration and audit committees should be entirely comprised of non-executive directors. Chairmanship and membership of the committees should be decided with due regard to the need to ensure that committee membership is refreshed and that undue reliance is not placed on particular individuals.	39%	18%	39%	4%
4.12. Recommendation with regard to Nomination Committee	7%	0%	71%	21%
4.13. Recommendation with regard to Remuneration Committee	7%	7%	61%	25%
4.14. Recommendation with regard to Audit Committee	79%	11%	7%	

Source: Nasdaq Vilnius

SOE recognition of stakeholder rights and SOE supervisory boards

This section assesses Lithuania's position against **Guideline V.A** (recognising and respecting stakeholders' rights); **Guideline V.B** (reporting on stakeholder relations); **Guideline V.C** (internal controls, ethics and compliance programmes or measures); and **Guideline VII.C** (board composition and exercise of objective and independent judgment).

Recognition of and respect for stakeholder rights (Guideline V.A)

Guideline V.A calls on governments, state ownership entities and SOEs to recognise and respect stakeholders' rights established by law or through mutual agreements. The Lithuanian Ownership Guidelines do not stipulate any specific SOE responsibilities towards stakeholders. They do, however, establish certain disclosure requirements. SOEs are requested to report on material issues affecting employees and other stakeholders.

Applicable to all corporations, the Lithuanian Labour code establishes the rights of all employees, and is applicable to the employees of SOEs. It notably establishes employees' right to information and consultation (Art. 47) and to authorise representatives to negotiate on their behalf with employers about "improvements in occupational safety and health".

Reporting on stakeholder relations (Guideline V.B)

Guideline V.B recommends that listed or large SOEs report on stakeholder relations, including where relevant and feasible with regard to labour, creditors and affected communities. SOEs are required to report on "material issues regarding employees and other stakeholders", as per the information disclosure standards of the Nasdaq Vilnius Corporate Governance Code (which, as mentioned earlier, SOEs are required by the Transparency Guidelines to respect, on a mandatory basis for 13 large SOEs and on a comply-or-explain basis for the rest). The Code further recommends that when companies have material information to disclose regarding employees and other stakeholders, they disclose "information about the links between the company and its stakeholders, including employees, creditors, suppliers and the local community, as well as the company's policy with regard to human resources, employee participation schemes in the company's share capital, etc." (Principle X.4). According to information provided by the Lithuanian authorities in the context of the 2015 SOE review, 110 SOEs report regularly on stakeholder relations. Most reporting relates to relations with employees, while the largest SOEs also report on broader stakeholder relations (OECD, 2015).

Internal controls, ethics and compliance programmes or measures (Guideline V.C)

Guideline V.C calls on SOE boards to develop, implement, monitor and communicate internal controls, ethics and compliance programmes or measures, including those which contribute to preventing fraud and corruption. There is no general requirement for the boards of SOEs to develop internal controls, ethics or compliance programmes specifically relating to the prevention of fraud and corruption. However, most large SOEs are required by applicable legislation to establish either an internal control system or an audit committee. As of amendments to the Law on Audit of Financial Statements which entered into force on 1 March 2017, all large SOEs are required to establish an audit committee. For fully corporatised SOEs, the Ownership Guidelines furthermore require that state ownership entities "ensure that an effective internal control system is put in place" which monitors, among others, "compliance with contractual and other obligations to third parties and the management of all related risk factors". The Ownership Guidelines also require that state ownership entities ensure SOEs' observance of the sections of the Law on Internal Control and Audit relating to internal control, which means that statutory SOEs must establish an internal control function.

Of note, all listed companies, including listed SOEs, are required to establish audit committees which, under the Law on Audit, must monitor the efficiency of internal control and risk management systems. According to the 2015 aggregate report, among the SOEs required to establish an audit committee, only two – Lithuanian Energy and Klaipėda Oil – had complied. However, according to the Bank of Lithuania, in 2015 all listed SOEs had established audit committees.

Board composition (Guideline VII.C)

Guideline VII.C recommends that SOEs' board composition allow the exercise of objective and independent judgment and that all board members—including any public officials—be nominated based on qualifications and have equivalent legal responsibilities.

The sub-sections that follow discuss (i) the formal qualifications criteria for SOE board members; (ii) their individual legal responsibilities; and (iii) the composition of SOE boards in practice, all with a view to assessing the impact of these elements on the ability of SOE boards to exercise objective and independent judgement. The information that follows complements – and should be read in parallel with – the assessment contained in the Chapter 3.3 section on SOE operational autonomy. As highlighted in that section, according to the legislation in place, the boards of statutory SOEs are accorded relatively weak powers compared to the state, which effectively limits their ability to exercise independent judgement. The Lithuanian authorities' plans to convert 11 commercially-oriented statutory SOEs to limited liability companies would help to address this concern by according their boards greater powers as compared to the state and leading to concomitant increases in their independence from the state. Another important element limiting SOE boards' ability to exercise independent and objective judgement – and which the Lithuanian authorities are also in the process of addressing – is the practice of verbal or written "instructions" from representatives of ownership ministries concerning how civil servants should vote at SOE board meetings. As mentioned in the Chapter 3.5 assessment section on the rights, duties and responsibilities of boards, amendments to the Law on Civil Service, foreseen for enactment in the first half of 2018, would eliminate a provision requiring that civil servants obtain a written authorisation to serve on SOE boards. Eliminating this provision could help reduce the perception that civil servants are expected to act "on behalf of" the state in fulfilling their board duties. Regardless of its legal or formal basis, the practice of written or verbal instructions on how SOE board members should vote is not consistent with the *SOE Guidelines*.

(i) Formal qualifications criteria for SOE board members

In establishing a board that is able to exercise objective and independent judgement, the annotations to **Guideline VII.C** highlight the importance of a transparent nomination process and recommend that SOE board members have sufficient commercial, financial and sector-specific expertise to effectively carry out their duties. In this regard, the state has established a nomination process, involving an inter-ministerial selection committee, which was previously applicable only to the boards of six large fully corporatised SOEs and has since been made more broadly applicable, notably to also include statutory SOEs.[37] The Lithuanian authorities reported in early 2018 that the process, using the selection criteria, was being implemented in 43 "active" SOEs, taken to mean SOEs not undergoing, or expected to undergo, near-term reorganisations. As of February 2018, 30 SOEs had completed their nomination processes, while eight were under way, three remained to be initiated and two were "to be decided" (see Annex 2 for a status update on the board nomination process in all SOEs as of February 2018). The boards of those SOEs must notably include members with financial expertise, strategic planning and management expertise, and sector-specific knowledge and experience. Furthermore, amendments to the related rules were enacted in March 2017 to increase the mandated proportion of independent directors to ½ and to bar politicians from serving on SOE boards. These formal requirements would appear to be in line with the relevant standards of the *SOE Guidelines* concerning board composition.

The state's SOE board composition rules also involve more general selection criteria, including the requirement that all candidates to SOE boards: possess a university education; have the right to occupy the position in question; have not been disqualified from the board of a legal person over the preceding five years. For statutory SOEs, general qualifications for board members (if a board is established) are further outlined in the Law on State and Municipal Enterprises. The Law notably stipulates that in order to become a board member, a natural person must fulfil a number of general criteria, including (i) holding a university degree; (ii) being of "good repute"; and (iii) not having any connections with other legal persons that could cause a conflict of interest (Art. 10). The Law also states that "special requirements for board members shall be set" by the ownership entity, and outlines the general procedure for board member nominations.

(ii) Legal responsibilities of board members

The annotations to **Guideline VII.C** also highlight the importance of ensuring that all board members – including any state representatives – act in the interests of the enterprise, and not the constituencies that nominated them. In this regard, the respective laws applicable to fully corporatised and statutory SOEs establish a general requirement that all boards must act in the interest of the enterprise (and its shareholders for limited liability companies).

Concerning the legal responsibilities of individual board members, the Civil Code of Lithuania (Articles 2.86 and 2.87) provides explicitly for equal rights and obligations of the "members of a legal person's managing body". It also stipulates that a member of a managing body of a legal person who fails to perform or performs improperly his duties specified in article 2.87 or the certificate of incorporation must redress all damage incurred on the legal person except as otherwise provided by law, incorporation documents or an agreement. For fully corporatised SOEs, the Law on Companies does not make mention of the individual liability of board members but does provide for shareholders to engage in legal action against board members in case of malfeasance in the carrying out of their board duties (Art. 16). For statutory SOEs, the Law on State and Municipal Enterprises establishes the individual liability of board members as follows: "the board members, if the board is formed, who fail to perform or improperly perform their duties set out in the Civil Code, this Law and other laws as well as the articles of association of the enterprise must redress all damage incurred on the enterprise" (Art. 9). This provision is also applicable to the CEO.

According to information obtained from Lithuanian corporate governance practitioners, the fact that Lithuanian SOEs did not generally offer liability insurance to board members was initially an impediment to attracting independent board members. However, nowadays independent board members are generally accorded individual liability insurance on an *ad-hoc* basis.

(iii) Board composition in practice

As outlined in the Chapter 2.8 sections dealing with, respectively, the board composition of Lithuania's largest SOEs and recent or ongoing reforms in the SOE sector, since 2015 Lithuania has undertaken a number of reforms to equip boards with more independent directors and shield them from political interference. These include the March 2017 requirement mandating at least ½ proportion of independent directors on

SOE boards and barring politicians from serving on SOE boards. As of February 2018, this requirement had been implemented in 30 SOEs and related nomination procedures were under way in an additional eight SOEs. Of the remaining 28 SOEs that did not comply with the requirements, nearly all are slated for reorganisation, privatisation, liquidation or conversion to another legal form and, of those, 14 have no board in place. Furthermore, the boards of Lithuania's largest SOEs currently have no acting politicians and with only one exception fully comply with the state's SOE board composition rules (the exception is the Lithuanian Oil Products Agency, which the Lithuanian authorities assert will be undergoing re-organisation in the near future). As implementation of the rules on board composition continues, SOE board independence can be expected to improve more in the near future.

Historically, the composition of SOE boards has raised questions regarding both their ability to exercise independent judgment and their capacity to effectively perform their board duties. In the recent past, the state's requirements for independent directors on SOE boards (previously only applicable to large, fully corporatised SOEs, before they were made more broadly applicable in March 2017) were not fully implemented in practice. From 2014 to 2015, the number of SOEs with at least one independent director on the board increased from 11 to 27, out of 73 SOEs with boards. The historical presence of vice ministers on the boards of several of Lithuania's largest SOEs has also been a cause for concern, given the risk that they act on behalf of their constituencies rather than in the long term interest of the enterprise.

Many boards have also traditionally mostly consisted of civil servants from the ownership ministries, who do not receive compensation for their board service. This could create incentives for such board members to act in the interests of their employers (e.g. state ownership entities) rather than the enterprise. Related to this, according to information provided by non-governmental sources in the context of the 2015 SOE review, although board members of SOEs are fully liable by law for their actions while performing their board duties (as outlined above), there is not a broad-based understanding of this individual responsibility among public officials serving on SOE boards, who may in practice feel obliged to make decisions purely on behalf of their state employers (OECD, 2015).

Finally, the fact that a number of SOE board members apparently hold multiple posts could jeopardise their ability to effectively fulfil their board duties. According to the 2015 state aggregate report, 27 SOEs during that period had at least one board member serving on more than four boards. 18 of those SOEs were overseen by the Ministry of Agriculture and six by the Ministry of Transport and Communications. As has been the case in other OECD accession candidate countries, the Lithuanian authorities might encounter some difficulties in identifying a sufficient number of qualified (and interested) candidates to serve as independent members on the boards of SOEs, particularly while in the early stages of instilling a "culture" of independence within these governance organs. However, according to independent board members interviewed for this review, trends in this respect are positive.

Notes

1. See online here: http://www.nasdaqbaltic.com/market/?pg=news&news_id=211228. Bank Snoras was granted the right by the Vilnius Stock Exchange board in 2006 to issue on the secondary list 2 million registered preference shares (each at 10 Lithuanian Litas [EUR 2.94] with 10% non-cumulative dividend) valuing in total 20 million Litas.

2. Regulations issued by the Bank of Lithuania are binding legal acts adopted by the Board of the Bank of Lithuania, which within its remit as stipulated under law (i.e. the Law on Bank of Lithuania, Law on Securities, Law on Markets in Financial Instruments, Law on Companies and other legal acts), provides the Bank with the right to set legal regulation in certain areas.

3. The Lithuanian authorities explain that this situation pertains to cases where a person (or persons) directly or indirectly holds financial instruments, which at the maturity of the buy-up term, and in accordance with the official agreement, grant the person(s) the right or opportunity to acquire already-issued shares of the issuer with voting or similar rights.

4. The rules for mandatory takeover bids are provided in Section IV of the Law on Securities. Paragraph 1 of Art. 36 of the Law on Securities ("Obligation to Announce a Takeover Bid and the Procedure for the Information about the takeover Bid") states: "where a person, acting independently or in concert with other persons, acquires shares that in connection with the holding held by him or by other persons acting in concert entitles him to more than 1/3 of votes at the general meeting of shareholders of an offeree company, he must either: (1) transfer securities exceeding this threshold, or (2) announce a mandatory takeover bid to buy up the remaining shares granting the voting rights of the offeree company and the securities confirming the right to acquire securities granting the voting rights".

5. Resolution of the Board of the Bank of Lithuania on Approval of the Rules on the Notifications of Transactions in the Issuer's Securities Concluded By Managers Of Issuers (28 February 2013 No. 03-51) was repealed by the Resolution on the Approval of the Rules on the Disclosure of Information (22 August 2017 No 03-127).

6. The Civil Code applies the term "managing body". This term is described in Article 2.82[2], "Authority and Functions of the Bodies of Legal Persons", which states that a managing body can mean "a collegial managing body" operating in conjunction with the company manager and the general meeting of shareholders", or in certain companies, "a managing body and the general meeting of members may be considered to be the same body of a legal person". The Lithuanian authorities explained that, in practice, the term "managing body" under the Civil Code refers to either the CEO or the board of directors. It does not include the supervisory board (where one exists), as the supervisory board does not undertake management functions.

7. The Law on Markets in Financial Instruments, for example, includes conflicts of interest provisions applicable to financial brokerage firms (Art. 21), the operator of the regulated market (Art. 52), the Central Depository (Art. 68) and the supervisory institution (Art. 72).

8. Regulation (EU) No. 596/2014 of the European Parliament and of the Council of 16 April 2014 on market abuse (market abuse regulation) and repealing Directive

2003/6/EC of the European Parliament and of the Council, and Commission Directives 2003/124/EC, 2003/125/EC and 2004/72/EC came into force on 3 July 2016. Since these regulations are binding, they must be applied in their entirety across the EU. In general, these changes will require increasing sanctions currently available in Lithuanian law.

9. As of mid-2016, 21 out of 28 listed companies were in a group situation, providing consolidated financial statements.

10. While the Ministry of Finance is ultimately responsible for changes to the Business Accounting Standards, the Authority is responsible for undertaking public consultations on possible changes to these standards. The Ministry of Finance has convened a new Business Accounting Standards Committee (replacing the old Accounting Standards Committee), which consists of representatives of state institutions, academia and auditor and/or professional accountant organisations.

11. See online here: https://www.ifac.org/publications-resources/2013-handbook-code-ethics-professional-accountants

12. For statutory SOEs, the narrative annual and quarterly reports are called "activity statements".

13. See the "State Audit Report on the Commercial Activities of State Forests", 31 March, 2010 (in Lithuanian): http://vkc.turtas.lt/static/uploads/-_Misku_ataskaita_8.pdf.

14. Minister of Economy Decree of 20 December 2013 "On the Approval of the Recommendations on Identifying and Providing Information on SOEs' Special Obligations".

15. Specifically, Article 10.1 of the code states: "The company should disclose information on: [...] Members of the company's supervisory and management bodies, chief executive officer of the company and their remuneration". It further states "It is also recommended that information about the amount of remuneration received from the company and other income should be disclosed with regard to members of the company's supervisory and management bodies and chief executive officer".

16. State regulations concerning the remuneration of SOE executives are presented in a Government Resolution "On the Remuneration for Work of Executives, their Deputies and Chief Accountants in State Enterprises and State-Controlled Limited Liability Companies".

17. The Ownership Guidelines require the 24 large SOEs in categories I and II to establish an internal control committee, if they are not otherwise required by the Law on Audit to establish an audit committee. Article 52 of the Law on Audit requires public interest entities to establish an audit committee, responsible notably for monitoring "the effectiveness of the entity's internal control, internal audit where applicable, and risk management systems". Statutory SOEs are required to establish a system of internal control according to the requirements set out in the Law of the Republic of Lithuania on Internal Control and Internal Audit.

18. Prior to the Law on Companies amendments, listed companies were required to disclose information on related party transactions, but without such detailed criteria on the contents.

19. The previously applicable Resolution of the Board of the Bank of Lithuania on the Approval of the Rules on Preparation and Submission of Periodic and Additional Information (No 03-48) was repealed by a 22 August 2017 Resolution of the Board of the Bank of Lithuania on the Approval of Rules on the Disclosure of Information. This was undertaken in implementation of EU Regulation No 596/2014 on Market Abuse.

20. Box 3.2 includes the IAS 24 definition of a related party transaction and a related party. The Lithuanian authorities report that the applicable definition of "materiality" derives from IAS 1 – "Presentation of Financial Statements", which states that "material omissions or statements of items are material if they could, individually or collectively, influence the economic decisions that users make on the basis of the financial statements. Materiality depends on the size and nature of the omission or misstatement judged in the surrounding circumstances. The size or nature of the item, or a combination of both, could be the determining factor". (See online here: http://www.ifrs.org/IFRSs/Pages/IFRS.aspx)

21. While most of this core principle focuses on Guideline II, which recommends the clarification of the state's role as owner, Guidelines I.B and I.D recommend further clarification of how the state expects to carry out its role as owner by defining and disclosing its rationales for enterprise ownership. In doing so, these Guidelines help to establish whether the ownership function of the government is sufficiently developed and active to credibly handle the ownership function separately from regulation.

22. The OECD Secretariat did not attempt to undertake an exhaustive review of any formal mechanisms underpinning the instructions system. Provisions requiring that decisions by the ownership ministry be executed in written form were notably identified in the articles of association of the statutory SOEs Klaipėda State Seaport Authority and Lithuanian Airports, but these are just examples. For statutory SOEs, the instructions system itself is perhaps merely a means of further formalising the authority over corporate decision-making that is already granted to the state by the Law on State and Municipal Enterprises.

23. Indirect financial support for SOEs can include, for example, preferential financing terms, tax arrears or other preferential trade credits from other SOEs. It can also involve SOEs receiving inputs (such as energy, water or land) at prices or conditions more favourable than those available to private competitors.

24. More information on the state guarantee granted to Nordic Investment Bank for its loan to Klaipėda Oil is available online here http://www.lithuaniatribune.com/69958/parliament-guarantees-lng-loan-to-ab-klaipedos-nafta-201469958/.

25. Possible amendments include changes to the Labour Code to increase employee participation in the taking of major company decisions (i.e. company reorganisations, liquidation, etc.); strengthening the information-sharing and consultation function with employee representatives; and strengthening the role of women on company boards.

26. Lithuanian authorities refer to, in particular, Civil Code Art. 2.82 ("Authority and Functions of the Bodies of Legal Persons") and 2.83 ("Contracts Concluded in Overstepping the Authority of Managing Bodies of a Private Legal Person").

27. Specifically, the Lithuanian authorities cited the following provisions from the Law on Companies (the referenced article numbers relate to the version of the Law on

Companies prior to the November 2017 amendments): Art. 16.1.5, Art. 18.1, Art. 19.10, Art. 38.3-4, Art. 53, and Art. 55.5-6.

28. Illegal work is as defined in Article 98 of the Labour Code, including for example work carried out by foreigners or non-EU citizens without complying with regulatory or statutory employment procedures, or without informing the State Social Insurance Fund office.

29. This includes the capital requirements regulation and directive (CRR/CRD IV), updated rules for markets in financial instruments (MiFID 2) and the EU market abuse regulation (MAR).

30. See, for example: European Bank for Reconstruction and Development (EBRD) (2012), *Commercial Laws of Lithuania: An Assessment by the EBRD* (www.ebrd.com/documents/legal-reform/lithuania-country-law-assessment.pdf), and EBRD (2009), *EBRD Insolvency Law Assessment Project – 2009* (http://www.ebrd.com/downloads/legal/insolvency/lithuania_ia.pdf).

31. The Enterprise Bankruptcy Act does not apply to "budgetary institutions, political parties, trade unions and religious communities and associations" (Art. 1.2). The Law on Restructuring of Enterprises does not apply to "budgetary institutions, political parties, trade unions, religious communities and associations, credit institutions, payment institutions, electronic money institutions, insurance and reinsurance companies, management companies, investment companies and intermediaries of public trading in securities" (Art. 1.4).

32. In addition, the company manager, or CEO, is required under the Law on Companies to "be guided by laws and other legal acts, the articles of association of the company, decisions of the general meeting of shareholders, decisions of the supervisory board and the [management] board, and his job description".

33. For more on company directors in Lithuania and their fiduciary duty, see: LSE Enterprise (2013), "Annex to Study on Directors' Duties and Liability in Lithuania", prepared for the European Commission DG Market, p. A 522 (see online here: http://ec.europa.eu/internal_market/company/docs/board/2013-study-reports_en.pdf).

34. LSE Enterprise (2013), "Annex to Study on Directors' Duties and Liability in Lithuania", prepared for the European Commission DG Market, p. A 522 (See online here: http://ec.europa.eu/internal_market/company/docs/board/2013-study-reports_en.pdf).

35. The Code includes a note to Principle III.6 stating: "The Code does not provide for a concrete number of independent members to comprise a collegial body. Many codes in foreign countries fix a concrete number of independent members (e.g. at least 1/3 or 1/2 of the members of the collegial body) to comprise the collegial body. However, having regard to the novelty of the institution of independent members in Lithuania and potential problems in finding and electing a concrete number of independent members, the Code provides for a more flexible wording and allows the companies themselves to decide what number of independent members is sufficient. Of course, a larger number of independent members in a collegial body is encouraged and will constitute an example of more suitable corporate governance".

36. For more information about Lithuanian Energy's supervisory and management board composition, see online here: http://www.le.lt/en/about-us/408#parent-company.

37. The inter-ministerial SOE board selection process was previously outlined in the Ownership Guidelines and has since been revised and transferred to Government Resolution 631 "On the Approval of the Description of the Selection of Candidates to the Board of a State Enterprise [...]", which itself was revised to be made applicable also to fully corporatised SOEs.

References

Baltic Institute of Corporate Governance (2013), *CEOs in Lithuanian State-Owned Enterprises*, Baltic Institute of Corporate Governance, Vilnius, www.bicg.eu/wp-content/uploads/2016/02/CEOs-in-Lithuanian-State-Owned-Enterprises.pdf.

Bank of Lithuania (2010), "Corporate Governance Practices Overview" (in Lithuanian), https://old.lb.lt/bendroviu_valdymo_praktikos_apzvalga.

Nasdaq Baltic (2015), *Review of Corporate Governance Practices in the Baltics in 2015*, Nasdaq, www.nasdaqbaltic.com/files/baltic/CG%20review/Review%20of%20CG%20practices%20in%20the%20Baltics%20in%202015.pdf.

Klaipėdos Nafta (2015), "Financial Statements Prepared in Accordance with International Financial Reporting Standards as Adopted by the European Union, Independent Auditors Report and Annual Report for the Financial Year Ending on 31 December 2014", http://www.nasdaqomxbaltic.com/upload/reports/knf/2014_ar_en_ltl_solo_ias.pdf.

Litgrid (2015), "Consolidated Annual Report of Litgrid AB and its Subsidiaries for 2014", http://www.nasdaqomxbaltic.com/upload/reports/lgd/2014_ar_en_ltl_con_ias.pdf.

Lithuanian Energy (2015), "Annual Report 2014", https://issuu.com/lietuvosenergija/docs/annual_report_2014.

OECD (2017), *Phase 2 Report on Implementing the OECD Anti-Bribery Convention in Lithuania: December 2017*, OECD Working Group on Bribery, OECD, Paris, www.oecd.org/corruption/anti-bribery/Lithuania-Phase-2-Report-ENG.pdf.

OECD (2015), *OECD Review of the Corporate Governance of State-Owned Enterprises: Lithuania,* OECD, Paris, www.oecd.org/corporate/oecd-review-corporate-governance-soe-lithuania.htm.

OECD (2014), *OECD Review of the Corporate Governance of State-Owned Enterprises: Latvia*, OECD, Paris, http://www.oecd.org/daf/ca/oecd-review-corporate-governance-soe-latvia.htm.

State-Owned Enterprises Governance Coordination Centre (2016), *State-Owned Enterprises in Lithuania: Annual Report 2015*, State-Owned Enterprises Governance Coordination Centre, Bank of Property, Vilnius, http://www.vkc.sipa.lt/static/uploads/VKC_2016_EN_A4_WEB.pdf.

World Bank (2007), *Report on the Observance of Standards and Codes (ROSC), Lithuania: Accounting and Auditing,* International Bank for Reconstruction and Development/The World Bank, Washington DC, http://documents.worldbank.org/curated/en/291391468054236962/Lithuania-Report-on-the-Observance-of-Standards-and-Codes-ROSC-accounting-and-auditing.

World Bank (2002), *Report on the Observance of Standards and Codes (ROSC), Lithuania: Accounting and Auditing*, International Bank for Reconstruction and Development/The World Bank, Washington DC, http://documents.worldbank.org/curated/en/468561468270570341/Report-on-the-Observance-of-Standards-And-Codes-ROSC-Lithuania-accounting-and-auditing.

Chapter 4

Conclusions and recommendations for strengthening corporate governance in Lithuania

This chapter presents the conclusions of the assessments made by the OECD Corporate Governance Committee and the OECD Working Party on State Ownership and Privatisation Practices regarding Lithuania's position relative to the G20/OECD Principles of Corporate Governance and the OECD Guidelines on Corporate Governance of State-Owned Enterprises. In this context, it provides an overview of the strengths and weaknesses of Lithuania's corporate governance framework for listed and state-owned enterprises, including the potential impact of recent or prospective reforms. The chapter ends with a set of recommendations to further align Lithuanian policies and practices with OECD corporate governance standards.

This report assesses Lithuania's corporate governance framework for listed companies and state-owned enterprises with respect to the five "core corporate governance principles" set out in *the Roadmap for the Accession of Lithuania to the OECD Convention*,which draws upon the *G20/OECD Principles of Corporate Governance* (*Principles*) and the *OECD Guidelines on Corporate Governance of State-Owned Enterprises* (*SOE Guidelines*). It also recommends measures to further align with the *Principles* and the *SOE Guidelines*.

4.1 Conclusions

This report reaches a positive overall view of Lithuania's corporate governance framework for listed and state-owned enterprises and of Lithuania's ability and willingness to implement OECD corporate governance standards, namely the *Principles* and the *SOE Guidelines*. While some challenges remain, Lithuania has responded to most concerns raised over the course of the review process, via new and/or pending legislation and other reforms. The strengths and weaknesses of Lithuania's corporate governance framework, including the potential impact of recent and pending reforms, can be summarised as follows.

Lithuania's corporate governance landscape

Lithuania, like many other small markets, appears to lack a critical mass of listed and actively traded companies. Its 27 listed companies (as of February 2018) tend to have highly concentrated ownership and quite low liquidity (equity turnover volume for the Nasdaq Vilnius Exchange was just 0.3% of GDP in 2015). Yet, it is worth noting that Lithuania has the most listed companies and highest market capitalisation among Baltic countries. It has an institutional structure in place for capital market oversight, including active market surveillance by an independent regulator, the Bank of Lithuania, and a court system that has ruled in favour of protection of minority shareholder rights in a number of important cases. On the other hand, enforcement cases are relatively rare and tend to be limited to verbal warnings or warning letters, while court cases generally require appeals to Supreme Court level before they are resolved, making it expensive and time-consuming for minority shareholders to seek remedies through private actions. The legal framework generally establishes requirements for corporate governance structures and protections consistent with the recommendations of the *Principles*. However, attempts to influence Lithuanian companies to adopt best practices through the comply-or-explain reporting mechanism of the Nasdaq Vilnius Corporate Governance Code appear to have had limited success, with low compliance rates on some important measures, particularly related to the functioning of boards of directors and their independence. Moreover, the Code is currently out of date following numerous and significant recent legal reforms. Implementation weaknesses have been exacerbated by the fact that the legal framework has also historically allowed for considerable flexibility regarding listed companies' chosen board structure, responsibilities and composition. In practice, these factors lead to significant shortcomings in boards' independent and objective oversight of management decisions, particularly in the case of single-tier management boards. Amendments to the Law on Companies enacted in November 2017 mitigate these fundamental concerns by requiring that the single-tier management boards of listed companies undertake some supervisory responsibilities – including oversight of material related party transactions – and comprise a minimum proportion of independent directors.

Lithuania has substantial state ownership, with SOEs accounting for 3.2% of national employment, well above the OECD average of 2.4%, and in line with the top ten OECD countries with the largest SOE sectors relative to national employment. While the number of SOEs in Lithuania has dropped from 128 in 2015 to 66 as of February 2018, this reduction is largely attributable to mergers and restructurings, while the basic characteristics (value, employment and sectoral distribution) have remained stable during this period. Lithuania has a predominantly decentralised state ownership model, with line ministries simultaneously exercising ownership and regulatory functions in most cases. The Lithuanian authorities have adopted a number of whole-of-government policies to harmonise SOE governance and disclosure standards, which are generally of a high standard. Lithuanian SOEs are not as a rule exempt from the application of laws and regulations applicable to private companies, including those bearing on competition. However, the legal framework for statutory SOEs (applicable to 40% of SOEs by value) results in non-trivial differences in their corporate governance requirements and notably accords the state a number of decision-making powers that are the purview of boards of directors in limited liability SOEs. Examples of differences in the legal framework for statutory SOEs include: (i) the fact that their boards must include civil servants and can include the CEO, which – together with the aforementioned decision-making powers accorded to the state – weakens the oversight capacity of boards; and (ii) the fact that statutory SOEs do not legally own the assets entrusted to them, which could potentially hinder creditors' ability to initiate insolvency procedures against those SOEs and access collateral. The recently adopted requirement that the boards of all SOEs comprise at least half independent members (for which implementation was mandatory in SOE boards by January 2018) along with plans to corporatise most statutory SOEs could go quite some way in addressing concerns regarding limitations to the statutory SOE framework.

Ensuring the enforcement of shareholder rights and equitable treatment

Lithuania has legal requirements in place to ensure enforcement of shareholder rights and equitable treatment with respect to most of the relevant recommendations of the *Principles.* Beyond the legal framework, it is notable that the Supreme Court has repeatedly ruled in favour of minority shareholder rights, including in five court cases involving enforcement of takeover provisions that have generally reinforced minority shareholders' claims to receive mandatory offers for their shares. Lithuania has also recently strengthened its framework and sanctioning authority for enforcement against insider trading and market abuse cases, and issued significant fines related to one recent insider trading case. Over the course of Lithuania's corporate governance accession review process, some departures from the *Principles'* standards in areas related to minority shareholders' rights and equitable treatment were identified. The Lithuanian authorities have since enacted legislative reforms or established rules that appear to largely address the related shortcomings. The recent reforms notably: (i) eliminated a Law on Companies provision granting controlling shareholders' explicit right to access company documents upon request, subject to signing a confidentiality pledge; (ii) established the requirement, through November 2017 amendments to the Law on Financial Statements of Entities, for all limited liability companies to disclose the contents of shareholders agreements (and not just their existence) in annual reports, making it easier for all shareholders to understand the corporate control landscape; and (iii) introduced amendments to the Law on Companies requiring board and audit committee review of material related party transactions, complemented by new Bank of Lithuania rules on audit committee independence.

Concerning the minority shareholders of SOEs, while many of the same concerns apply as for non-state-owned companies, they can be exacerbated in SOEs. This applies, for example, to concerns about shareholders' equitable access to information, which can in practice be hindered by the fact that most listed SOEs have a very small free float (less than 5%), leading to low involvement of minority shareholders in corporate decisions, including appointment of board members. The requirement to increase the number of independent directors on SOE boards should help address this concern, since independent members may in practice be more likely to consistently act in the interests of all shareholders, including minority shareholders (although legally all board members are required to do so).

Timely and reliable disclosure in accordance with international standards

Lithuania has a robust legal framework for disclosure of extensive company information, including for annual reports, annual audited financial statements, quarterly financial reports, as well as an annual report on corporate governance practices in compliance with the Nasdaq Vilnius Corporate Governance Code. Beyond legally required disclosure, reports on compliance with the voluntary recommendations of the Corporate Governance Code indicate weaker disclosure practices in relation to the composition and practices of the board and executive remuneration policies. However, amendments to the Law on Financial Statements of Entities enacted in November 2017 require that all companies include information on board remuneration in their annual reports.

Concerning accounting practices, until a recent amendment to the Law on Accounting, Lithuanian companies were required to follow IFRS and International Accounting Standards, and all listed companies were reported to have implemented IFRS. However, starting 1 January 2016, Lithuanian listed companies may also choose to follow local Lithuanian Business Accounting Standards, which is permitted under EU regulations as long as local standards are consistent with IFRS and EU acquis. This only applies to separate financial statements, whereas consolidated financial statements still must be prepared in accordance with IAS/IFRS. The Lithuanian authorities report that local accounting standards are closely aligned with international standards, and that they are moving to harmonise the most significant remaining differences. In practice, all currently listed companies disclose according to IFRS, but the option to use national accounting standards could impact future listings.

While Lithuanian companies were previously required to follow IFRS IAS 24 standards for the disclosure of related party transactions, and all companies in practice reported information on RPTs, there has not been active enforcement to ensure that all companies provide sufficient descriptions of the conditions and facts necessary to assess whether the transactions were conducted on market terms at arms' length. With the enactment of new Law on Companies amendments on related party transactions, the Bank of Lithuania has asserted that it will review company annual reports to ensure that they are fully complying with RPT-related disclosure requirements. Finally, the Law on Audit was amended in December 2016, with its new provisions entering into force on 1 March 2017. The amendments establish more stringent requirements for independence, objectivity and professional ethics of auditors and audit firms. These amendments to the Law on Audit were complemented with a January 2017 Resolution of the Bank of Lithuania establishing requirements for the composition and functions of audit committees of listed companies, notably establishing independence criteria for audit committee members and strengthening the audit committee's role in selecting auditors and audit firms.

The state has developed high standards of disclosure specifically for SOEs (the Transparency Guidelines) which are mandatory for large SOEs and optional (comply-or-explain) for the remainder. SOEs generally comply with reporting requirements on financial and operating results, but this review has identified some issues regarding the accounting and auditing practices of SOEs, in particular concerning (i) the valuation of state assets entrusted to statutory SOEs; (ii) the non-trivial number of SOEs that received conditional opinions from external auditors; and (iii) the ability of small audit firms, which reportedly audit the accounts of some of Lithuania's largest SOEs, to credibly and reliably do so. While making the disclosure standards mandatory for large SOEs is in line with the Working Party's recommendations, it could nonetheless be useful for the Lithuanian authorities to clarify and disclose the rationale for selecting the 13 enterprises for mandatory compliance. As of January 2018, eight SOEs were reported to be implementing IFRS. According to the Lithuanian authorities, following the mergers in the state-owned road maintenance and forestry sectors, these enterprises now meet the size threshold that triggers mandatory compliance with the disclosure standards. Concerning disclosure at the level of the state, Lithuania produces an annual aggregate report on SOEs which reports extensively on the governance and performance of SOEs, including estimates for the costs and funding arrangements of SOEs' public policy obligations. The content, scope and frequency of aggregate reporting are of a high standard.

Effective separation of the government's role as owner and its regulatory role

While the government has taken steps to strengthen its ownership co-ordination function, the lack of a clear separation of ownership and regulatory roles still constitutes a vulnerability in the Lithuanian framework. In many cases, ministries responsible for sectoral policy or regulation also exercise ownership over SOEs that operate in the relevant markets. Lithuania has nonetheless made significant progress in professionalising the exercise of state ownership, including through the development of a whole-of-government ownership policy and the creation of an agency – the Governance Coordination Centre – tasked notably with monitoring its implementation. However, the GCC has historically not had the institutional power or the resources to enforce the state ownership policy (and other state policies or decisions bearing on SOEs) when ownership ministries or SOEs do not comply. Similarly, no whole-of-government remedial measures are foreseen in cases of non-compliance. Its recent transfer from an SOE to a public institution under the Ministry of Economy has the potential to strengthen its institutional independence. The approximate doubling of its budget for 2018-19 could increase its capacity to positively influence practices by line ministries and SOEs. In this respect, it should be noted that the GCC plays a non-trivial role in harmonising state ownership practices across the SOE sector, for example through its participation in the inter-ministerial committee on SOE board nomination and its role in advising on SOEs' yearly operational strategies and on the content of line ministries' shareholder expectation letters.

Lithuania goes some way towards disclosing the rationales for state ownership through a classification of SOEs according to objectives (in brief, primarily profit-seeking, primarily public policy-oriented, or mixed objectives). However, for enterprises that undertake primarily profit-seeking activities, the rationale for continued state ownership should be more defined and disclosed.

Lithuania has made progress in improving SOEs' operational autonomy, including through the introduction of a greater number of independent members on SOE boards. The March 2017 resolution barring acting politicians from serving on SOE boards and requiring at least one half independent directors– for which compliance by SOE boards was required by January 2018 – constitutes a significant step forward in this regard. SOEs' operational autonomy has historically been limited by the predominance of ministerial representatives – in some cases vice-ministers – on boards, as well as the apparent use of "instructions" from ministries. (The Lithuanian authorities have clarified that a provision in the Law on Civil Service requiring that civil servants obtain an approval from their minister to serve on SOE boards does not constitute an "instructions" system, since the approval does not contain any directions concerning how to vote at board meetings. Nevertheless, the provision was in the process of being amended at the time of writing. Its removal would constitute an improvement, since it contributes to the perception that civil servants are expected to act only on behalf of their state employers.)

Concerning SOEs' legal and corporate forms, Lithuania maintains a sizeable portfolio of "state enterprises", for which the applicable law accords the state certain decision-making rights that would normally be the purview of a board of directors (e.g. the right to hire and fire the CEO) and entrusts asset ownership to the state rather than to the enterprise, underscoring corporate governance weaknesses associated with this legal form. The state has developed a "State Enterprise Reorganisation Plan" which proposes the conversion of 11 commercially-oriented statutory SOEs into limited liability companies by the end of 2019, building on a review undertaken by a Ministry of Economy working group. Consolidation of the multiple forestry and road maintenance enterprises into single SOEs has been completed and efforts are under way or planned to implement internal restructurings with a view to improving corporate efficiency, while ensuring that the new, larger SOEs respect high standards of governance and transparency.

Ensuring a level playing field

Lithuanian SOEs are not formally exempt from the application of general laws, tax codes and regulations. However, in practice differences in the operational conditions between SOEs and private enterprises can create distortions in the competitive landscape. These include: public policy obligations, for which funding is not always calibrated to the cost of their fulfilment; rate-of-return requirements that are not market consistent; and (in at least one documented case) preferential loans between SOEs. The fact that public procurement rules are not applicable to SOE subsidiaries, while in line with EU rules on in-house procurement, can in practice result in irregular procurement practices. Other elements affecting the level playing field are specific to statutory SOEs, which are notably subject to tax obligations (or their functional equivalent) that exceed those placed on private competitors. State enterprises also do not legally own the state assets entrusted to them, which could limit the ability of lenders to access collateral in case of non-payment. The proposed conversion of 11 statutory SOEs to limited liability companies, mentioned above, has the potential to lead to significant improvements in this regard. However, amendments to the Law on Companies and the Law on State and Municipal Enterprises enacted in April 2017 that introduce maximum term limits and reappointment criteria specifically for the CEOs of SOEs are of some concern. These provisions limit the flexibility available to SOE boards to re-appoint CEOs who are performing well but have reached the now legally imposed two-term limit or may have failed to achieve certain objectives due to extenuating circumstances.

Recognising stakeholder rights and the duties, rights and responsibilities of boards

A number of legal protections are in place to facilitate resolution of disputes between employers and employees, to ensure protection of consumers, and to provide protections for whistle-blowers. A new Law on the Protection of Whistle-blowers was enacted in November 2017 and provides for the protection of both public and private sector whistle-blowers. SOEs are in principle not exempt from the application of these broader laws bearing on respect for stakeholder rights. The authorities have not established any SOE-specific requirements concerning stakeholder rights, but SOEs are explicitly required by the Ownership Guidelines to report on material issues affecting employees and stakeholders. The 2015 SOE review found that the majority of SOEs do report on stakeholder relations, with most related disclosure focusing on employees and the largest SOEs also reporting on broader stakeholder issues (OECD, 2015). The Lithuanian government has devoted considerable attention to reforming its insolvency framework, with several recent amendments made to the Enterprise Bankruptcy Act and the Law on Restructuring of Enterprises. Amendments to both laws submitted to the Parliament in December 2015 were returned to the initiators for improvement in May 2016. A unified law governing both bankruptcy and enterprise restructuring (which would replace the two aforementioned laws) is reportedly planned for submission to the Parliament in 2018.

Amendments to the Law on Companies enacted in November 2017 introduce some important new requirements concerning the responsibilities and composition of listed companies' boards of directors. While Lithuanian companies are still accorded great flexibility to establish either two-tier boards or different forms of single-tier boards, once the amendments enter into force in July 2018, it will no longer be possible for listed companies to be overseen by single-tier management boards with no supervisory authority and no outside directors. All single-tier management boards will be required to undertake some supervisory functions and to comprise a minimum proportion of independent directors. Traditionally, most Lithuanian companies, including most SOEs, have elected to use the single-tier executive board model, which has left the AGM in charge of supervision while delegating most responsibilities to management via the management board. This has constituted a significant departure from international good practice. For SOEs, the newly established requirement that boards comprise at least half independent directors, once fully implemented, has the potential to strengthen independent scrutiny over the management and operations of these enterprises. For (other) listed companies that are currently overseen by an executive management board, the new requirement concerning independent directors could strengthen the incentive of boards to serve the interests of all shareholders. The fact that the audit committees of listed companies, must (as of 1 March 2017) comprise at least one half independent directors, may offer some further protections in this regard. Moreover, the November 2017 Law on Companies amendments grant audit committees a strengthened role in listed company oversight, by requiring CEOs to request an audit committee assessment of, *inter alia*, whether a related party transaction is entered into under market conditions. The Lithuanian authorities appear to have addressed concerns highlighted during the corporate governance accession review process (based on draft legislation that was previously under discussion in Parliament), regarding the criteria for determining which transactions should undergo review.

Concerning SOE boards of directors, they are not systematically required to establish internal controls, ethics and compliance measures, including those dedicated to combatting fraud and corruption. However, most large SOEs are required by applicable legislation to establish either an audit committee or an internal control system. The composition of SOE boards (and notably the predominance of government representatives, discussed above) can limit their ability to exercise independent and objective judgment in the interest of the enterprise, particularly evident in cases where written instructions have been given. Furthermore, in practice under the current legal framework, SOE boards often remain extensions of their ownership ministries. This issue is particularly exacerbated in statutory SOEs, whose boards are accorded weak powers compared to the state, effectively limiting their independence. However, there has certainly been progress in this respect, with the aforementioned resolution increasing the requirement for independent members on SOE boards from one-third to one-half and barring politicians from serving on SOE boards. SOEs were required to comply with these new requirements by January 2018. If fully implemented, these new requirements would constitute a significant step forward in (i) protecting SOE boards from political interference; and (ii) strengthening their ability to exercise independent judgement, based on clear objectives communicated by the state. In addition, government plans to corporatise 11 additional statutory SOEs within the next two years, if implemented, would also go a long way towards alleviating these concerns.

4.2 Recommendations

The Corporate Governance Committee and the Working Party on State Ownership and Privatisation Practices note that Lithuania has made considerable progress in its implementation of the *Principles* and the *SOE Guidelines*. Nevertheless, they have identified areas where further improvements are recommended following accession to the Organisation.

To address remaining challenges in the implementation of the *G20/OECD Corporate Governance Principles*, the Corporate Governance Committee addresses the following **priority recommendation** to Lithuania:

- **Monitor implementation of reforms to the Law on Companies with a view towards clarifying and further strengthening the responsibilities of companies' boards of directors.** Lithuania's Law on Companies and related laws have gone through several waves of recent reforms, making it important to work with market participants to ensure a common understanding of their implementation, and to identify areas where further clarification may be needed to ensure effective implementation in practice. In the medium term, there remains scope for further clarification and strengthening of board responsibilities within the Law on Companies with reference to relevant provisions of the *G20/OECD Principles of Corporate Governance* not only for listed companies, but also for non-listed and corporatised state-owned enterprises.

The Corporate Governance Committee addresses the following **additional recommendations** to Lithuania:

- **Updating the Nasdaq Vilnius Corporate Governance Code.** Update the Nasdaq Vilnius Corporate Governance Code to ensure consistency and complementarity between its voluntary recommendations and recent legislative reforms.

- **Reforming the insolvency framework.** Move forward with reforms to establish an effective and efficient insolvency framework that enforces creditors' rights.

To address remaining challenges related to the corporate governance of state-owned enterprises and further align national practices with the *OECD Guidelines on Corporate Governance of State-Owned Enterprises*, the Working Party on State Ownership and Privatisation Practices addresses the following **priority recommendations** to Lithuania:

- **Strengthening the ownership function.** Improve the GCC's capacity to effectively monitor compliance with – and support enforcement of – the state's SOE governance and disclosure standards. Its advisory role should also be strengthened, including through requirements for more systematic input to shareholding ministries' ownership decisions and actions, such as the preparation of shareholder letters of expectations. Move forward with appointing a permanent head of the institution and hiring additional staff so that the GCC can effectively fulfill its functions.

- **Increasing the operational independence of SOE boards of directors.** Ensure that the state's requirements on SOE board composition are fully and consistently implemented. To address remaining concerns regarding SOEs' limited autonomy from ownership ministries, priority should be given to (i) abolishing the use of voting instructions from ministries to public officials; (ii) further improving the board selection process to enhance efficiency while maintaining requirements for transparency and to ensure that board members meet criteria based on experience and qualifications; and (iii) proceeding with the corporatisation of statutory SOEs engaged in economic activities, recommended below.

- **Streamlining SOEs' legal and corporate forms.** Move forward with plans to convert statutory SOEs engaged in economic activities to limited liability companies. As plans for corporatisation and other consolidation of statutory SOEs advance, the Lithuanian authorities are encouraged to consider corporatising any remaining statutory SOEs that undertake economic activities.

- **Ensuring that SOEs are subject to high quality accounting and auditing standards.** Ensure timely compliance with the state's disclosure standards by the SOEs for which they have become mandatory. This includes completing the transition to IFRS in financial statements for 2019 (published in 2020). The authorities should clarify and disclose the rationale for determining for which SOEs the disclosure standards are mandatory.

- **Enacting amendments to the Law on Companies**. Remove the provision in the Law on Companies stipulating maximum term limits and reappointment criteria for the CEOs of SOEs. In the medium term, as the Lithuanian authorities consider other ways to clarify and strengthen the role and responsibilities of boards of directors within the Law on Companies, they are also encouraged to consider the scope for applying such changes to non-listed SOE boards.

The Working Party on State Ownership and Privatisation Practices addresses the following **additional recommendation** to Lithuania:

- **Rationalisation of sectors with multiple SOEs**. Ensure that the newly consolidated state-owned forestry and road maintenance enterprises are organised with a view to maximising corporate efficiency, ensuring sufficient oversight and subjecting the concerned SOEs to high standards of governance and disclosure.

References

OECD (2015), *OECD Review of the Corporate Governance of State-Owned Enterprises: Lithuania,* OECD, Paris, www.oecd.org/corporate/oecd-review-corporate-governance-soe-lithuania.htm.

Annex 1

List of Lithuanian state-owned enterprises according to objectives (end 2015)

Size class (I-V) Transparency Guidelines mandatory (♦)	Group	Name (Lithuanian)	Name (English)	State ownership entity	Board structure	Legal form
I♦	1B	UAB EPSO-G	EPSO-G	Ministry of Energy	Two-tier	Private LLC
Subsidiaries of EPSO-G	-	AB Amber Grid	Amber Grid	Ministry of Energy	One-tier management	Public LLC, listed
	-	AB Litgrid	Litgrid	Ministry of Energy	Two-tier	Public LLC, listed
I♦	1B	AB Klaipėdos Nafta	Klaipėda Oil	Ministry of Energy	Two-tier	Public LLC, listed
I	2	VĮ Lietuvos Naftos Produktų Agentūra	Lithuanian Oil Products Agency	Ministry of Energy	One-tier management	SE
I♦	1B	UAB Lietuvos Energija	Lithuanian Energy	Ministry of Finance	Two-tier	Private LLC
Subsidiaries of Lietuvos Energijia	-	AB Lietuvos Energijos Gamyba	Lithuanian Energy Production	Ministry of Finance	Two-tier	Public LLC, listed
	-	AB LESTO	Lithuanian Electricity Distribution Network Operator	Ministry of Finance	Two-tier	Public LLC, listed
	-	AB Lietuvos Dujos	Lithuanian Gas	Ministry of Finance	Two-tier	Public LLC, listed
I♦	1B	AB Lietuvos Geležinkeliai	Lithuanian Railways	Ministry of Transport and Communications	One-tier management board	Public LLC
I♦	1B	AB Lietuvos Paštas	Lithuanian Post	Ministry of Transport and Communications	One-tier management board	Public LLC

Size class (I-V) Transparency Guidelines mandatory (♦)	Group	Name (Lithuanian)	Name (English)	State ownership entity	Board structure	Legal form
I ♦	1B	VĮ Klaipėdos Valstybinio Jūrų Uosto Direkcija	Klaipėda State Seaport Authority	Ministry of Transport and Communications	One-tier management board	SE
I ♦	1B	VĮ Lietuvos Oro Uostai	Lithuanian Airports	Ministry of Transport and Communications	One-tier management board	SE
II	1A	VĮ Visagino Energija	Visaginas Energy	Ministry of Economy	One-tier management board	SE
II	2	VĮ Regitra	Regitra	Ministry of Interior	One-tier management board	SE
II ♦	2	VĮ Registrų Centras	Centre of Registers	Ministry of Justice	One-tier management board	SE
II ♦	1B	AB Lietuvos Radijo ir Televizijos Centras	Lithuanian Radio and Television Centre	Ministry of Transport and Communications	One-tier management board	Public LLC
II ♦	2	VĮ Oro navigacija	Air Navigation	Ministry of Transport and Communications	One-tier management board	SE

Note: The new Road Maintenance SOE, created through a consolidation of the 11 below enterprises in November 2017, is considered "large" and thus subject to the state's mandatory disclosure standards and is also planned for conversion to a limited liability company in the State Enterprise Reorganisation Plan.

II	2	VĮ Automagistralė	Expressway	Ministry of Transport and Communications/Lithuanian Road Administration	One-tier management board	SE
II	2	VĮ Alytaus Regiono Keliai	Alytus Regional Roads	Ministry of Transport and Communications/Lithuanian Road Administration	One-tier management board	SE
II	2	VĮ Kauno Regiono Keliai	Kaunas Regional Roads	Ministry of Transport and Communications/Lithuanian Road Administration	One-tier management board	SE
II	2	VĮ Klaipėdos Regiono Keliai	Klaipėda Regional Roads	Ministry of Transport and Communications/Lithuanian Road Administration	One-tier management board	SE

Size class (I-V) Transparency Guidelines mandatory (♦)	Group	Name (Lithuanian)	Name (English)	State ownership entity	Board structure	Legal form
II	2	VĮ Marijampolės Regiono Keliai	Marijampolė Regional Roads	Ministry of Transport and Communications/Lithuanian Road Administration	One-tier management board	SE
II	2	VĮ Panevėžio Regiono Keliai	Panevėžys Regional Roads	Ministry of Transport and Communications/Lithuanian Road Administration	One-tier management board	SE
II	2	VĮ Šiaulių Regiono Keliai	Šiauliai Regional Roads	Ministry of Transport and Communications/Lithuanian Road Administration	One-tier management board	SE
II	2	VĮ Tauragės Regiono Keliai	Tauragė Regional Roads	Ministry of Transport and Communications/Lithuanian Road Administration	One-tier management board	SE
II	2	VĮ Telšių Regiono Keliai	Telšiai Regional Roads	Ministry of Transport and Communications/Lithuanian Road Administration	One-tier management board	SE
II	2	VĮ Utenos Regiono Keliai	Utena Regional Roads	Ministry of Transport and Communications/Lithuanian Road Administration	One-tier management board	SE
II	2	VĮ Vilniaus Regiono Keliai	Vilnius Regional Roads	Ministry of Transport and Communications/Lithuanian Road Administration	One-tier management board	SE
III	2	UAB Žemės Ūkio Paskolų Garantijų Fondas	Agricultural Loan Guarantees Fund	Ministry of Agriculture	Two-tier	Private LLC
III	1A	AB Giraitės Ginkluotės Gamykla	Giraitė Armament Factory	Bank of Property	One-tier management board	Public LLC
III ♦	2	VĮ Ignalinos Atominė Elektrinė	Ignalina Nuclear Power Plant	Ministry of Energy	One-tier management board	SE

Size class (I-V) Transparency Guidelines mandatory (♦)	Group	Name (Lithuanian)	Name (English)	State ownership entity	Board structure	Legal form
III	1B	VĮ Panevėžio Miškų Urėdija	Panevėžys Forest Enterprise	Ministry of Environment/Directorate General of State Forests	No board	SE
III	1B	UAB Būsto Paskolų Draudimas	Housing Loan Insurance	Ministry of Finance	One-tier management board	Private LLC
III	2	VĮ Indėlių ir Investicijų Draudimas	Deposit and Investment Insurance	Ministry of Finance	One-tier management board	SE
III	2	VĮ Turto Bankas	Bank of Property	Ministry of Finance	One-tier management board	SE
III	1B	VĮ Infostruktūra	Infostructure	Ministry of Interior	One-tier management board	SE
IV	1B	UAB Lietuvos Monetų Kalykla	Lithuanian Mint	Bank of Lithuania	One-tier management board	Private LLC
IV	1B	AB Jonavos Grūdai	Jonava Grains	Ministry of Agriculture	One-tier management board	Public LLC
IV	2	VĮ Pieno Tyrimai	Dairy Research	Ministry of Agriculture	No board	SE
IV	2	VĮ Valstybės Žemės Fondas	State Land Fund	Ministry of Agriculture	No board	SE
IV	2	VĮ Lietuvos Paminklai	Lithuania Sights	Ministry of Culture/Department of Cultural Heritage	One-tier management board	SE
IV	1A	UAB Toksika	Toksika	Ministry of Economy	One-tier management board	Private LLC
IV	1A	UAB Lietuvos Parodų ir Kongresų Centras LITEXPO	Lithuanian Exhibition and Congress Centre LITEXPO	Ministry of Economy	One-tier management board	Private LLC
IV	2	UAB Investicijų ir Verslo Garantijos	Investment and Business Guarantees	Ministry of Economy	Two-tier	Private LLC
Note: The new State Forest Enterprise, which was legally created in January 2018 through mergers of 42 individual forest enterprises (including those listed directly below) and the State Forest Management Institute, is considered "large" and thus subject to the state's mandatory disclosure standards. It is not planned for conversion to a limited liability company in the State Enterprise Reorganisation Plan.						
IV	1B	VĮ Biržų Miškų Urėdija	Biržai Forest Enterprise	Ministry of Environment/Directorate General of State Forests	No board	SE

Size class (I-V) Transparency Guidelines mandatory (♦)	Group	Name (Lithuanian)	Name (English)	State ownership entity	Board structure	Legal form
IV	1B	VĮ Jurbarko Miškų Urėdija	Jurbarkas Forest Enterprise	Ministry of Environment/Directorate General of State Forests	No board	SE
IV	1B	VĮ Kaišiadorių Miškų Urėdija	Kaišiadorys Forest Enterprise	Ministry of Environment/Directorate General of State Forests	No board	SE
IV	1B	VĮ Kazlų rūdos mokomoji Miškų Urėdija	Kazlų Rūda Training Forest Enterprise	Ministry of Environment/Directorate General of State Forests	No board	SE
IV	1B	VĮ Kėdainių Miškų Urėdija	Kėdainiai Forest Enterprise	Ministry of Environment/Directorate General of State Forests	No board	SE
IV	1B	VĮ Kretingos Miškų Urėdija	Kretinga Forest Enterprise	Ministry of Environment/Directorate General of State Forests	No board	SE
IV	1B	VĮ Kuršėnų Miškų Urėdija	Kuršėnai Forest Enterprise	Ministry of Environment/Directorate General of State Forests	No board	SE
IV	1B	VĮ Mažeikių Miškų Urėdija	Mažeikiai Forest Enterprise	Ministry of Environment/Directorate General of State Forests	No board	SE
IV	1B	VĮ Nemenčinės Miškų Urėdija	Nemenčinė Forest Enterprise	Ministry of Environment/Directorate General of State Forests	No board	SE
IV	1B	VĮ Prienų Miškų Urėdija	Prienai Forest Enterprise	Ministry of Environment/Directorate General of State Forests	No board	SE
IV	1B	VĮ Radviliškio Miškų Urėdija	Radviliškis Forest Enterprise	Ministry of Environment/Directorate General of State Forests	No board	SE
IV	1B	VĮ Raseinių Miškų Urėdija	Raseiniai Forest Enterprise	Ministry of Environment/Directorate General of State Forests	No board	SE

Size class (I-V) Transparency Guidelines mandatory (♦)	Group	Name (Lithuanian)	Name (English)	State ownership entity	Board structure	Legal form
IV	1B	VĮ Rietavo Miškų Urėdija	Rietavas Forest Enterprise	Ministry of Environment/Directorate General of State Forests	No board	SE
IV	1B	VĮ Šakių Miškų Urėdija	Šakiai Forest Enterprise	Ministry of Environment/Directorate General of State Forests	No board	SE
IV	1B	VĮ Šalčininkų Miškų Urėdija	Šalčininkai Forest Enterprise	Ministry of Environment/Directorate General of State Forests	No board	SE
IV	1B	VĮ Šiaulių Miškų Urėdija	Šiauliai Forest Enterprise	Ministry of Environment/Directorate General of State Forests	No board	SE
IV	1B	VĮ Šilutės Miškų Urėdija	Šilutė Forest Enterprise	Ministry of Environment/Directorate General of State Forests	No board	SE
IV	1B	VĮ Švenčionėlių Miškų Urėdija	Švenčionėliai Forest Enterprise	Ministry of Environment/Directorate General of State Forests	No board	SE
IV	1B	VĮ Tauragės Miškų Urėdija	Tauragė Forest Enterprise	Ministry of Environment/Directorate General of State Forests	No board	SE
IV	1B	VĮ Telšių Miškų Urėdija	Telšiai Forest Enterprise	Ministry of Environment/Directorate General of State Forests	No board	SE
IV	1B	VĮ Trakų Miškų Urėdija	Trakai Forest Enterprise	Ministry of Environment/Directorate General of State Forests	No board	SE
IV	1B	VĮ Ukmergės Miškų Urėdija	Ukmergė Forest Enterprise	Ministry of Environment/Directorate General of State Forests	No board	SE
IV	1B	VĮ Valkininkų Miškų Urėdija	Valkininkai Forest Enterprise	Ministry of Environment/Directorate General of State Forests	No board	SE

Size class (I-V) Transparency Guidelines mandatory (♦)	Group	Name (Lithuanian)	Name (English)	State ownership entity	Board structure	Legal form
IV	1B	VĮ Vilniaus Miškų Urėdija	Vilnius Forest Enterprise	Ministry of Environment/Directorate General of State Forests	No board	SE
IV	-	UAB Viešųjų Investicijų Plėtros Agentūra	Public Investment Development Agency	Ministry of Finance	Two-tier	Private LLC
IV	1A	AB Problematika	Problematika	Ministry of Transport and Communications	One-tier management board	Public LLC
IV	1B	AB Smiltynės Perkėla	Smiltynė Ferry Terminal	Ministry of Transport and Communications	One-tier management board	Public LLC
IV	2	VĮ Vidaus Vandens Kelių Direkcija	Inland Waterways Authority	Ministry of Transport and Communications	One-tier management board	SE
IV	1A	UAB Geoterma	Geoterma	Bank of Property	One-tier management board	Private LLC
V	1A	UAB Respublikinė Mokomoji Sportinė Bazė	Republican Instructional Sports Base	Government of the Republic of Lithuania/Department of Physical Education and Sports	One-tier management board	Private LLC
V	2	UAB Sportininkų Testavimo ir Reabilitacijos Centras	Athletes Testing and Rehabilitation Centre	Bank of Property	One-tier management board	Private LLC
V	-	UAB Mokslas ir Technika	Science and Technique	Lithuanian Academy of Sciences	No board	Private LLC
V	1A	UAB Panevėžio Veislininkystė	Panevėžys Breeding	Ministry of Agriculture	One-tier management board	Private LLC
V	1A	UAB Šilutės Polderiai	Šilutė Polders	Ministry of Agriculture	One-tier management board	Private LLC
V	1A	UAB Valstybinė Projektų ir Sąmatų Ekspertizė	The State Expertise of Projects and Estimates	Ministry of Agriculture	No board	Private LLC
V	1A	UAB Aerogeodezijos Institutas	Aerogeodesy Institute	Ministry of Agriculture	One-tier management board	Private LLC

Size class (I-V) Transparency Guidelines mandatory (♦)	Group	Name (Lithuanian)	Name (English)	State ownership entity	Board structure	Legal form
V	1A	UAB Dotnuvos Eksperimentinis Ūkis	Dotnuva Experimental Farm	Ministry of Agriculture	One-tier management board	Private LLC
V	1A	UAB Upytės Eksperimentinis Ūkis	Upytė Experimental Farm	Ministry of Agriculture	One-tier management board	Private LLC
V	2	UAB Gyvulių Produktyvumo Kontrolė	Animal Productivity Control	Ministry of Agriculture	One-tier management board	Private LLC
V	2	UAB Lietuvos Žirgynas	Lithuanian Horse Stable	Ministry of Agriculture	One-tier management board	Private LLC
V	2	UAB Šeduvos Avininkystė	Šeduva Sheep Breeding	Ministry of Agriculture	One-tier management board	Private LLC
V	2	UAB Šilutės Veislininkystė	Šilutė Breeding	Ministry of Agriculture	One-tier management board	Private LLC
V	2	UAB Klaipėdos Žuvininkystės Produktų Aukcionas	Klaipėda Fisheries Product Auction	Ministry of Agriculture	One-tier management board	Private LLC
V	2	AB Lietuvos Veislininkystė	Lithuanian Breeding	Ministry of Agriculture	One-tier management board	Public LLC
-	2	AB Kiaulių Veislininkystė	Swine Breeding	Ministry of Agriculture	One-tier management board	Public LLC
V	2	VĮ Lietuvos Žemės Ūkio ir Maisto Produktų Rinkos Reguliavimo Agentūra	Lithuanian Agricultural and Food Market Regulation Agency	Ministry of Agriculture	No board	SE
V	2	VĮ Žemės Ūkio Informacijos ir Kaimo Verslo Centras	Agricultural Information and Rural Business Centre	Ministry of Agriculture	No board	SE
V	2	VĮ Distancinių Tyrimų ir Geoinformatikos Centras Gis-Centras	Remote Sensing and Geoinformatics Centre Gis-Centras	Ministry of Agriculture/National Land Service	One-tier management board	SE
V	2	UAB Lietuvos Kinas	Lithuanian Cinema	Ministry of Culture	No board	Private LLC
V	1A	UAB Poilsio Namai Baltija	Vacation Home Baltija	Bank of Property	One-tier management board	Private LLC

Size class (I-V) Transparency Guidelines mandatory (♦)	Group	Name (Lithuanian)	Name (English)	State ownership entity	Board structure	Legal form
V	1B	AB Klaipėdos Metrologijos Centras	Klaipėda Metrology Centre	Ministry of Economy	No board	Public LLC
V	1B	AB Šiaulių Metrologijos Centras	Šiauliai Metrology Center	Ministry of Economy	No board	Public LLC
V	1B	AB Vilniaus Metrologijos Centras	Vilnius Metrology Centre	Ministry of Economy	One-tier management board	Public LLC
V	1B	AB Kauno Metrologijos Centras	Kaunas Metrology Centre	Ministry of Economy	No board	Public LLC
V	1B	AB Panevėžio Metrologijos Centras	Panevėžys Metrology Centre	Ministry of Economy	No board	Public LLC
V	2	UAB Kauno Petrašiūnų Darbo Rinkos Mokymo Centras	Kaunas Petrašiūnai Job Market Training Centre	Ministry of Education and Science	No board	Private LLC
V	1A	AB Mintis	Mintis (Publishing House)	Bank of Property	One-tier management board	Public LLC
V	2	VĮ Energetikos Agentūra	Energy Agency	Ministry of Energy	No board	SE
V	2	VĮ Radioaktyviųjų Atliekų Tvarkymo Agentūra	Radioactive Waste Management Agency	Ministry of Energy	No board	SE
V	1A	UAB Projektų Ekspertizė	Project Expertise	Ministry of Environment	No board	Private LLC
V	1A	VĮ Valstybinis Miškotvarkos Institutas	State Forest Management Institute	Ministry of Environment	No board	SE
V	1B	VĮ Statybos Produkcijos Sertifikavimo Centras	Building Production Certification Centre	Ministry of Environment	No board	SE
V	1B	VĮ Alytaus Miškų Urėdija	Alytus Forest Enterprise	Ministry of Environment/Directorate General of State Forests	No board	SE

Size class (I-V) Transparency Guidelines mandatory (♦)	Group	Name (Lithuanian)	Name (English)	State ownership entity	Board structure	Legal form
V	1B	VĮ Anykščių Miškų Urėdija	Anykščiai Forest Enterprise	Ministry of Environment/Directorate General of State Forests	No board	SE
V	1B	VĮ Druskininkų Miškų Urėdija	Druskininkai Forest Enterprise	Ministry of Environment/Directorate General of State Forests	No board	SE
V	1B	VĮ Dubravos eksperimentinė mokomoji Miškų Urėdija	Dubrava Experimental Training Forest Enterprise	Ministry of Environment/Directorate General of State Forests	No board	SE
V	1B	VĮ Ignalinos Miškų Urėdija	Ignalina Forest Enterprise	Ministry of Environment/Directorate General of State Forests	No board	SE
V	1B	VĮ Jonavos Miškų Urėdija	Jonava Forest Enterprise	Ministry of Environment/Directorate General of State Forests	No board	SE
V	1B	VĮ Joniškio Miškų Urėdija	Joniškis Forest Enterprise	Ministry of Environment/Directorate General of State Forests	No board	SE
V	1B	VĮ Kauno Miškų Urėdija	Kaunas Forest Enterprise	Ministry of Environment/Directorate General of State Forests	No board	SE
V	1B	VĮ Kupiškio Miškų Urėdija	Kupiškis Forest Enterprise	Ministry of Environment/Directorate General of State Forests	No board	SE
V	1B	VĮ Marijampolės Miškų Urėdija	Marijampolė Forest Enterprise	Ministry of Environment/Directorate General of State Forests	No board	SE
V	1B	VĮ Pakruojo Miškų Urėdija	Pakruojis Forest Enterprise	Ministry of Environment/Directorate General of State Forests	No board	SE
V	1B	VĮ Rokiškio Miškų Urėdija	Rokiškis Forest Enterprise	Ministry of Environment/Directorate General of State Forests	No board	SE

Size class (I-V) Transparency Guidelines mandatory (♦)	Group	Name (Lithuanian)	Name (English)	State ownership entity	Board structure	Legal form
V	1B	VĮ Tytuvėnų Miškų Urėdija	Tytuvėnai Forest Enterprise	Ministry of Environment/Directorate General of State Forests	No board	SE
V	1B	VĮ Utenos Miškų Urėdija	Utena Forest Enterprise	Ministry of Environment/Directorate General of State Forests	No board	SE
V	1B	VĮ Varėnos Miškų Urėdija	Varėna Forest Enterprise	Ministry of Environment/Directorate General of State Forests	No board	SE
V	1B	VĮ Veisiejų Miškų Urėdija	Veisiejai Forest Enterprise	Ministry of Environment/Directorate General of State Forests	No board	SE
V	1B	VĮ Zarasų Miškų Urėdija	Zarasai Forest Enterprise	Ministry of Environment/Directorate General of State Forests	No board	SE
V	2	VĮ Lietuvos Prabavimo Rūmai	Lithuanian Assay Office	Ministry of Finance	No board	SE
V	1A	UAB Universiteto Vaistinė	University Pharmacy	Ministry of Health	No board	Private LLC
V	1A	UAB Senevita	Senevita	Ministry of Social Security and Labour	One-tier management board	Private LLC
V	1B	AB Detonas	Detonas	Ministry of Transport and Communications	One-tier management board	Public LLC
V	2	VĮ Seimo Leidykla Valstybės Žinios	Seimas Publisher State Journal	Office of the Parliament	One-tier management board	SE
V	1A	AB Autoūkis	Autoūkis	Bank of Property	Two-tier	Public LLC
V	1A	AB Informacinio Verslo Paslaugų Įmonė	Business Information Services Company	Statistics Lithuania	One-tier management board	Public LLC
III	1B	VĮ Mūsų Amatai	Mūsų Amatai	Ministry of Justice/Prison Department	No board	SE

Size class (I-V) Transparency Guidelines mandatory (♦)	Group	Name (Lithuanian)	Name (English)	State ownership entity	Board structure	Legal form
V	-	VĮ Mašinų bandymo stotis	Machinery Testing Station	Ministry of Agriculture	No board	SE
Enterprises undergoing liquidation or bankruptcy						
III	2	VĮ Vilniaus Pilių Direkcija	Vilnius Castle Directorate	Ministry of Culture	No board	SE
II	1A	AB Lietuvos Jūrų Laivininkystė	Lithuanian Shipping Company	Ministry of Transport and Communications	Two-tier	Public LLC

Annex 2

Status of board appointments in Lithuanian state-owned enterprises (February 2018)

	Name (Lithuanian)	Name (English)	State ownership entity	Board structure	Number of independent members*	Number of board members*	Notes
		Enterprises that comply with state rules on SOE board composition					
1	Lietuvos energija, UAB	Lithuanian Energy	Ministry of Finance	Two-tier	3	5	
2	AB Smiltynės perkėla	Smiltynė Ferry Terminal	Ministry of Transport and Communications	One-tier management board	2	3	
3	UAB Gyvulių produktyvumo kontrolė	Animal Productivity Control	Ministry of Agriculture	One-tier management board	3	6	Planned for reorganisation and merger with another SOE
4	AB Lietuvos veislininkystė	Lithuanian Breeding	Ministry of Agriculture	One-tier management board	3	6	Planned for reorganisation and merger with another SOE
5	UAB Šilutės veislininkystė	Šilutė Breeding	Ministry of Agriculture	One-tier management board	3	6	Planned for reorganisation, merger with another SOE and privatisation
6	UAB Panevėžio veislininkystė	Panevėžys Breeding	Ministry of Agriculture	One-tier management board	3	6	Planned for reorganisation and merger with another SOE
7	AB Kiaulių veislininkystė	Swine Breeding	Ministry of Agriculture	One-tier management board	3	6	Planned for reorganisation, merger with another SOE and privatisation
8	UAB Dotnuvos eksperimentinis ūkis	Dotnuva Experimental Farm	Ministry of Agriculture	One-tier management board	3	6	Planned for liquidation
9	UAB Lietuvos žirgynas	Lithuanian Horse Stable	Ministry of Agriculture	One-tier management board	3	6	Planned for reorganisation, merger with

	Name (Lithuanian)	Name (English)	State ownership entity	Board structure	Number of independent members*	Number of board members*	Notes
							another SOE and privatisation
10	AB Vilniaus metrologijos centras	Vilnius Metrology Centre	Ministry of Economy	One-tier management board	3	5	Planned for privatisation
11	UAB Toksika	Toksika	Ministry of Economy	One-tier management board	2	3	
12	UAB Lietuvos parodų ir kongresų centras LITEXPO	Lithuanian Exhibition and Congress Centre LITEXPO	Ministry of Economy	One-tier management board	3	5	
13	VĮ Kelių priežiūra	Road Maintenance	Ministry of Transport and Communications	One-tier management board	4	5	Planned for conversion to private/public limited liability company
14	UAB Upytės eksperimentinis ūkis	Upytė experimental farm	Ministry of Agriculture	One-tier management board	3	6	Planned for reorganisation, merger with another SOE and privatisation
15	AB Lietuvos paštas	Lithuanian Post	Ministry of Transport and Communications	One-tier management board	4	5	
16	UAB Žemės ūkio paskolų garantijų fondas	Agricultural Loan Guarantees Fund	Ministry of Agriculture	Two-tier	2	4	Planned for reorganisation
17	VĮ Lietuvos oro uostai	Lithuanian Airports	Ministry of Transport and Communications	One-tier management board	3	5	Planned for conversion to private/public limited liability company
18	UAB Šeduvos avininkystė	Šeduva Sheep Breeding	Ministry of Agriculture	One-tier management board	3	6	Planned for reorganisation, merger with another SOE and privatisation
19	UAB Investicijų ir verslo garantijos	Investment and Business Guarantees	Ministry of Economy	Two-tier	3	5	Planned for reorganisation
20	AB Detonas	Detonas	Ministry of Transport and Communications	One-tier management board	2	3	
21	VĮ Oro navigacija	Air Navigation	Ministry of Transport and Communications	One-tier management board	3	5	Planned for conversion to private/public limited liability company
22	VĮ Ignalinos atominė elektrinė	Ignalina Nuclear Power Plant	Ministry of Energy	One-tier management board	3	5	
23	VĮ Klaipėdos valstybinio jūrų uosto direkcija	Klaipėda State Seaport Authority	Ministry of Transport and Communications	One-tier management board	2	4	Planned for conversion to private/public

	Name (Lithuanian)	Name (English)	State ownership entity	Board structure	Number of independent members*	Number of board members*	Notes
							limited liability company
24	UAB EPSO-G	EPSO-G	Ministry of Energy	Two-tier	2	4	
25	UAB Lietuvos monetų kalykla	Lithuanian Mint	Bank of Lithuania	One-tier management board	3	5	
26	AB Klaipėdos nafta	Klaipėda Oil	Ministry of Energy	Two-tier	2	3	
27	AB Lietuvos geležinkeliai	Lithuanian Railways	Ministry of Transport and Communications	One-tier management board	5	7	
28	VĮ Regitra	Regitra	Ministry of the Interior	One-tier management board	5	10	
29	AB Lietuvos radijo ir televizijos centras	Lithuanian Radio and Television Centre	Ministry of Transport and Communications	One-tier management board	4	5	
30	VĮ Valstybinių miškų urėdija	State Forest Enterprise	Ministry of Environment	One-tier management board	4**	7**	
	Enterprises for which SOE board nominations are under way						
31	VĮ Registrų centras	Centre of Registers	Ministry of Transport and Communications	One-tier management board	4**	5**	
32	AB Problematika	Problematika	Ministry of Transport and Communications	One-tier management board	2**	3**	Planned for privatisation
33	VĮ Vidaus vandens kelių direkcija	Inland Waterways Authority	Ministry of Transport and Communications	One-tier management board	3**	5**	Planned for conversion to private/public limited liability company
34	AB Giraitės ginkluotės gamykla	Giraitė Armament Factory	VĮ Turto bankas	One-tier management board	3**	5**	
35	VĮ Turto bankas	Bank of Property	Ministry of Finance	One-tier management board	3**	5**	Planned for conversion to private/public limited liability company
36	AB Jonavos grūdai	Jonava Grains	Ministry of Agriculture	One-tier management board	3**	6**	
37	UAB Šilutės polderiai	Šilutė Polders	Ministry of Agriculture	One-tier management board	3**	6**	
38	VĮ Visagino energija	Visaginas Energy	Ministry of Economy	One-tier management board	3**	5**	Planned for conversion to private/public limited liability

	Name (Lithuanian)	Name (English)	State ownership entity	Board structure	Number of independent members*	Number of board members*	Notes
							company and transfer to the authority of the municipality of Visaginas
	Enterprises for which board nominations are foreseen to commence in the near-term						
39	UAB Viešųjų investicijų plėtros agentūra	Public Investment Development Agency	Ministry of Finance	Two-tier	2	5	Planned for reorganisation
40	UAB Būsto paskolų draudimas	Housing Loan Insurance	Ministry of Finance	One-tier management board	0	5	Planned for liquidation
41	VĮ Infostruktūra	Infostructure	Ministry of National Defence	One-tier management board	0	5	Planned for conversion to other legal form. Decision postponed until July 2018.
	Enterprises for which compliance with state rules on SOE board composition is to be decided						
42	UAB Universiteto vaistinė	University Pharmacy	Ministry of Health	One-tier management board	0	2	
43	AB Informacinio verslo paslaugų įmonė	Business Information Services Company	Statistics Lithuania	One-tier management board	0	5	Planned for privatisation
	Enterprises not required to comply with state rules on SOE board composition due to foreseen reorganisation or partial economic activity						
44	UAB poilsio namai Baltija	Vacation Home Baltija	VĮ Turto bankas	One-tier management board	0	4	Partial or no economic activity/under privatisation
45	UAB Aerogeodezijos institutas	Aerogeodesy Institute	VĮ Turto bankas	One-tier management board	0	3	Partial or no economic activity/under privatisation
46	UAB Klaipėdos žuvininkystės produktų aukcionas	Klaipėda Fisheries Product Auction	VĮ Turto bankas	One-tier management board	0	5	Partial or no economic activity/under privatisation
47	UAB Geoterma	Geoterma	VĮ Turto bankas	One-tier management board	0	3	Partial or no economic activity
48	VĮ Energetikos agentūra	Energy Agency	Ministry of Energy	One-tier management board	1	2	Planned for conversion to other legal form (public institution)
49	VĮ Lietuvos naftos produktų agentūra	Lithuanian Oil Products Agency	Ministry of Energy	One-tier management board	1	2	Planned for reorganisation
50	VĮ Lietuvos paminklai	Lithuania Sights	Department of Cultural Heritage	One-tier management board	0	6	Planned for conversion to other legal form
51	UAB Respublikinė mokomoji sportinė bazė	Republican Instructional Sports Base	Department of Physical	One-tier management	0	3	Planned for privatisation

	Name (Lithuanian)	Name (English)	State ownership entity	Board structure	Number of independent members*	Number of board members*	Notes
			Education and Sports	board			
52	VĮ Distancinių tyrimų ir geoinformatikos centras "Gis-centras"	Remote Sensing and Geoinformatics Centre "Gis-Centras"	Ministry of Agriculture	One-tier management board	0	5	Board will be removed. Planned for conversion to private/public limited liability company (after foreseen merger with Agricultural Information and Rural Business Centre)
	Enterprises not required to comply with state rules on board composition because they have no board						
53	VĮ Žemės ūkio informacijos ir kaimo verslo centras	Agricultural Information and Rural Business Centre	Ministry of Agriculture	No board			Planned for reorganisation, merger with another SOE
54	VĮ Pieno tyrimai	Dairy Research	Ministry of Agriculture	No board			Planned for conversion to private/public limited liability company following merger with another SOE
55	VĮ Valstybės žemės fondas	State Land Fund	Ministry of Agriculture	No board			Planned for conversion to private/public limited liability company and privatisation
56	VĮ Lietuvos žemės ūkio ir maisto produktų rinkos reguliavimo agentūra	Lithuanian Agricultural and Food Market Regulation Agency	Ministry of Agriculture	No board			Planned for conversion to other legal form (public institution)
57	VĮ Mašinų bandymo stotis	Machinery Testing Station	Ministry of Agriculture	No board			Planned for conversion to private/public limited liability company and privatisation
58	VĮ Lietuvos prabavimo rūmai	Lithuanian Assay Office	Ministry of Finance	No board			Planned for conversion to other legal form (public institution)
59	VĮ Radioaktyviųjų atliekų tvarkymo agentūra	Radioactive Waste Management Agency	Ministry of Energy	No board			Planned for reorganisation, merger with another SOE
60	UAB Projektų ekspertizė	Project Expertise	Ministry of Environment	No board			Planned for reorganisation, merger with another SOE
61	VĮ Statybos produkcijos sertifikavimo centras	Building Production Certification Centre	Ministry of Environment	No board			Planned for reorganisation

	Name (Lithuanian)	Name (English)	State ownership entity	Board structure	Number of independent members*	Number of board members*	Notes
							(to public institution)
62	UAB Valstybinė projektų ir sąmatų ekspertizė	The State Expertise of Projects and Estimates	Ministry of Agriculture	No board			Planned for reorganisation, merger with another SOE
63	VĮ Mūsų amatai	Mūsų Amatai	Prison Department	No board			Planned for conversion to other legal form. Decision postponed until July 2018.
64	UAB Kauno Petrašiūnų darbo rinkos mokymo centras	Kaunas Petrašiūnai Job Market Training Centre	VĮ Turto bankas	No board			Under privatisation
65	UAB Lietuvos kinas	Lithuanian Cinema	Ministry of Culture	No board			Planned for liquidation
66	VĮ Indėlių ir investicijų draudimas	Deposit and Investment Insurance	Ministry of Finance	No board			Planned for conversion to other legal form. Decision postponed until January 2019

Notes: In some cases, the reported number of board members reflects the nomination committee's decision prior to the final nomination. *Based on preliminary data, February 2018. ** Foreseen number of board members after final
Source: Information provided by the Lithuanian authorities.

ORGANISATION FOR ECONOMIC CO-OPERATION AND DEVELOPMENT

The OECD is a unique forum where governments work together to address the economic, social and environmental challenges of globalisation. The OECD is also at the forefront of efforts to understand and to help governments respond to new developments and concerns, such as corporate governance, the information economy and the challenges of an ageing population. The Organisation provides a setting where governments can compare policy experiences, seek answers to common problems, identify good practice and work to co-ordinate domestic and international policies.

The OECD member countries are: Australia, Austria, Belgium, Canada, Chile, Colombia, the Czech Republic, Denmark, Estonia, Finland, France, Germany, Greece, Hungary, Iceland, Ireland, Israel, Italy, Japan, Korea, Latvia, Lithuania, Luxembourg, Mexico, the Netherlands, New Zealand, Norway, Poland, Portugal, the Slovak Republic, Slovenia, Spain, Sweden, Switzerland, Turkey, the United Kingdom and the United States. The European Union takes part in the work of the OECD.

OECD Publishing disseminates widely the results of the Organisation's statistics gathering and research on economic, social and environmental issues, as well as the conventions, guidelines and standards agreed by its members.

OECD PUBLISHING, 2, rue André-Pascal, 75775 PARIS CEDEX 16
(26 2018 01 1 P) ISBN 978-92-64-30260-0 – 2018

www.ingramcontent.com/pod-product-compliance
Ingram Content Group UK Ltd.
Pitfield, Milton Keynes, MK11 3LW, UK
UKHW051502290926
15471UKWH00008B/1367

9 789264 302600